INSTITUTIONAL INVESTORS IN GLOBAL MARKETS

Institutional Investors in Global Markets

GORDON L. CLARK AND
ASHBY H. B. MONK

OXFORD
UNIVERSITY PRESS

OXFORD
UNIVERSITY PRESS

Great Clarendon Street, Oxford, OX2 6DP,
United Kingdom

Oxford University Press is a department of the University of Oxford. It furthers the University's objective of excellence in research, scholarship, and education by publishing worldwide. Oxford is a registered trade mark of Oxford University Press in the UK and in certain other countries

First Edition published in 2017

Published in the United States of America by Oxford University Press
198 Madison Avenue, New York, NY 10016, United States of America

British Library Cataloguing in Publication Data
Data available

Library of Congress Control Number: 2016959011

ISBN 978–0–19–879321–2

For our families and friends—supporters of our project in so many ways.

Preface

This book is about what institutional investors do, how they do it, and when and where they do it: it is about the production of investment returns in the global economy. Being a book about the production process, it also tackles some of the key issues found in the academic literature on the theory of the firm. This literature is rooted in studies of manufacturing firms in the heartland of the English Industrial Revolution. In many respects, given their interest in the underlying principles framing the organization of firms and in situating firms in context, Adam Smith and Alfred Marshall were both economists and economic geographers. During the twentieth century, the academic literature on the theory of the firm brought into focus industrial corporations and then the management revolution that resulted in re-engineering integrated corporations through intermediation as found in supply chains and global production networks.

Our book shares with other treatments of the modern corporation an abiding interest in the management and organization of the production process. In our case, we focus on the global financial services industry, where the building blocks underpinning the study of industrial corporations are less relevant. In fact, they can be blind alleys when seeking to understand the organization of the production process and its results as expressed in global financial markets. One of the goals of our book is to explain how and why the production of investment returns differs from that of manufactured goods. Another is to provide an analytical framework that situates financial institutions within the complex web of the intermediaries that dominate developed financial markets. As such, the book is more than an analysis of the organization and management of institutional investors; it is also an analysis of the global financial services industry.

We came to the topic after having been involved in a variety of projects that dealt with the role of endowments, insurance companies, pension funds, and sovereign wealth funds in global financial markets. Over the past couple of decades, we have come to realize that these types of organizations deserve more recognition in the academic literature and, perhaps obviously, a degree of engagement that can allow us to understand better how and why they do what they do. As a result, our approach begins with the organization and management of these institutions rather than with their place in the structure and performance of global financial markets. In doing so, we share with Coase (1992) and Davis (2015) an interest in what might be referred to as the 'substance' of firms and markets. In other words, we work from the inside of financial institutions to the outside, instead of imposing the theories of modern management studies and microeconomics on them. Nonetheless, we take seriously the imperatives driving global financial markets in home jurisdictions and offshore. We could hardly do otherwise.

In developing our project, we have been privileged to work with many individuals and organizations in the global financial services industry. In our acknowledgements, we give heartfelt thanks to those who have taken us inside the industry. Like other academics able to report on what they observe in firms and industries, we recognize that being privileged in this manner carries with it certain obligations. Most obviously, we set aside detailed knowledge of specific organizations to report on the logics or analytical principles that give shape to an institutional investor and its place in the global financial services industry. As importantly, we explain the interaction between institutions and financial markets with reference to the management of the production process rather than to the theory of financial market performance and structure.

One thing we have learnt from writing up our research is that it is too easy to idealize the management and organization of institutional investors. Had we chosen simplicity and parsimony as the guiding principles underpinning our analytical framework, we would have risked allowing abstract logic to submerge the analysis instead of giving pride of place to the complex interplay between manager authority and the domain-specific skills and expertise of investment managers. We have tried as much as possible to walk a fine line between analytical logic and the messy world of organizations, the apparent competition for authority in them and the necessary compromises that any organization must make if it is to reconcile the competing claims of interest inside and outside its jurisdiction. In writing the book, we have been mindful of what has gone on before, especially in organization theory and in the theory of the firm. Here, then, is an opportunity to read our book, which we have located at the intersection between the works of Coase, March and Simon, Marris, and related theorists of organization and contract theory, as well as between Williamson's transaction cost economics and scholars like Bathelt and Glückler, who emphasize relationships over formal contracts.

Acknowledgements

This book was made possible by the support of numerous organizations and we would, in particular, like to acknowledge that of our home institutions. For Gordon Clark, these are the Smith School of Enterprise and the Environment, the Saïd Business School at Oxford University and, further afield, the Department of Banking and Finance in the Monash Business School at Monash University. For Ashby Monk, they are the Global Projects Center (GPC) in the Faculty of Engineering at Stanford University, and the Regents of the University of California. Without the administrative and organizational support of our home institutions and, in particular, the editorial support of Alice Chautard, Angelika Kaiser, and Jennifer Sabourin, this book would have never seen the light of day.

When developing a research programme based on in-depth knowledge of the life of institutions and organizations, any researcher relies on whatever access, information, and insights these organizations can offer. We were privileged to have been taken into a wide range of investment institutions around the world, including endowments, family offices, pension funds, and sovereign wealth funds. It would be invidious to pick out specific organizations and individuals while leaving others unidentified. We can, however, acknowledge the open door provided to us by the Swedish government through its review of the AP funds to which we contributed. We would like to thank the panel for its interest in our ideas and members of the enquiry staff, including Mats Langensjo and Åsa Sterte.

Closer to home, we would like to thank Roger Urwin from Willis Towers Watson for his insights into pension fund governance and investment management. He is one of the stars in the field and it is difficult to imagine how we could have become involved in these issues without his help and advice. He was also heavily involved in the formulation of Chapter 9 of this book; we are grateful for his willingness to share his ideas, resources, and key informants. We are also conscious of the help provided by many other industry advisers and executives over the past decade or so, including Keith Ambachtsheer, Jagdeep Singh Bachher, Mark Burgess, Peter Curtis, John Evans, Don Ezra, Eduard van Gelderen, Divyesh Hindocha, Heribert Karch, Mike Orszag, Nick Sykes, and John Whiteman. Along the way, we have also benefited from collaborating with industry groups such Allianz Global Investors (Elizabeth Corley), Arabesque Asset Management (Omar Sharif), Conexus (Amanda White), and *Pensions & Investments* (Chris Battaglia), as well as EuroMoney Institutional Investor (Diane Alfano, Scott Kalb, and Michael Peltz) and participants in the GPC's research club.

This book began life through two related projects. Keith Ambachtsheer of the Rotman School of Management's International Centre for Pension Management (ICPM) at the University of Toronto sponsored one on the governance and management of pension reserve funds. He has followed our research with interest, provided encouragement, and underwritten the significance of what we have sought to achieve. The other project to underpin this particular book, which the Leverhulme Trust sponsored, was on the governance, management, and legitimacy of sovereign wealth funds. The Leverhulme Trust also funded the book that resulted from it, which involved a number of our colleagues, including Adam Dixon. In combination, these two projects gave us the opportunity to scour the world and talk to investment organizations, sponsors, intermediaries, and governments.

We have also been fortunate in being able to present our research at academic forums, industry conferences, various institutions' board and senior executive meetings, government-sponsored enquiries, and various roundtables convened by interested groups. We were able to test out our ideas, hear people's comments on them, and, over time, refine and then further refine our central message. We have relied on the support, ideas, and critical comments of many academic colleagues, notably Harald Bathelt, Christine Brown, Adam Dixon, Sabine Dörry, Dorothee Franzen, Eric Knight, Ray Levitt, Phillip O'Neill, Debra Ralston, W. Richard Scott, Rajiv Sharma, and Dariusz Wójcik. Most importantly, Sarah McGill provided key insights, argument, and enthusiasm during the latter stages of the project, which involved translating ideas into this book. Without our colleagues' support and advice, we would have been unable to develop the project in all its dimensions.

Along the way, we published a number of articles on the project, some of which formed the basis of chapters developed in this book. For permissions to use material from our work previously published in their journals, we therefore thank the following:

Pion Ltd—'Financial institutions, information, and investing-at-a-distance', *Environment and Planning A* (2013) 45: 1318–36; and 'The geography of investment management contracts: The UK, Europe, and the global financial services industry', *Environment and Planning A* (2014) 46: 531–49.

Oxford University Press—'The scope of financial institutions: In-sourcing, outsourcing, and off-shoring', *Journal of Economic Geography* (2013) 13: 279–98.

Regional Studies Association—'State and local pension fund governance and the process of contracting for investment services: The scope of diversity and the problem of embeddedness', *Territory, Politics, and Governance* (2014) 2: 150–72.

Association of American Geographers—'The production of investment returns in spatially extensive markets', *The Professional Geographer* (2015) 67: 595–607.

Taylor and Francis—'Information, knowledge, and investing in offshore markets', *Journal of Sustainable Finance and Investment* (2014) 4: 299–320.

Sage—'Ambiguity, contract and innovation in financial institutions', *Competition and Change* (2016) 20: 187–203.

Institutional Investor Journals—'The outsourced chief investment officer model of management and the principal-agent problem', *Journal of Retirement* (2017) 4(3).

Since we have relied on research sponsors for engagement and funding—some of which are commercial entities—we declare that this book neither serves the interests of any specific commercial party nor has provided the authors with any direct financial benefit.

Finally, any long-running project such as this incurs many debts—specifically the patience of our families and friends. We are grateful that Shirley and Courtney, and Henry and Bea, have given life to our personal and professional commitments. Likewise, we are very grateful for the help and support that Peter B. Clark provided in getting us to be more serious about what we can learn from institutions and how we might frame the conversation in ways that can promote institutions' long-term development.

Gordon L. Clark and
Ashby H. B. Monk

Oxford and Stanford,
August 2016

Table of Contents

List of Figures xvii
List of Tables xix
List of Acronyms and Abbreviations xxi

1. Introduction 1
   - Institutional Investors 2
   - Financial Risk and Uncertainty 6
     - Theory and Practice 6
     - Risk and Uncertainty 7
     - Learning by Doing 9
   - Methodology and Exposition 10
   - Outline of the Book 14

2. Institutions and Organizations 19
   - Nomenclature 20
   - Institutions in the Social Sciences 23
   - Organizations, Inside and Out 25
   - Organizations, Networks, and Resources 28
   - Building Blocks 31

3. The Architecture of Information 37
   - The Information–Industry Nexus 38
   - Institutional Size and Scope 40
   - Governance of Financial Institutions 42
   - The Architecture of Financial Information 45
   - Investment on the Margin 48
     - Pipeline Extensions 50
     - Pipelines and Buzz 51
     - Buzz 52
   - Conclusions 53

4. Production of Investment Returns 58
   - Coase, Contract, and Location 60
   - Financial Institutions: Building Blocks 62
     - Ecology of Finance 63
     - Managers and Workers 63
     - Coordination 64
   - Producing Investment Returns 66
     - Stocks and Flows 67
     - Small and Large Institutions 67
     - Flexibility and Adaptation 68
   - Global Financial Centres and Markets 72

The Base Case: Co-location 73
The Base Case (Redux): Co-location on the Margin 73
The Intermediate Case: Global Market Integration 74
The Limit Case: Realizing Value in Emerging Markets 76
Implications and Conclusions 78

5. Scope of Financial Institutions 82
Theory of the Firm 83
Governance, Contract, and the Firm 85
The Institution and its Industry 89
Tasks and Functions 92
Insourcing 92
Outsourcing 94
Geographical Reach: Offshoring 95
Implications and Conclusions 98

6. Investment Management Contracts 102
The Nature of Contract 103
Financial Institutions and Financial Markets 105
Agents, Principals, and Fiduciaries 105
Geographical Structure of the Industry 106
Products Sought and Produced 107
Product and Financial Markets 108
Investor Strategy and Skill 109
Contract: Form, Functions, and Performance 109
Form 110
Functions 111
Performance 112
Choice of Jurisdiction 112
In Situ or Default Contracting 112
Contracting in London 114
Contracting in Offshore Jurisdictions 115
The Map of Contract 116
Implications and Conclusions 118

7. Public-sector Contracting for Investment Services 122
State and Local Pension Institutions 124
Pension Funds: Form and Functions 126
Governance and Management 126
Norms and Conventions 127
Contractual Relationships 128
Employment Contracts 128
Pre-contract Screening 129
Commercial Contracts 129
Contracts and Templates 130
Content of RFPs 130
Templates, Terms, and Conditions 132
Community Norms 135

Commonalities and Differences 136
Implications and Conclusions 139
Appendix 143

8. Advisers and Consultants 145
Theory of Intermediation 147
Financial Intermediation 147
Capabilities and Resources 148
Organizational Form 149
What Do Advisers Do? 150
Case 1: Small Fund, Representative Board, Wholly Outsourced 150
Case 2: Medium Fund, Representative Board, Mixed Sourcing Strategy 151
Case 3: Large Fund, Representative Board, Reliant on Insourcing 152
Contracts and Services 153
Ambiguity, Contract, and Financial Markets 157
Modes of Innovation 160
Market Disjuncture 160
Innovation in Form and Function 162
Innovation in Products and Services 163
Implications and Conclusions 164

9. Outsourcing and the Principal–Agent Problem 169
Convention and Financial Markets 170
Board Authority and Governance 171
Investment Models and Expectations 172
Market Position and Performance 172
Models of Management 173
Economies of Scale and Scope 174
Outsourcing Strategy 174
Four Ideal Types 175
Principles and Practices 177
Nine Principles 177
Practice as Contract 180
The Principal–Agent Problem 181
Identity and Responsibility 182
Two Institutional Factors 182
Governing OCIO Management 183
Implications and Conclusions 185

10. Cooperation and Collaboration 189
Returning to Fundamentals 190
Persistence and Competition 190
Economies of Scale and Scope 191
Contingency and Response 192
Objectives, Contract, and Authority 193
Objectives and Constraints 193
The Employment Relation 194

Service Contracts 194
Authority and Convention 196
Modes of Innovation 196
Cooperation 197
Collaboration 198
Agency and Governance 200
Transforming Home Bias 201
Conferences and Research Clubs 201
Seeding-related Ventures 202
Partnerships, Informal and Formal 203
Investment Clubs and Shared Equity 204
Implications and Conclusions 205

11. Reframing Finance 208
A Reason for Being 209
The Case for Innovation 211
Prudent Innovation 213
Catalysts for Innovation 214
Extra-financial Objectives 215
Fees and Cost Transparency 215
Collaboration and Cooperation 216
Competitive Advantages 216
Innovation Implemented 217
Sensing 219
Seizing 219
Transforming 219
A Real-World Example 220
Some Final Thoughts 221

Bibliography 223
Index of Names 241
General Index 245

List of Figures

1.1.	Mapping risk and uncertainty	8
3.1.	Financial institutions—pipelines of information	47
3.2.	UK monthly thirty-year bond yields, 1996–2016	49
3.3.	Expected and realized returns	50
4.1.	Management strategies by the nature of labour contracts	66
4.2.	Size of a financial institution and the inflows of assets	72
5.1.	Contractual regimes	88
5.2.	Sourcing options	88
5.3.	Intangible assets	91
5.4.	Strategic scope	96
7.1.	Word count and clauses in IMAs	133
8.1.	Stylized account of the consultant–client relationship	157
9.1.	Models of governance	176
9.2.	Models of management	184

List of Tables

7.1. Contractual items shared by state and local pension funds (per cent) 134

7.2. Contractual items *not* shared by state and local funds 135

List of Acronyms and Abbreviations

401(k)	name of a retirement investment plan
AIG	American International Group
AP	Swedish National Pension Fund
AUM	assets under management
Brexit	Britain's exit from the European Union
BRICS	Brazil, Russia, India, China, and South Africa
CalPERS	California Public Employees' Retirement System
CDO	collateralized debt obligation
CEM	Customer Experience Management
CEO	chief executive officer
CIO	chief information officer
DAC	divide-and-conquer
DB	defined benefit
DC	defined contribution
DCIO	delegated chief investment officer
DNA	Deoxyribonucleic Acid
EMH	efficient markets hypothesis
ERISA	Employee Retirement Income Security Act of 1974
FM	fiduciary management
FOI	freedom of information
FOIA	Freedom of Information Act
FTSE	Financial Times Stock Exchange
GAO	Government Accountability Office
GFC	global financial crisis
GP	general partner
GPC	Global Projects Center
HPI	horizontal process of incorporation
ICPM	International Centre for Pension Management
IMA	investment management agreement
IMCA	Investment Management Consultants Association
IT	information technology

LACERS	Los Angeles City Employees' Retirement System
LP	limited partner
LTCM	long-term capital management
MoU	memorandum of understanding
MPT	modern portfolio theory
OCIO	outsourced chief investment officer
OECD	Organisation for Economic Co-operation and Development
OIC	Oregon Investment Corporation
PBGC	Pension Benefit Guaranty Corporation
PERF	Public Employees Retirement Fund
PERS	public employee retirement systems
PPP	public–private partnership
PSERS	Public School Employees' Retirement System
R&D	research and development
REE	rational expectations equilibrium
RFP	request for proposal
RTK	right to know
SDF	sovereign development fund
SERS	State Employees' Retirement System
TMT	technology, media, telecommunications

1

Introduction

Institutional investors come in many forms, shapes, and sizes. Throughout the book, we work at different levels, looking at institutional investment vehicles (endowments, family offices, insurance companies, pension funds, and sovereign wealth funds), the intermediaries who serve them, and the asset managers of commercial organizations who often place assets in global financial markets. We know more about asset managers than about asset owners. Nonetheless, in many respects, asset owners deserve pride of place in any analysis of financial market structures and their performance, for they are the clients, whereas intermediaries like asset managers provide services to realize their clients' goals and objectives. In this chapter, we provide a brief overview of the role and significance of institutional investors. We begin with asset owners and extend our discussion to asset managers.

It is widely acknowledged that institutional investors underpin the structure and performance of global financial markets. Whereas arguments are made for and against viewing their investment strategies in terms of long-term commitments as opposed to short-term opportunism—witness the UK *Kay Review* (Kay 2012)—there is no doubt that the growth of institutional investors over the past fifty years has given global financial markets a remarkable depth of liquidity and scope of activities. At the same time, institutional investors rely heavily on financial markets to frame and implement their investment strategies. Therefore, it is important to understand what is distinctive about this environment compared with other industry environments, especially manufacturing. In this chapter, we explain the significance of financial risk and uncertainty in the production of investment returns and provide a brief overview of what can be termed the map of financial risk and uncertainty.

In subsequent chapters, these issues are developed in more detail using conceptual building blocks from economics, economic geography, and finance. In this chapter, we also provide a brief overview of our research methods and mode of exposition. In short, we deliver a stylized representation of institutional investment, the relationships between institutional investors and intermediaries, and the logic and principles underpinning the production of investment returns. We hardly ever refer to specific institutions or organizations. It is worth noting that in Chapter 2 we not only directly tackle the conceptual status of institutions and organizations, but also provide a rationale for our use of terms. Meanwhile, however, we shall use the terms as they are used in the industry, among regulators, and in a number of academic disciplines. Institutional investors typically have a distinctive legal status, whereas organizations can be thought of as assemblages of people and resources collected together to realize certain objectives.

INSTITUTIONAL INVESTORS

Institutional investors are a key component of modern economies; they mobilize savings to invest in traded and untraded securities (Davis and Steil 2001). In many cases, they are portfolio investors, as opposed to direct investors who are willing and able to apply their considerable resources to a specific investment facility or option in which they own a majority or controlling stake. Much has been written about the significance of institutional investors for global stock markets, for they are the people who map the flows of assets around the world in relation to opportunities at home and abroad. Likewise, considerable academic research has focused on the role of institutional investors in facilitating global financial integration. There was a time, not so long ago, when it was meaningful to suggest that global financial integration would be so profound that the investment and risk management activities of institutional investors would come up with an organizational framework able to place assets around the world against an unproblematic metric of risk and return, thus replacing both space and time.

Notwithstanding the rhetoric accompanying the 'end of geography', institutional investors have learnt to deal with a world best understood as a patchwork of heterogeneous expectations, rules, and regulations rather than an undifferentiated surface of investment opportunities (cf. O'Brien 1992). Moreover, institutional investors normally maintain a continuing commitment to invest in their home jurisdictions. Investment is typically anchored in the origin of the funds under management and in the immediate opportunities for investment available in home markets. In part, the intimate connection between the origin of funds and their investment destinations reflects the fact that, as the volume of funds grew in the Anglo-American world over the middle and later years of the twentieth century, the inflow of funds to financial markets reinforced the significance of these markets for their nation-states and beyond. If we add the global economic success of Japan in the decades immediately after the Second World War, this gives us three global markets—Tokyo, London, and New York—which became the switch points for flows of financial assets around the world.

As these markets grew in significance over the second half of the twentieth century, memories of the financial crises of the late nineteenth and early twentieth centuries faded to be replaced by growing confidence in the stability of these financial markets, especially compared with the margins of the world (for example, Asia and Latin America). Underpinning the emerging hegemony of these markets was an intellectual programme that sought to formalize and systematize investment norms and conventions into an overarching set of rules for investment. This movement has been described in many ways (see Bernstein's 1996 treatment of risk management). Modern portfolio theory (MPT), followed by the ready acceptance of the Sharpe ratio, the efficient market hypothesis (EMH), the Black–Scholes theorem, and much else besides, all played a part in the emerging paradigm of investment theory and practice. This paradigm was so significant that it drove a wedge between the primarily asset-owning institutional investors who acted on behalf of others, including beneficiaries, and the asset managers who provided the capabilities and resources necessary to realize the benefits of modern investment theory.

It was widely accepted that best-practice investment management was to be attained through intermediation. Here, asset owners, such as pension funds, endowments, and foundations, would contract out the strategic and tactical investment decision-making (along with the investment of assets) to asset- and style-specific investment managers. At the limit, the investment-related activities of asset owners were conceived and implemented through a network of service providers whose contracts were notionally performance related but were, in fact, more often based on convenience and past commitment than on a long-term value proposition. In time, risk management via portfolio diversification was extended to service provision, with the result that both large and small asset owners tended to hold numerous providers with overlapping mandates. In the vernacular of the industry, the search for better performance was conducted through 'beauty parades'—namely presentations by service providers to fund boards and executives loath to fire incumbent providers. When contracts were standardized, fees normalized and markets grew, everyone became a winner.

Just as the golden era appeared to have no end in sight, problems were emerging. Harbingers of the future came in different guises. The Asian financial crisis of 1997, while significant for the core markets of the global financial system, was absorbed and the moment of instability explained by reference to something that had happened elsewhere. The failure of long-term capital management (LTCM) in 1998 surprised the market in part because the principals of the fund were so reputable; in this case, a rescue package was quickly put in place and, once again, markets absorbed the costs of instability. The technology, media, telecommunications (TMT) bubble of the first years of the twenty-first century was home grown and represented converging expectations on the promise of technological invention and innovation for sustained high levels of economic growth. Public recognition of the causes and consequences of the bubble were, however, smothered by the terrorist attacks of 11 September 2001 and the ensuing war on terror. Thereafter, Chinese economic growth masked the softening of the US economy. Just around the corner, however, with the onset of the global financial crisis (GFC) and now the Brexit crisis, the euro crisis profoundly disrupted confidence in the virtues of developed financial markets. It has now become commonplace to speak about the systemic risks apparent in developed markets around the world (Haldane and May 2011).

Sophisticated institutional investors have drawn a variety of lessons from the past twenty years. An obvious one has been that risk management is an essential ingredient in a successful long-term investment strategy and that financial markets do not always price risk in ways that reflect underlying factors. A second lesson has been that risk management through portfolio diversification works well in 'normal' conditions, but may be quite inadequate in extreme conditions when risk management is, in fact, at a premium. A third lesson has been that the interests of asset owners and asset managers are not symmetrical: during good times, when markets are on the rise, both parties benefit from a standard contract, even if relatively poor performance may come at the same cost as relatively good performance. During moments of crisis, when markets are dysfunctional and risk pricing fails, asset owners can lose a large portion of the value of their assets, while asset managers continue to claim fees for an investment performance that is not as bad as that of their competitors. A fourth lesson has been that the size of an institutional investor is no guarantee of superior performance—there is a premium to be had from effective governance and management in crisis conditions not otherwise evident in 'normal' conditions (Clark and Urwin 2010).

Our book takes as given the evident tensions between asset owners and their service providers in the aftermath of the GFC and continuing global financial uncertainties. Sources of uncertainty are to be found, for example, in the euro crisis and in the growth prospects of China and emerging markets. At issue is whether the model of intermediation, conceived and put in place in the second half of the twentieth century, is a viable blueprint for institutional investors over the first half of the twenty-first century. We show that one response to recent events has been disintermediation—in other words, the paring back of service providers to allow asset owners more control over (and oversight of) the formation and implementation of investment strategy. A related response has been for asset owners to insource the formation and implementation of investment strategy—thereby becoming investors in their own right. Yet another response has been reintermediation—managing the formation and implementation of investment strategy through partnerships and relationships with external providers whose interests and incentives are aligned with those of the asset owners.

Crucially, our research is framed with reference to institutional investors with long-term commitments, but notwithstanding the ever-present temptation to maximize short-term investment returns. In this regard, we include asset owners like pension funds, endowments, family offices, foundations, sovereign wealth funds, and, on the edge, insurance companies. We do not ignore the issue of short-term returns, but set it in the context of how best to realize long-term objectives through effective investment governance and management. Equally important for our research has been a concern to situate institutional investors in their home markets *and* in what we term spatially as extensive financial markets. As we show, one of the challenges that institutional investors face when pursuing strategies of disintermediation, insourcing, and reintermediation has been the spatial disconnect between their home bases and national and international financial markets. A related challenge has been to realize the evident opportunities to be found in emerging markets otherwise controlled by global asset managers. In this respect, we place explicit emphasis on time and space for the governance and management of institutional investors wanting to refashion how they manage themselves and their partnerships.

Our book is about a world being turned upside down—intermediation has become an important political issue and an issue of governance and management. Even so, many asset owners have been around for decades; they are embedded in particular economic and political environments with attendant expectations and constraints on innovation. Few asset owners face competitors over their obligations and responsibilities; in many cases, they have a legal right to represent the interests of 'captive' beneficiaries. Likewise, the largest asset managers tend to dominate the global investment management industry; they absorb competitors when seeking to innovate, while allowing redundant or yet-to-be-proven tasks and functions to be spun off into the market for investment management. We are interested in the leading edge of the investment management industry, the search for organizational innovation and the reconfiguration of existing institutions given what is possible. This book is about how to meet long-term commitments by investing away from an institution's home base in a world increasingly dominated by investment opportunities at a distance from either established institutions or accepted norms and conventions.

To frame our analysis, we return to first principles. Most obviously, we explain how and why institutional investors are different from other kinds of organizations—notably those that dominate microeconomic textbooks. This includes consideration of what counts as a productive 'asset' in an investment house. It also includes distinguishing between the tangible assets of plant and equipment used to characterize manufacturing firms, and the intangible assets of human capital, as well as the decision-making protocols and procedures that are so important to investment institutions. Learning is obviously important in both kinds of organizations. Nonetheless, as we show, formal and tacit knowledge in investment houses are contingent on the structure and performance of financial markets and cannot be honed to perfection as is often the case in manufacturing companies. We focus on how investment returns are produced in these types of organizations. We explain the difficulties facing senior managers in promoting innovation in the production of investment returns. Inspired by Coase (1937, 1992) and others interested in the internal logic of economic organizations, we emphasize the organizational logic underpinning the production of investment returns and the ways in which intermediation, disintermediation, and reintermediation may play roles in that process.

FINANCIAL RISK AND UNCERTAINTY

Like other industries, the production of financial services, including investment management, relies on economies of scale and scope within and between markets for financial products. These markets are regional, national, and international in scope, for financial institutions pool dispersed financial assets and liabilities in a handful of global financial centres to reap economies of scale in processing and placement (Wójcik 2011). For many years, insurance companies and pension funds employed external asset managers to produce planned returns through various financial strategies and products. As we show, large asset owners have begun to bring the production of investment returns in-house, partly because of the high costs of intermediation associated with outsourcing. To appreciate our approach to this issue better, in this section we provide a schematic overview of three key factors affecting the production process.

Theory and Practice

The EMH dominated financial theory and practice for more than a generation. In sum, it stood for the idea that market prices incorporate all available information and thereby sustain rational expectations (Fama 1970, 1991). It justified a presumption in favour of markets in the sense that behaviour inconsistent with rational expectations would be priced accordingly and driven out of the market. In the first instance, behaviourists disputed the EMH by demonstrating the persistence of behaviour at odds with theoretical expectations (Akerlof and Shiller 2009; Shiller 2005). Informed by a research programme led by Kahneman and Tversky (1979), others suggested that the EMH could not account for behavioural biases and anomalies evident in patterns of securities' pricing. In the aftermath of the GFC, it has been argued that there are systemic tendencies in financial markets that drive markets away from a sustainable equilibrium (Haldane and May 2011; Stiglitz 2014).

Yet, markets vary around the world according to their transparency, the significance or otherwise of third-party information, and the mechanisms that transmit information among agents in markets (Clark and Wójcik 2007). The value attributed to information in developed markets need not apply to emerging ones. Dealing with the issue of investing offshore when market structure and performance fail to match the experience of home markets is an important theme of the book. We take seriously the geography of finance. The EMH was also framed by reference to a representative agent—an unencumbered market participant. These individuals exist and play a role in the formation of market prices and expectations (Barber and Odean 2001). However, in developed markets, many traders are the employees of institutional investors who not only limit the former's discretion but also impose upon them a 'house view' related to the products they manage and sell. There is, in this sense, an agency problem in that managers may be less well placed than their traders to understand the flux and flow of market expectations.

Institutional investors operate in a distinctive environment. A risk-adjusted rate of return is a stream of income realized repeatedly at the end of each trading term, and is summed together over a period to be reported at designated points in time. Trading strategies and periods typically map onto the rhythm of daily life in the relevant jurisdictions. Three implications follow and are vital when we come to explaining how and why the management 'problem' is so important for institutional investors. First, agents (employees and/or service providers) often time the stream of returns to match reporting dates. Second, switching mandates between the managers of investment products representing specific asset classes, sectors, and/or geographies, need not result in superior rates of return net of switching costs (Ellis 2012; Litterman et al. 2004). Third, herding around certain times, events, and metrics is—at least for senior managers—a challenge in that the interests of the client may be quite different from those of the portfolio managers.

Risk and Uncertainty

Financial markets are subject to risk and uncertainty. Risk refers to the probability of a certain outcome or set of outcomes, and uncertainty to either an inability to attribute a risk premium to a class of possible future events, or an inability to foretell what is likely to be salient in the future—a distinction owed, among others, to Keynes (1948) and Knight (1921). Some analysts treat risk and uncertainty as synonymous and seek to reduce uncertainty to risk.

While risk and uncertainty are related, the two concepts are best treated as distinctive and different (Diebold et al. 2010). At any point in time, events anchored in recognized market processes show that risk models are effective tools for estimating their likely occurrence and impact. It is also possible to use skill and expertise to extend the applicability of these tools to related or analogous situations. As events unfold, and as new information becomes available, risk models can be updated and re-estimated. In these ways, risk models 'colonize' uncertainty in the sense that they work until they fail—whereas unanticipated events disturb the status quo.[1]

These elements of risk management—models, skill, and expertise—are represented in Figure 1.1 (at a particular point in time and space). To the extent that risk models are effective, they can be applied repeatedly by machine and/or agents. To the extent that these models can be extended to analogous or related situations (X–Y), trading systems dominate (Gilboa et al. 2014). Where skill and expertise are required in the application and assessment of risk models (Y–Z) will depend, in part, on experience. Expertise can facilitate judgement, in the sense that pattern recognition systems can aid assessment and choice between models. However, as unanticipated events disturb risk models, and as market expectations are increasingly violated in ways that challenge experience and pattern recognition systems, skill and expertise come to the fore. Put slightly differently, inherited decision rules and cognitive biases in favour of known conditions may trip the unwary and the inexperienced in the manner suggested by Barber and Odean (2001), among others. This takes analysts to instances where models begin to fail

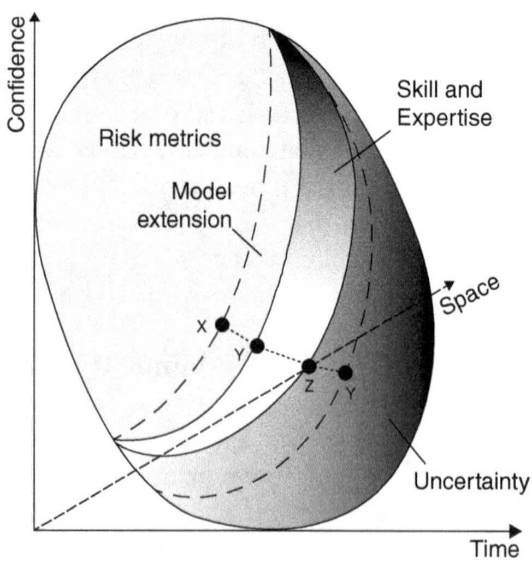

Figure 1.1. Mapping risk and uncertainty

Source: Authors and John Whiteman

(Z–Y) and then to uncertainty, represented in Figure 1.1 by the darkly shaded area to the right of skill and expertise, which grows and shrinks as less or more stability dominates market expectations.

Time has been emphasized in the context of a particular market environment in a shared jurisdiction. Figure 1.1 is, of course, in three dimensions, representing the risks and uncertainties associated with investment at home and abroad. So, for example, it is widely recognized that investors at home tend to be better in the sense that their ability to colonize uncertainty is more effective; this is because they are either better informed or more knowledgeable about the market at hand (Wójcik 2009). Expectations are formed at a point in time and space, even if the home domain of clients anchors their 'location', which may be virtual insofar as it is at the intersection of transaction-related market agents.[2] It is also apparent that some markets are more stable than others due to the nature of regulation, the depth of liquidity, and scope and reliability of market information. In some markets, the trade-off between risk and return implies a premium on market position that is more important than in other financial markets. In these circumstances, it is difficult to colonize uncertainty with any confidence because of the difficulties in identifying, collecting, and valuing salient information.[3]

Here, risk and uncertainty are treated as fundamental attributes of financial markets. It should also be acknowledged that the risks associated with an investment strategy are related to the rate of return, to the objectives of institutions, and to the mandates allocated to portfolio managers. An investment strategy may produce a relatively predictable but lower stream of returns with relatively less risk than some other strategies. On the other hand, a higher-return target implies greater risk. In the first instance, a low risk/low return product is likely to be found at the centre of the market, while a high risk/high return product is likely to be found on the margin of the market, where the boundary between risk and uncertainty is more permeable and returns are reliant on judgement. In these ways, models of market performance and their investment strategies can be translated into investment products.

Learning by Doing

Recent research on learning by doing in manufacturing companies suggests that knowledge management can be quite effective. Levitt et al. (2012) show that shift-based learning in an automobile plant can be rapid, and the lessons learned from process innovation are readily transferred between shifts without an appreciable loss of efficiency. Three assumptions underpin their analysis. First, the production process is replicable time after time. Second, learning by doing is viable because its effects are directly measurable. Third, the process of innovation is incremental and additive rather than disruptive of the existing configuration of production. An interesting aspect of the Levitt et al. study is the authors' silence about how learning is organized so that lessons are transferred between shifts. They are also, given the ever-present temptation to backslide or 'forget' lessons gleaned from earlier experiences, silent on how the lessons learned are sustained over time.

Alevy et al. (2007), by contrast, suggest that finance professionals know that producing investment returns is not entirely predictable. Learning by doing is contingent on one's place in the market (time and space) and unanticipated events can profoundly disrupt expectations. Models of the market can be both calibrated against the past *and* used to predict the future (against limits or parameters). The ready availability of relevant information—expressed through key variables, estimated relationships, and measures of goodness of fit—does, of course, reinforce confidence in these models of markets. However, when analysts look forward, these models become sets of beliefs—hypotheses or expectations—about the future.[4] Expectations may be realized and confidence in their robustness reinforced. Inevitably, in the future and/or in some other market, expectations will not be met. The issue is whether past success can be set aside in the interests of exercising judgement in ways that are relevant to current circumstances (Fox and Tversky 1995).

In a stable financial environment, skilled market participants are better able than their less skilled counterparts to improve their trading skills and capacity to realize return objectives (Campbell et al. 2011). However, where unanticipated events conspire to disrupt expectations, processing information becomes more important than the knowledge of the agent or institution (expressed as informed judgement and expertise). Weitzman (2007) observed that the world of financial markets is fraught with uncertainty: 'the way-too-large empirical volatility of equity prices seems badly disconnected from the basic spirit of a real-economy-driven REE (rational expectations equilibrium). Instead of self-confident REE investors with sure expectations of objective frequencies generated by an already known stochastic structure (about which nothing further remains to be learned), the whole situation looks and feels like skittish investors nervously reacting to unsure expectations of unknown deeper forces of shifting structure.'[5] Learning by doing is probably only a momentary 'fix' on a system in motion—never going backwards and always going forward in unexpected ways.

METHODOLOGY AND EXPOSITION

Our book provides an analytical framework for understanding the governance and management of financial institutions. This mode of presentation is one among many in the cognate fields of economic geography, finance, and management (Amin and Cohendet 2004; Baker et al. 2002; Storper and Salais 1997). Our systematic approach to the principles underpinning the structure and performance of institutional investors provides a way of understanding the nature and scope of industry practice. This strategy can be justified in many ways. For instance, it is a necessary first step in guiding the empirical analysis of specific instances and industry formations. Nonetheless, as our discussion on the significance of risk and uncertainty indicates, our framework is sensitive to the environment in which financial institutions operate. As such, our approach has a higher level of specificity than many theory-led models of the firm.

While, throughout the book, we desist from identifying particular organizations, service providers, and intermediaries, this should not be taken as implying that details do not matter. They do matter, as Chapters 5 and 6 on the nature and scope of contractual relationships between the buy side and the sell side of the market indicate. Here, we show that the nature and regulation of commercial relationships, the negotiation and governance of contracts, and the accountability of the financial services industry at home and abroad are embedded in geography (McCormick 2010). One contribution of the book is its recognition of the degree to which being embedded frames the governance and management of financial institutions. There is already a large and extensive body of research on commodity-producing and -distributing industries with extensive global footprints (see Durand and Wrigley (2009) on the global retailing industry). The contribution of this book, however, is to the growing research programme and cognate disciplines looking at the nature and significance of the global financial services industry, advanced business services, and related institutional formations of policy and governance.[6]

Our analytical framework draws on extensive fieldwork and brings together related literature from geography, economics, and finance to provide an informed assessment of the fundamental logics driving organizational behaviour in global financial markets. We utilize, at times, a comparative perspective that crosses the United Kingdom, Europe, North America, Australasia, the Middle East, and beyond. However, where we might have limited our focus to the intersection between financial institutions and their 'home' jurisdictions, we place the former in a global context. In so doing, we rely on participant observation in the global financial services industry, involving, among others, asset owners, asset managers, intermediaries such as custodians and brokers, and the providers of consulting and legal services—in short, the ecology of the industry (for related research, see Faulconbridge (2006); Faulconbridge et al. (2007); Wójcik (2009)). As such, knowledge and experience of the industry and, in particular, of the management problem facing asset owners in relation to the asset management industry are distilled into linked propositions, industry conditions, and key dilemmas.

Fieldwork can be linked to long-standing traditions in economic geography and economics. For example, Clark (1998) refers to 'close dialogue' as a form of bilateral engagement with the organizational principals that emphasize the importance of understanding one's own perspective, as well as the key issues, dilemmas, and industry settings of one's organization. In many respects, the senior managers of institutional investors are quite aware of how their organizations function, including the constraints that affect organizational performance and innovation. Drawing on Adam Smith and the research practices associated with modern industrial economics, Helper (2000) makes a series of related points to justify the usefulness of so-called 'factory visits'. As will become obvious, we believe that fieldwork provides an invaluable means of understanding how organizations function more or less effectively, which is a point we amplify in Chapter 2. We also demonstrate that fieldwork does not stand on its own: the insights gleaned from engagement with organizations and their principals allow us to interrogate and develop theoretical principles.

Fieldwork also comes in many forms. It was made possible by access to key decision makers inside and outside a wide variety of financial institutions and organizations. Without adequate access, fieldwork can become sterile in terms of insight and theoretical sophistication. In some instances, the sponsorship of major research organizations made access possible. Our previous book on sovereign wealth funds (Clark et al. 2013) represents this type of approach. Over the years, in Oxford and Stanford, we have convened the informal and formal research clubs of financial institutions and organizations with a view to building up networks of contacts and providing a venue for senior managers to meet one another. We have used clubs to foster the exchange of ideas and research projects on governance and management. In some cases, we have become involved in these organizations as advisers, board members, and paid employees. As a result, readers of our previously published papers will have noted that we tend to present our findings from the inside (the practice of governance and management) to the outside (the theoretical principles of organizational design and performance).

This type of engagement comes with obligations. Sponsoring and participating in the research clubs of an industry's organizations presupposes a degree of confidentiality and non-disclosure, which is more consistent with the Chatham House rule than with the attribution of expressed views to individuals and their sponsoring organizations. As for giving advice, under these circumstances, it is as important to listen to senior managers as it is to make specific recommendations. Consistent with our intellectual project, we were keen to identify and distribute best practice and solve specific problems. Here, of course, there is a fine line between research, advice, and implementation. While implementation is key, we were conscious of the need to honour the principles of confidentiality and so disclose, where appropriate, actual or possible conflicts of interest. We have placed our exposition of the principles and practices of industry within a framework of academic norms and conventions. Our insights and conclusions are intended neither to advance the cause of any organization nor to do anything other than contribute to a richer understanding of the industry.

In the first five of our chapters, we focus on the nature and role of contracts in the global financial services industry. Our analytical strategy is grounded in a particular market environment. As noted, risk and uncertainty are pervasive aspects of financial markets and are arguably deeply embedded in the contractual relationships that bring together financial institutions and their suppliers. Likewise, we suggest that the geography of a contract is important, for jurisdictions such as the United Kingdom and the United States serve as bridges between geographically dispersed financial institutions and centralized market providers. In these ways, our approach is more akin to Macauley's (1963, 1985) sociology of contractual relations and to Bathelt and Glückler's (2011) relational economic geography than it is to standard treatments of contract. We are more concerned with the reality of contracting in the global financial services industry than with the theory of optimal contracting, even if we are mindful of the value of such a reference point (Bolton and Dewatripont 2005).

Any treatment of a private contract is necessarily abstract because contracts are proprietary documents. As such, they are subject to confidential clauses designed to limit third-party disclosure of the form, terms, and conditions of the agreement. In a number of instances, we encountered situations in which disclosure of contractual terms and conditions was strictly limited between functions, even *within* organizations. It is not surprising, therefore, that most studies of contract in the social sciences, including economics, sociology, and management studies, do not disclose the sites of fieldwork, the nature and content of the documents analysed, or the parties involved. For example, the seminal studies of the practice of contract by Macauley (1963, 1985) and Macneil (1985) make no mention of the terms and conditions of specific contracts or of who was involved in them. Empirical research on contracts tends to rely on US court cases, which lay bare the issues, arguments, and points of dispute; even here, however, court opinions do not report the substance of the contracts in dispute. These documents are unobtainable for public viewing, even in the court in which the dispute was heard.

Consequently, how contractual relationships in the industry are portrayed in this book should be treated as provisional rather than definitive. Despite having conducted numerous interviews and compared diverse types of contractual frameworks across asset classes, different kinds of financial institutions (for example, public and private pension funds and sovereign wealth funds), and service providers in the United Kingdom, Europe, and the United States, we are unable to violate confidentiality. Our research suggests that the shackles of confidentiality tend to favour the provider side of the market because few clients have either the legal resources or the information needed to challenge the terms and conditions of proffered contracts. As many legal scholars have noted, the ideal contract is a chimera in which the practice of contract involves the exercise of power (Shiffrin 2007). Likewise, the choice of jurisdiction in relation to the exercise of a contract can also be intimately related to the relative powers of the contractual parties.

Making sense of the form and content of public-sector contracts is also challenging. In Chapter 7, we consider US state and local government contracts for financial services in some detail. While state and local governments may disclose the basic terms of a service contract, it is difficult to gain access to either an RFP (request for proposal) or actual contract. In some cases, despite most RFPs and contracts being proprietary documents, we were able to report on public employee retirement systems (PERS), RFPs, and investment management agreements (IMAs). Legal penalties can be invoked if confidentiality is violated. That PERS contracts are often subject to partisan commentary and debate reinforces caution about public disclosure. Interviews with senior managers of US public-sector pension institutions, covering a range of topics and stretching over more than a decade, sustained our research on the governance and management of PERS (Clark 2008; Hagerman et al. 2006). We also had opportunities to investigate the governance and management of related public and private financial institutions and their service providers on both sides of the Atlantic.

As in the related research on contracts, our analysis, which is cross-sectional rather than time-dependent, is driven by specific institutions and their documents (Argyres et al. 2007; Mayer and Argyres 2004). Furthermore, problems of access have prevented us from commenting on the evolution of sector- or jurisdiction-specific contractual norms and conventions. Our focus is on how the process of contracting is organized and substantiated in the manner suggested by, among others, Deakin and Michie (2000). Following Macauley (1985), and those inspired by his sociology of contract, we have drawn our insights from detailed studies of the substantive content of RPFs, IMAs, and contracts, as well as from British and European research on the structure and logic of contract law as it pertains to the investment management industry. As such, our analysis of contract in this book is an exercise in analysis and clarification grounded in knowledge of service agreements and contracts gleaned from fieldwork, freedom of information (FOI) requests, and intensive searches of state and local PERS websites.

OUTLINE OF THE BOOK

In Chapter 2, we turn to the issue of the status of institutional investors in the global economy. We discriminate between different types of institutional investors—endowments, family offices, and pension funds on the one hand, and the conventional roles and responsibilities of asset owners, holders, and managers working in banks and stand-alone asset-management companies on the other. We begin with the issue of intermediation, which indicates that an important function of asset owners and holders is to collect savings and financial commitments from dispersed individuals and to place them in financial markets to reap a risk-adjusted rate of return. Both institutions and intermediaries, like asset managers, can place collected assets. Most importantly, we explain how the use of the term '*institutional* investors', with reference to the current debate in the social sciences on institutions and organizations, emphasizes the legal status of many institutional investors, as well as the fact that they are organizations that must be governed and managed. These are key issues for the entire book.

In Chapter 3, we show that information systems are fundamental to the production of investment returns. At one level, this involves collecting information from financial markets to transmit to institutional investors with a view to informing investment strategy and its implementation. At another level, of course, it involves sharing information within an organization to facilitate the investment process and the coordination of the various component parts that make up an institution's investment strategy. Many institutional investors utilize the information systems of third-party providers and face considerable challenges in coordinating those systems with respect to managing the investment process. More recently, some institutional investors have introduced their own organization-wide information management systems with a view to imposing order on the flow of information that otherwise may be chaotic. Investments in spatially extensive financial markets are a demonstration of the significance of this issue.

Turning to Chapter 4, we introduce the reader to the most basic of issues—how institutional investors produce investment returns over time and space. In doing so, senior managers coordinate the investment process in relation to the institution's goals and objectives. We demonstrate how and why the powers of senior managers are contingent rather than absolute: because of the significance of human capital in the investment process, the market for skill and expertise may compromise the authority of senior managers to set investment strategies, as well as asset-specific risk and return investment objectives. Strategies of management, like divide-and-conquer (DAC) or incorporation, are used to address these issues. It is also demonstrated that a growing volume of assets under management (AUM) can significantly affect senior managers' capacities to innovate.

Having established a framework through which to understand the production of investment returns, in Chapter 5 we expand on the significance of two types of intangible assets crucial to realizing the mission of institutional investors. One is the human capital of the organization and its related partners and providers, the other the decision-making protocols and procedures used to formulate and implement investment strategy. Whereas some commentators suggest that the production of risk-adjusted rates of return can, or should, be understood by reference to the production of any other type of manufactured product, we contend that this type of analogy is unhelpful in understanding what is distinctive about the global financial services industry. Specifically, we tackle the issue of insourcing and outsourcing—the make or buy question—and the matter of producing investment returns at home rather than offshore.

Chapters 3 to 5 adopt an internal perspective on the production process. In Chapters 6 and 7 we looked more closely at relationships between asset owners and asset managers and, specifically, the formulation and governance of service contracts binding institutional investors to their providers. In Chapter 6, we draw on our field research to explain the role of contract in relationships between asset owners and asset managers, referencing current practice in the United Kingdom, Europe, and North America. We show that these relationships appear symmetrical in that this type of service contract can be terminated at will. However, appearances are deceptive. In many cases, such contracts are asymmetrical in that asset owners often rely on asset managers because they lack the capabilities and resources to do otherwise. It is noted that the laws of England and Wales figure prominently in industry practice worldwide and bind together clients and providers across spatially extensive financial markets.

In Chapter 7, the focus shifts from private to public agents and we look closely at the process of contracting for financial services in US state and local pension funds. This chapter addresses the costs and consequences of institutional governance and management in the US state and local pension-fund sector. Although the protocols and procedures of state governments dominate contracting in this sector, the formulation of investment contracts in accordance with the conventional model of intermediation can be highly idiosyncratic. It is shown that 'standard practices' hide the considerable diversity among US state and local pension funds, especially in the terms and conditions of investment contracts, and in the substance of specific service agreements for more or less significant services. In the penultimate section of the chapter, we refer to an idealized model of institutional design and the governance and management of the investment management process.

The conventional model of intermediation depends on a couple of key actors, namely consulting actuaries and asset consultants. In Chapter 8, we look at their roles and responsibilities in relation to asset owners and holders and the process of investment management. In doing so, we provide a baseline from which to understand these roles and responsibilities; we also differentiate between small, medium, and large owners and holders of assets.

In a conventional model of intermediation, consulting actuaries and asset consultants claim influence by virtue of their access to knowledge about and understanding of the investment management process. Here, we provide a framework through which to understand consultants' value in the framing of investment strategies and their implementation, emphasizing issues of process as well as substance. As financial markets have become more challenging environments in which to produce investment returns, and as larger asset owners have moved towards disintermediation, insourcing, and reintermediation, the role of consultants in sustaining innovation in the practice of investment has become an issue.

In Chapter 9, we extend our discussion of intermediation and the role of consultants to focus on the so-called outsourced chief investment officer (OCIO) model of investment strategy and implementation. We explain how and why this is a desirable mode of organization; and we emphasize issues of size and scope that are either unavailable internally or available at a price that is inconsistent with the best interests of beneficiaries. Here, we also identify the principles and practices associated with best practice, as well as the challenges associated with governing relationships with entities that are charged with responsibility for managing the entire value chain.

As suggested in Chapter 8, there is a premium on innovation in the production of investment returns. This premium can be realized in a number of ways, which include promoting different methods of framing investment strategy and its implementation, as well as different ways of governing and managing intermediaries. In Chapter 10, our focus is on strategies of cooperation and collaboration between similar types of institutional investors. We set out the advantages and disadvantages of different kinds of cooperation and collaboration, as well as issues concerning the governance and management of these types of semiformal arrangements. We note that these arrangements can empower senior managers in their own organizations and so facilitate long-term solutions to the formulation and implementation of an investment strategy. We also note that cooperation and collaboration are likely to be only partial solutions to the costs and consequences of organizational inertia and the entrenchment of common interests.

Chapter 11 is the final chapter of the book. It looks forward, emphasizing the forces motivating institutional innovation and the imperatives driving institutional investors towards different forms of management. We note the urgency behind reintermediation, arguing that it is unlikely that financial markets will return to 'normal' if normal is to be understood as the 1980s and 1990s where a balanced portfolio was a winning formula for investment strategy. This chapter is also about the different ways in which institutional innovation can take place in the sector given the nature of many institutions and their political constituencies.

NOTES

1. There is considerable interest in the nature and significance of unanticipated events, with some theorists, notably Barro (2006), arguing that these events are so significant that they reframe market structure, beliefs, and expectations. Rather than treating these events as anomalous, and excluding them as such, Barro suggests that these events reset market dynamics and, after some time, become incorporated into market behaviour.
2. Time and space are inextricably bound together. In the initial stages of a financial crisis, to cope with uncertainty agents and institutions tend to retreat from other markets to focus on just one. In later phases of a crisis, agents and institutions tend to reach out to other markets to compensate for the limits apparent in the home one. Therefore, the relationship between time and space is strategic rather than antagonistic (cf. Murdoch et al. 2000 with Clark and Thrift 2005).
3. Cognitive scientists distinguish between encoding data and attributing meaning to information, thus suggesting that meaning making is a higher-order cognitive function (Bor 2012: 53). Some authors, including Gabaix and Laibson (2006), suggest that sorting through received information according to salience is commonplace; otherwise, data from the environment are likely to overwhelm the decision-making (Aragones et al. 2005).
4. Recent research on the nature and stability of beliefs and their status in theory and practice can be found in Ellsberg (1961); Kurz (1994); Manski (2004); and Rook (2014).
5. Weitzman (2007: 1103) goes on to remark 'in a *nonergodic* situation where hidden parameters are *evolving*, everyone is perennially uncertain about current structure and learning is *not* converging to an REE because no matter how the data are filtered there are not "true" REE structural-parameter values to converge to'. Emphasis is in the original text, excluding a footnote.
6. See, for example, Coe (2014); Faulconbridge and Muzio (2009); French et al. (2011); Maurer (2008); and Wójcik (2013).

2

Institutions and Organizations

One response to the global financial crisis (GFC) was to look afresh at the role and significance of financial institutions, whatever their organizational forms. Inspired by interventions from Haldane (2009) and Haldane and May (2011), policymakers have sought to better understand the behaviour of banks, as well as their interactions with one another. Caught up in the net cast by financial regulators have been large asset managers, banks, insurance companies, pension funds, and sovereign wealth funds. Given their size and significance for their host economies, and given their importance for the structure and performance of global financial markets, it is not surprising that some regulators have deemed these organizations systemically important financial institutions.

In this chapter, we explain how and why we apply the phrase 'financial institutions' to asset owners of various types whose purpose is the realization of target risk-adjusted rates of return on assets under management (AUM).[1] We note that these types of asset owners are typically 'beneficial' in conception and by intent; that is, they act on behalf of those whose long-term welfare is served by their investment strategies and decisions. We could use the phrase 'beneficial institutions' to label these organizations, for to do so would be consistent with their goals and objectives. Notwithstanding their ultimate purpose, it is also important to see them as they function—as financial institutions that are as important as banks in terms of the scope and significance of their activities and, perhaps, more important than many banks in terms of their influence over the long-term shape of capitalist economies. It is apparent that many nation-states have broadened the scope of their statutory and regulatory frameworks to take account of these institutions' financial functions and activities.

Financial institutions are also organizations in that they govern and manage their activities in ways that the theory of organizations and their distinctive attributes by sector and jurisdiction can explain. This point is made by comparing banks with asset owners, isolating their formal differences while bringing to the fore their commonalities. As such, we take on the challenge of explaining how and why asset owners are organized in the ways they are and the implications to be drawn from their performance in global financial markets. We begin with March and Simon (1958) because their approach to analysing large organizations resonates with our experience of observing the activities of asset owners around the world. However, as we suggest, it is insufficient simply to rely on their theory of organizations as if the logic of organizational design were set in stone. Senior managers of large asset owners have sought to vary organizational form *and* functions in ways that serve the overarching goals of their host institutions—hence, the emphasis we place on recent research on the make-or-buy issue in economics, which we frame here in terms of insourcing versus outsourcing and disintermediation versus reintermediation.

NOMENCLATURE

As observed in Chapter 1, we focus on the organization of financial institutions commonly referred to as institutional investors (Davis and Steil 2001). Broadly speaking, institutional investors include asset owners and asset managers. The former are often deemed to include endowments, family offices, foundations, pension funds, and sovereign wealth funds, whereas the latter include companies such as BlackRock, JP Morgan Chase, and State Street. As briefly mentioned in the Introduction, these asset owners and asset managers are also organizations; that is, they are sets of people, capabilities, and resources established and managed for a purpose or set of purposes (Helfat et al. 2007). As organizations, institutional investors face significant coordination and management challenges in the face of market risk and uncertainty. Whereas much of the academic literature on banking and finance uses the terms 'institutions' and 'organizations' interchangeably, in the social science literature these types of entities are labelled and their forms and functions analysed in a variety of ways. Here, we aim to be transparent about the use of these terms.

Being an 'owner' is to have a legally enforceable property right. Pension funds are not really asset owners but asset 'holders'; that is, they act on behalf of those who have transferred their property rights or entitlements to the pension fund (Morrison and Wilhelm 2007). Pension-fund participants are the ultimate owners of funds invested and managed on their behalf. Nonetheless, let us be clear about the powers of pension and sovereign wealth funds. These entities normally have an exclusive right to invest and manage financial assets, powers that their sponsors (businesses and governments) rather than the participants (individuals and citizens) assign. Using the terms Hirschman (1971) made popular, participants more often than not have no effective voice in the investment and management of their assets and rarely have the option to exit from such an entity. Where governments allow pension-fund participants the right to exit should they so wish, they rarely exercise that option. In many cases, loyalty is taken for granted.

We use the terms 'asset owners' and 'asset managers' as they are in everyday life. We also observe that it is commonplace to refer to them as institutional investors as well as financial institutions. People using these terms rarely consider their epistemological status as concepts underpinned by certain theoretical frameworks or modes of explanation. Being labelled a financial institution is another way of describing an institutional investor, assuming the latter shares with other entities a similar organizational form and similar types of functions. For example, banks are sometimes described as financial institutions *and* sometimes as institutional investors. This blurs the definition of what a bank is, or is not, to include entities that perform bank-like functions, such as taking deposits, lending, and investing. This broad-gauged use of the phrase 'financial institutions' is found in recent studies devoted to explaining the status of, and possible regulatory reform of, systemically important financial institutions (Čihák and Nier 2012; Haldane and May 2011).

For many years, banks were seen as archetypical financial institutions insofar as they could take on a variety of forms, conduct a number of related activities, and provide a well-defined range of services. Their single most important function was to act as an intermediary between savers and investors (Diamond 1984). In so doing, banks and related financial institutions were located at the very centre of modern economies: without financial intermediaries transforming savings into investments, modern economies would not exist, at least not as we know them (Mayer and Vives 1993). Of course, many banks became more than intermediaries and took on significant investment management functions. Saving and investing organizations, financial institutions, and financial intermediaries are therefore all institutional investors. Whatever their label, the difference between a commercial entity and a financial institution is surely the importance of the latter for the growth and stability of market economies (King and Levine 1995).

Many Organisation for Economic Co-operation and Development (OECD) governments define 'financial' institutions by statute and regulation. One US definition includes insured depository institutions, credit unions insured by the federal government, federal home loan banks, mortgage companies, and much else besides. Also included are Federal Reserve banks, the branches or agencies of foreign banks, and 'any person or entity that makes in whole or in part a federally related mortgage loan'.[2] These entities can claim support from the US federal government should they come close to, or default on, their commitments. See *US Code Title 18 Crimes and Criminal Procedure*. Under *US Code Chapter 53, Subchapter II Records and Reports on Monetary Instruments and Transactions*, a 'financial institution' includes the entities listed as well as credit card providers, dealers in commodities, and any 'person' or 'network of persons' engaged in the business of transferring money 'domestically or internationally'. Furthermore, the secretary of the Treasury is provided with powers to treat any business as a 'financial institution' if need be.[3] In this context, institutional investors are, or can be, officially designated financial institutions.

More recent official definitions distinguish between financial services and financial institutions. For example, the Swiss government leaves unspecified what counts as a financial service and/or financial instrument, thereby providing regulatory agencies with the powers to respond to product innovation in financial markets. The Swiss Financial Institutions Act establishes a supervisory regime for organizations, like pension funds, deemed 'financial institutions' (Rapin and Pétermann 2015). The Canadian Office of the Superintendent of Financial Institutions Act treats pension funds in the same way as it treats financial institutions. Likewise, the Insurance Companies Act includes as a financial institution, whether incorporated federally or provincially, any entity 'primarily engaged in dealing securities, including portfolio management and investment counselling'. Note, however, that pension funds are also trust-based institutions in countries reliant on an English common-law heritage. As such, pension funds are not always subject to countries' and states' company laws and regulations, although they can directly own and be shareholders of listed and unlisted companies (Clark 2000).

One implication to be drawn from this discussion is that there is some confusion over the differences between an institutional investor and a financial institution. Given that there is general agreement about the significance of certain types of financial functions for modern economies, aside from differences in terms of their organizational forms and specific functions, the terms are often used interchangeably. It is also apparent that there is a certain history embedded in the use of these terms. For example, more often than not an institutional investor is, or has been, an asset owner or asset manager, whereas more often than not a financial institution is, or has been, a bank or deposit-taking and lending organization.

Over the past couple of decades, these distinctions have become blurred, partly because banks have extended their reach into functions normally associated with asset managers and partly because asset owners and managers have taken on functions typically associated with banks, like direct placements and lending. Some endowments, foundations, and pension funds now have such significant financial holdings that many countries have brought them into their systems of prudential regulation and supervision. Formally or by default, pension funds and entities such as foundations, insurance companies, and sovereign wealth funds that 'deal securities' are considered financial institutions.

INSTITUTIONS IN THE SOCIAL SCIENCES

In our discussion of institutional investors as financial institutions, we referred to the common use of the term 'institution' in banking and finance. To summarize, in this academic field, and in related public policy domains, institutional investors are a set of financial institutions located at the very heart of developed countries' financial systems. Indeed, by some accounts, because they act as essential intermediaries between savers and investors, these entities have made possible the growth and development of modern economies (King and Levine 1995a, 1995b). National and international rules and regulations underwrite their status and provide them with a licence to operate across a wide range of financial activities and services. Because they are a certain size, are essential to economic growth and development, and are deeply embedded in commercial transactions of all kinds, it is arguable that financial institutions are one of a select number of institutions that sustain modern societies around the world.

Our discussion to this point begs the question of what constitutes an institution beyond that suggested by the term 'financial institution'. Also left to one side was the relationship between institutions and organizations. At the outset, we suggested that financial institutions are also organizations that must be governed and managed to realize their objectives. This much is obvious. Nevertheless, the significance attributed to institutions suggests that they have a certain status or importance separate and different from organizations. In a similar manner, any reading or debate in the social sciences about institutions would quickly conclude that they have a distinctive status and are different from organizations. Whereas financial institutions are more often than not defined as such in government statutes and through regulations, the category of 'institution' in the social sciences is less about entities established for various reasons or purposes than it is an idea at the intersection between the individual and society (Scott 2008). In this section, we consider a number of the threads of argument in the social sciences about institutions and institutionalism.

Writers of surveys about research on institutions often begin by acknowledging the importance of Max Weber's late nineteenth-century bureaucracies. Sociologists often value Weber's work more than contemporary institutional theorists do and this is partly because Weber was more interested in the centralization of administrative functions in the state through the Industrial Revolution than in the ontological status of institutions in modern societies and economies. Nonetheless, his work inspired a research programme that has lasted for more than a century. Wilson (1989), for example, writes about the irrationalities of modern bureaucratic behaviour and provides various ethnographies of life lived within large pension funds and the financial services industry. O'Barr and Conley (1992) discuss the latter in their work on the culture of institutional investors, while Riles (2011) looks at the formalization of decision-making in global financial institutions. In part, this research tradition has focused on the mentality of bureaucracies and the persistence of institutions in the face of economic imperatives. Shonfield (1965) and Galbraith (1967), writing on the postwar experiences of the United Kingdom and United States respectively, reflect on the influence of this research tradition, so situate corporations in the context of the modern state rather than the market.

A break with this tradition came with North's (1990: 4) assertion that institutions, in the first instance, 'are perfectly analogous to the rules of the game in a competitive team sport'. More specifically, he had in mind formal systems of rules such as constitutions and regulatory frameworks that provide individuals with a well-defined action space through which to realize their objectives while imposing limits on individual behaviour that would violate, in some way, the collective interest in a well-functioning and predictable environment. Formal systems of rules are also general principles that may include, for example, the protection of private property and of freely made commitments or contracts between private agents. He also made reference to informal rules, or what others refer to as norms and conventions. For some theorists, like Brennan et al. (2014), norms and conventions come before formal systems of rules, for they form the basis of the subsequent codification of standards of conduct.

It is possible that formal and informal systems of rules can exist without an administrative apparatus. Rawls's (1971) theory of justice simply requires individuals in a state of nature or, as he described it, the original position, to conduct a series of thought experiments. In these they must imagine a set of rules that would be consistent with their long-term interests, but they would not know what particular social position they would occupy when the mind game turned into the experienced world. However, few theorists are so sanguine. Most believe that sanctions and incentives backed by coercion are necessary if people are to follow the rules in circumstances where some have more power than others (Milhaupt and Pistor 2008; Posner 1986). In our world, the nation-state provides these functions, distinguished, of course, by history and geography (past dependence) (Gertler 2017). Therefore, we can reasonably suppose that a set of rules can be given a specific organizational *form* over and above its existence as a set of ideals (Scott 2008). Insofar as the nation-state, along with its regulatory agencies, embodies these rules, something other than the state itself sustains their legitimacy.

We should notice, however, that the theory of rules as institutions has certain shortcomings. First, rules as institutions are only effective if they are parsimonious, coherent, and complementary. In other words, there are well-defined boundaries between rules; each is transparent in relation to the others; and, as a set, they complement and reinforce one another. Second, rules as institutions are only effective if they are salient and have a mechanism or mechanisms enabling them to evolve to remain relevant as circumstances change. Third, rules as institutions must, in some sense, be self-generative in application so that they do not require agents to interpret their salience, meaning, or relative status as events change. In other words, there is a degree of idealism embedded in rules as institutions, which, in effect, discounts the possibility that the institutions charged with realizing the virtues of agreed rules will dominate the meaning attributed to them and their application.

The theory of rules as institutions has some of the same shortcomings as H. L. A. Hart's (1961) positive theory of law. As Dworkin (1986) showed, the real world of 'hard cases' needs something more than rules if justice is to be done. He suggested that behind rules as institutions lie moral ideals. When rules conflict with one another, when complexity confounds their coherence, and when one rule is not enough to make a decision but a combination of them simply adds to the confusion, a higher order may be needed to bring resolution if not common agreement. By this logic, rules are insufficient; real institutions with authority and legitimacy are needed to make the decisions that rules by themselves are unable to produce. This is one way of explaining how and why the US Federal Reserve Bank jettisoned its rulebook during the GFC: it was, and still is, more than an agency designed to implement the rules of monetary policy-making. Quite literally, it claimed the authority and responsibility to act on behalf of society in the absence of effective rules.

While rules as institutions provide a rationale for the state and its administrative functions, the real world of institutions is more challenging. Here, there are two schools of thought. Roe (2006) and others argue that government agencies tend to be established to 'solve' problems not amenable to solution through established procedures, markets, or organizations. He suggests, however, that once established, these agencies have a life of their own and become a permanent feature of the institutional landscape. As such, the 'real' world of regulatory agencies is dominated by overlapping, competing, and inconsistent institutions that separately claim legitimacy but together complicate, even paralyse, effective decision-making and policymaking. Public choice theorists such as Steger (2002) go one step further by arguing that state agencies and institutions have 'constituencies' that sustain their powers and authority in return for favours. One way or another, conflict within and between institutions is commonplace. Often the reconciliation of such conflicts, while entirely commendable, is typically either partial or ineffective, so limiting what policymakers can accomplish.

ORGANIZATIONS, INSIDE AND OUT

In our discussion of the nature and status of institutional investors, we noted that these types of entities are normally identified as and labelled 'financial institutions'. As well, we have suggested that their status, in this regard, is due in part to their size and significance for modern economies. Standing between savers and investors, institutional investors provide a set of functions that are essential to contemporary market economies, and underwrite economic growth and development. We have also suggested that, in part, they owe their authority and legitimacy to the fact that they embody certain rules, or modes of performance, which in their organizational manifestations represent elements analogous to North's 'rules of the game'. Most importantly, we sought to discount the idealism of the new institutionalism in favour of a realist conception of these privileged entities, which matches Davis's (2015) interest in the lived life of organizations.

This returns us to the point made that institutions are also organizations. However, as suggested, not all organizations are institutions. In other words, not all organizations have the formal or informal status attributed to institutions—the status that embodies important social functions, rules, or objectives. To explain, consider the place of pension funds and sovereign wealth funds in modern societies. These entities have important economic, financial, and social functions consistent with their privileged locations between savers and investors. They also embody and, through their activities, underwrite the rules of the game, including the rules underwriting the process of intermediation. Finally, their privileged positions as the exclusive custodians of participants' and beneficiaries' welfare suggest that they carry significant social responsibilities over and above fulfilling important economic and financial functions in and between financial markets.[4]

If financial institutions are also organizations, how are we to conceptualize organizations? March and Simon's (1958) answer to the question has had a long-lived influence in the field of organization studies. They began with a distinction between so-called 'formal' and 'informal' organizations, supposing that the former have distinctive legal forms and boundaries that provide them with an identity. By implication, informal organizations are loose arrangements between people committed to collaboration and cooperation. March and Simon focus on the former. This is consistent with treatments of financial institutions as organizations, though we are mindful of the role that informal organizations can play in promoting institutional innovation (see Chapter 10). March and Simon suggested, in a strategy that Bowles (2004) also used, that it is easier to explain what an organization is by reference to examples. Their exemplars were US Steel, the Red Cross, and the New York State Highways Authority. By implication, organizations can be found in the private sector, the not-for-profit sector, and in government.

Their approach to the study of organizations broke with traditional studies of bureaucracies in a number of ways. Although not directly reported in their book and subsequent research, it is evident that they were keen observers of the life of 'real' organizations—how they arrange their activities, frame their decision-making, and evolve. Their work, along with that of their colleagues at Carnegie Mellon University, sought to characterize the internal logic of large organizations.[5] As the research programme progressed, they framed the study of organizations around routines and constraints, eschewing an optimization framework focused on rational agents in favour of behaviour in context (Simon 1956). This logic was expressed in a variety of ways, most obviously in Cyert and March's (1963) behavioural theory of the firm. Five key issues animated Cyert and March's analytical framework of organizations, namely their internal coordination, the motivations of their employees and participants, conflict, the assignment of decision rights within them, and innovation. These issues also underpin our book.

March and Simon (1958: 4) took as given what constitutes an organization and its attributes. Their definition is revealing: relying on a biological analogy, they suggested that 'organizations are assemblages of interacting human beings' with a 'high [degree of] specificity of structure and coordination within organizations—as contrasted with the diffuse and variable relations *among* organizations and among unorganized individuals'. We notice that this definition makes no reference to markets and hierarchies, the principal–agent problem, or the purpose or intended outcomes of organizations. These issues were brought to the fore by those who followed in their wake, notably Williamson (1975) on transaction costs, Lancaster (1975) on the objective function of firms, and Meckling and Jensen (1976) and Jensen (1993) on the principal–agent problem. Most importantly, March and Simon do not refer to the distinctive attributes of certain types of organizations. Later work sympathetic to their framework recognized that certain forces, including 'mimetic mechanisms', tend, as Scott (2008) suggested, to induce isomorphism within specific fields of endeavour.

Economic theories of organizations are based on the nexus between means and ends. Put slightly differently, given certain goals and objectives, it is assumed that economic agents choose an organizational form and related decision-making mechanisms to optimize those goals and objectives. By contrast, March and Simon and those inspired by their framework looked past organizational form and related decision-making mechanisms and sought to understand how, within those parameters, organizations go about their business and adapt (more or less) to changes in the external environment. If the environment in which a certain type of organization operates is stable and rewards routine practice, then the fit-for-purpose issue can be put aside in favour of a solely internal perspective. This is hardly the case for organizations like financial institutions, which operate in contemporary financial markets. As we noted, risk and uncertainty are ever present—because of the costs and consequences of dealing with risk and uncertainty, there is a premium on innovation, whether in organizational decision-making or in the actual form and functions of organizations.

The costs and consequences of organizational inertia were the subjects of Jensen's (1993) critique of the performance of major American corporations, and the theoretical frameworks of the time that failed to grasp the significance of global economic integration. For Jensen, the key issue was the entrenchment of senior managers more concerned about their prerogatives than about sustaining the adaptive potential of their organizations. He also suggested that senior managers were not nearly as sensitive as they should have been to the interests of shareholders who bore the brunt of financial markets discounting the shareholder value. His solution was to re-establish a connection between senior manager compensation and shareholder value, relying on financial markets to impose discipline on corporate strategy and decision-making. Whether or not this was an effective or desirable innovation is widely debated. For our purposes, it is apparent that the entrenchment of senior managers in financial institutions insulated from market competition can have significant long-term costs for beneficiaries and participants.

ORGANIZATIONS, NETWORKS, AND RESOURCES

Beginning with the issue of intermediation allowed us to locate the objects of our study (asset owners of various types, including pension funds and sovereign wealth funds) at the interface between savers and investors. The related academic research supposes that certain types of financial institutions are best placed to sustain the relationship between decentralized savers and the myriad investment opportunities available at home and abroad. This makes it easy to draw an analogy between banks and asset owners, such as pension funds and sovereign wealth funds, in relation to this particular function—see Mayer and Vives (1993) on the logic of intermediation. Having established the status of financial institutions, we were able to erect a bridge between these types of institutions and their organizational forms. Nonetheless, there are significant differences between banks and asset owners, particularly with regard to how they organize the process that produces risk-adjusted rates of returns.

A key difference between banks and asset owners is in the degree to which banks hold a wide range of services and functions internally, while both large and small asset owners tend to outsource many tasks and functions. In the interests of distinguishing between these two types of financial institutions rather than making a profound statement of fact, it could be said that, to reap the benefits of holding clients across a wide variety of transactions, banks tend to internalize services and functions. By this logic, banks seek to sell services to their account holders, for they recognize that the margins on core activities are low relative to the premiums they can charge for more specialized services. Asset owners, by contrast, normally provide just one 'product'—a risk-adjusted rate of return on AUM distributed to beneficiaries and participants according to their shares of AUM. However, there are other related services, including reporting on performance, providing information on investment options, and, in some cases, providing a platform through which participants make their own choices.

If banks sound like complex organizations and asset owners like simple ones, missing from this account are the various tasks and functions that go into producing a risk-adjusted rate of return. By convention, asset owners tend to outsource many of the tasks and functions needed to frame and implement an investment strategy. An archetypical organizational model is centred on a small controlling hub served by an extensive network of providers, each bound to the hub by a commercial contract that specifies the terms and conditions under which the provider produces the nominated service. By convention, it is assumed that a hub-and-spokes organization provides the hub control over each element or component in the production of risk-adjusted rates of return on AUM. As we explain in the book, it is widely assumed that this type of organization allows the controlling hub to minimize the costs of service provision by virtue of a threat that, should service providers shirk their responsibilities, the hub is able to terminate service contracts and employ other providers.

This is a highly stylized account of asset owners. It matches the argument that different types of organizations tend to be more similar within than between sectors; see, for example, Hannan and Freeman (1989) on organizational ecology. At the same time, there are banks that utilize a hub-and-spokes mode of organization and there are cases of asset owners choosing to insource rather than outsource. Whereas March and Simon and those who have followed in their wake focus on the internal logic of organizations, running in parallel has been a rather different perspective. In short, organizational form can be seen as an issue of competitive strategy as well as a response to the costs and benefits of different types of organizational strategies, including insourcing as opposed to outsourcing. Baker et al. (2001, 2002) have characterized the latter issue in terms of 'make or buy', or, to put it differently, whether to produce the service or set of services needed to create the final product within the organization (make), or to purchase the service or set of services from external providers (buy).

Coase's (1937) analytical framework has been revived by scholars seeking to understand how and why firms develop over time and space, grow in size but then unbundle their activities, sometimes internalize functions and at other times externalize them. One way or another, the boundaries are blurred between what March and Simon assumed to be stand-alone organizations and those, albeit related ones, that are intimately bound to a dominant or host organization or set of organizations. Coase's insight on the make-or-buy phenomenon has been developed in a number of ways, being represented, for example, in Oliver Williamson's (1975) distinction between markets and hierarchies. More recently, this issue has been reconceptualized in terms of networks, supply chains, and global production platforms. There are various ways of tackling these themes. Benkler (2002) develops an economic sociology of exchange and information networks; Grossman and Helpman (2004, 2005) integrate the economics of outsourcing with the patterns of international trade; and Coe and Yeung (2015) provide the definitive geography of global supply chains and production platforms.

It is worth noting that Coase, March, and Simon shared a number of common concerns, even if their respective approaches appear different. For Coase, the driving force behind the establishment and growth of the firm was the entrepreneur. In his analysis, property rights gave the entrepreneur the authority to set the agenda and the power needed to command others to carry it through. For March and Simon, there was no controlling central figure or person in authority able to exert control over the entire organization. In their world, authority and power were contested and conflict identified as an ever-present threat to the coherence of organizations. Coase acknowledged the significance of the issue but bypassed it, whereas March and Simon brought it to the centre of their analytical framework. In both cases, the coordination of organizations was the key issue, even if Coase was able to invoke a golden rule whereby diminishing returns to scale placed an upper limit on the size of firms. Issues of power, coordination, and organizational size are also evident in recent research on the organization of firms in the global economy (Helpman et al. 2008).

Like March and Simon, the model of the firm that Coase expounded was the product of close observation of the world around him. However, it is important to notice the differences. Coase systematically explained his knowledge and understanding of the growth and organizational development of firms in British cities prior to the Second World War. In this respect, his world was not that different from the world of 'industrial districts' that Alfred Marshall described in the late nineteenth and early twentieth centuries. By contrast, March and Simon focused on American corporate capitalism, which was a product of wartime industrial policy, managed development, and sustained economic growth in the 1950s. Globalization at first empowered major American corporations and then came to haunt them when overseas competitors began to infiltrate the domestic markets. As offshore markets developed and as communication technologies expanded their geographical reach, American companies responded to heightened competition at home by dissembling their production systems functionally and spatially. In effect, competitive pressures forced corporations to become more adept at managing themselves, including adapting their organizational forms and functions.

It is not surprising, therefore, that there was a revolution in how organizations were conceptualized. Simplistic ideas of settled organizational form and functions were left behind in favour of analytical frameworks that treated them as strategic variables. Attention has shifted from the study of organizations with well-defined boundaries to the study of the capabilities and resources available to senior managers (Helfat et al. 2007). At issue is the management of related tasks and functions within, between, and among organizations, which complement and compete with one another for a share of the value in sectors and industries. Throughout our book, we are mindful of the capabilities and resources available to the senior managers of financial institutions, situating the make-or-buy issue in the context of the ability of senior managers to realize their ambitions.

BUILDING BLOCKS

With a view to appreciating what follows in the book, in this section we identify the intellectual building blocks that underpin our analytical framework. Chapter by chapter, these building blocks will become familiar to organization theorists and practitioners alike. A number of distinctive elements or components to these building blocks, however, require recognition from the outset and, in summary terms, these are set out as follows.

A crucial building block is a model of how financial institutions like asset owners are governed and managed. The ultimate owners of an institution's AUM are the participants and beneficiaries of the institution (Morrison and Wilhelm 2008). Typically, the governing boards of these institutions represent the interests of the participants and beneficiaries, frequently nominated or elected because of their affiliations rather than their financial skills and expertise. More often than not, participants and beneficiaries are unable to exercise exit, voice, or loyalty. By design, the governing boards of these institutions fulfil these functions. The governing boards are also the employers of the senior executives charged with the responsibility of conceiving and implementing the asset owners' investment strategies. In short, 'principals' are silent and remote and 'representatives' are those with whom they have an affinity protect their interests; the latter, in turn, employ 'agents' to make good on their best interests. Senior managers then either outsource or insource the production of risk-adjusted rates of return subject to the approval of governing boards.

Setting the target risk-adjusted rate of return is the responsibility of governing boards, subject to fiduciary duty, the beneficiaries' underlying interests, and the organization's capabilities and resources. We could assume that there is a close match between the chosen target—the beneficiaries' interests—and the capacity of the organization to realize it. In fact, experience shows that target rates of return are often poorly specified and inadequate in terms of providing senior managers with a mandate to manage the investment process. Furthermore, an organizational form and an inherited set of functions that are inconsistent with rate-of-return objectives can encumber managers (Clark and Urwin 2008a). The persistence of such mismatches can be explained in a variety of ways. First, governing boards may have no incentive to change organizational form and functions. Second, these institutions may be poorly resourced, notwithstanding their responsibilities. Third, financial markets may be so unpredictable that target rates of return are inconsistent and misconceived in terms of the market environment (Clark 2014).

In setting targets and producing rates of return, financial institutions rely on three types of assets. Human capital, namely skills and expertise, and the organization's decision-making procedures are important 'intangible' assets. The electronic infrastructure that collects, distributes, and analyses market information is a fundamentally important 'tangible' asset. An institution's human capital can be of high quality, with a level of commitment that matches its goals and objectives. Equally, an institution's human capital could be relatively poor, and subject to a set of incentives and sanctions inconsistent with its goals and objectives. An institution may be well managed through decision-making protocols and procedures that enhance the performance of the investment management process. Then again, this need not be the case. Likewise, the electronic infrastructure of an organization can underpin employees' skills and expertise and facilitate investment decision-making. Yet, this is not always or everywhere the case. The participants and beneficiaries of an institution bear the costs and consequences of inadequate human capital, poor decision-making procedures, and antiquated information systems.

Throughout, our analysis plays off the significance of these three types of assets. We also refer to organizations' capabilities and resources, where the former can be defined in terms of the capacity of an organization to get things done and the latter refers to what is available within an organization to facilitate decision-making. There is some overlap between capabilities and resources in that the capacity to get things done relies on having the resources to do so (Helfat et al. 2007). We are mindful of our experience in this regard where, for example, it has been found that some financial institutions are able to get things done at a level of sophistication not expected given the resources available. Effective senior managers adapt to their environments, in some cases compensating for inadequate resources by varying the form and functions of their institution in relation to what is available outside the organization. We are also mindful that financial institutions are often resource poor but staffed by motivated individuals whose professional careers and reputations are dependent upon getting things done within a resource-constrained environment.

A key strategic decision is whether to produce the target rate of return within the organization or through the combination of external suppliers from the market for financial services. The make-or-buy issue was, for many years, resolved in favour of buying the suite of services needed to produce the target rate of return. The hub-and-spokes model of organization may provide the board and senior executives with the power and authority (respectively) to coordinate the processes of choosing external suppliers, negotiating contracts, and monitoring performance. In the final resort, the institution's capabilities and resources (augmented by consultants) determine the number of external providers and how frequently they are changed. Indeed, consultants have played a very important role in framing and implementing investment strategy. In these ways, intermediation has dominated the industry. More recently, however, larger asset owners have varied the mix between make and buy by introducing in-house functions related to the determination of investment strategy and its implementation.

Notice the way in which we represent the make-or-buy decision. Being a deliberate strategic decision made by an institution's board, it seeks to affect the organization's *form* as well as its functions. In doing so, it is a decision that affects the boundaries of an organization, what is inside and outside of an organization, and those aspects of the organization that are subject to employment contracts as opposed to service ones. We do not assume, and there is no evidence to suggest we should, the broader proposition that the boundaries of organizations in the sector are infinitely malleable. As in any organization, management entrenchment, resource budgets, and ongoing commitments inside and outside the organization limit make-or-buy options over the short and long term. In any event, the power and authority needed to manage the insourcing process and the resulting organization can be so significant that boards and senior managers may place limits on what they 'make' so as to protect their status as well as their future options. Reintermediation via selected partnerships and commitments is a strategic response to the probable costs associated with a wholly insourced strategy.

Throughout the book, we are mindful of the ever-present contests for power between boards and senior managers over the choice of organizational forms and functions, just as we are mindful of contests for power between senior managers and investment professionals. Given the premium on human capital in the industry, and the reliance of investment institutions on star performers by asset class and across the (internal and/or external) suppliers that make up an institution's investment programme, it is inevitable that insourcing places a premium on organizational performance. Realizing the advantages of insourcing over outsourcing depends on the effective coordination between different parts of the organization and on the authority of senior managers to make timely and effective decisions with respect to the institution's goals and objectives. By contrast, outsourcing carries with it the implication that the senior managers of an institution can vary the mix of external suppliers, relying on competition between suppliers for mandates to impose discipline on the market. However, the marketplace may be highly stratified and dominated by a limited number of suppliers.

Underwriting insourcing, outsourcing, and hybrid models that combine both is the theory and practice of contract. At one level, contract is entirely commonplace, being itself one of the most important institutions of modern capitalism. Contract can be seen as both a practice and a formal agreement subject to the costs of negotiation and enforcement (Greif 2006). In some cases, contracts are complete in the sense that these documents fully specify the obligations and commitments binding the parties together whatever transpires (Bolton and Dewatripont 2005). More often than not, however, contracts are incomplete in the sense that, whatever their formal legal status, they function as frameworks rather than recipe books for cooperation and implementation with ready-made options for exit should either party wish to terminate such a relationship. In our case, contracts are important across two dimensions—within organizations (employment contracts) and between organizations (service contracts). Given the scope and depth associated with intermediation in the global financial services industry, it should be apparent that contract is an important element in the process of producing risk-adjusted rates of return.

It is evident that contract is embedded in organization theory, including Coase's (1937) theory of the firm, Williamson's (1975) theory of transaction costs, and Grossman and Helpman's (2004, 2005) theory of outsourcing and offshoring. However, attempts have been made to distinguish between the norms and conventions underwriting commercial relationships, and the formal edifice of contract that carries with it legally codified obligations and commitments (see, for example, Macneil (1981) and, more recently, Bathelt and Glückler (2011) on relational conceptions of commercial exchange and transactions). In our treatment, we emphasize the processes and practices associated with contracting, whether inside or outside organizations. Whereas there is merit in recognizing that commercial relationships are bound together by societal expectations, we suggest that these types of relationships are, more often than not, framed in the shadow of law. Likewise, we suggest that the evident trust between parties to contracts in the financial services industry and other industries is made possible by the threat of law.

The final, but perhaps most important, building block underpinning our analysis is recognition of the distinctive environment in which financial institutions operate—global financial markets that are subject to risk and uncertainty. As indicated in the Introduction, we distinguish between risk, which is typically framed by reference to expectations based on experience, and uncertainty, which allows for events and circumstances that fundamentally stop our models integrating the past, present, and future. We recognize that the boundary between risk and uncertainty varies over time, especially if we look at the near future in relation to the long term. We also recognize that financial markets function in space and time—financial institutions have home jurisdictions; they are subject to home bias in terms of their investment strategies; and they frame expectations on experience that is itself anchored in a market or set of markets. One of the most important developments of the past twenty-five years has been the realization that ambitious target rates of return must inevitably take into account the opportunities on the margins of markets.

Here, then, is one of the key challenges facing Western financial institutions in the twenty-first century. These institutions relied on well-functioning markets, sustained by shared investment practices and expectations, and underpinned by regulatory institutions with a record of success in dampening irrational exuberance (Shiller 2005). Over the past couple of decades, doubts have been raised about the underlying stability of these markets. Furthermore, Western financial institutions have sought an investment premium, extending their reach to markets not nearly as transparent or efficient as their home ones. At issue is the degree to which financial institutions as organizations are capable of adapting to the new realities in home markets. Equally important is the degree to which financial institutions as organizations are able to be effective long-term investors in far-off markets that require new ways of organizing the governance and management of these institutions. Whereas much of the academic literature is concerned with the challenges of investing over time, we show that investing over space and time requires organizational innovation.

NOTES

1. Readers will note that the title of this chapter references Scott's (2008) book of the same title (excluding the subtitle). We are pleased to refer to his work, in part because he is a valued colleague and in part because of the clarity of his treatise. As will become clear, our purpose here is rather different from his—we are concerned to explain institutions as organizations whereas his goal was to bring clarity to the theoretical debate about the role of institutions in society.
2. See 18 US Code § 20, https://www.law.cornell.edu/uscode/text/18/20.
3. This was what the actions of the US Board of Governors of the Federal Reserve System indicated during the GFC. Although historically focused on banks and their default risks, the board extended its reach to multifunctional financial entities like Morgan Stanley, investment banks like Lehman Brothers, and insurance companies like American International Group (AIG) (Geithner 2014).
4. By virtue of statute and regulation, certain types of institutions, including financial ones, may be required to have specific governance structures and systems, as well as certain management functions. In addition, regulators may require certain types of decision-making procedures along with formal consultation with various shareholders and/or stakeholders.

5. In many respects, members of the Carnegie School had the advantage of being able to observe and be involved in large organizations in the Pittsburgh region, a city that then attracted the headquarters of many industrial corporations. There has been surprisingly little commentary on this aspect of their research, although it can be glimpsed in Williamson's (1975) theory of transaction costs. Subsequently, aspects of their research procedures were formalized by Clark's (1998) 'close dialogue' and Helper's (2000) 'field studies'.

3

The Architecture of Information

As suggested in Chapter 1, the map of finance was underwritten by the principles of finance and, in particular, the efficient market hypothesis (Wójcik et al. 2013). At base, this doctrine is framed by three assumptions or propositions (Litterman et al. 2004). First, the efficiency of financial markets depends on the volume and integrity of relevant information. Second, market prices fully reflect the available information, so promote the efficient allocation of resources between competing opportunities. Third, to the extent that information asymmetries exist, the search for market advantage will, inevitably, price those corners of the market leaving little opportunity for consistent abnormal returns. Even so, it has long been recognized that market agents do not have the same capacity to process information or, for that matter, make sense of information in a timely manner. The very idea of informationally efficient markets has been subject to trenchant criticism (Grossman and Stiglitz 1980).

In this book, we show that the scope of financial institutions depends on the processing of information internal to institutions, and between institutions and their market providers. Our concern is about the governance of financial institutions, with particular attention to the relationships between senior managers and portfolio managers in the context of strategic choices about insourcing, outsourcing, and offshoring. It was noted in Chapter 2 that these types of organizations have three kinds of intangible assets—human capital, institution-specific decision-making procedures, and the infrastructure for processing information. In this chapter, we focus on the design and management of financial institutions' information systems. We focus on the interface between geographically spread financial institutions, centralized financial markets, and return-seeking investment strategies on the margins of markets.

The next section of the chapter, 'The Information–Industry Nexus', provides a brief account of the growth of the global finance industry, emphasizing its autonomy from industrial capitalism. We argue that the premium on local knowledge was systematically discounted over the second half of the twentieth century by the intellectual apparatus accompanying portfolio management. This is followed by a discussion of the theory of the firm, and our own assessment of the applicability of this logic to financial institutions and to economic geography more generally (Dicken 2011; Taylor and Asheim 2001). Throughout, we emphasize the importance of information in the finance industry, the dependence of the industry on the valuation, and deployment of information within and outside financial institutions through return-seeking investment strategies. It is also emphasized that these institutions face an increasingly hostile market environment, which has prompted investment in systems of information processing aimed at exploiting opportunities on the margins of global financial markets.

Inspired by Storper and Venables (2004) and the distinction made by Bathelt and Glückler (2011) to the effect that information flows occur through either 'pipelines' (systems of information distribution) or 'buzz' (informal networks), in the penultimate section of the chapter, namely 'Investment on the Margin', we focus on the information-processing attributes of investment strategies aimed at realizing superior rates of return on the margins of markets. In the conclusion, we consider the implications of our analysis of the imperatives driving a representative investment institution and how this type of entity might deal with the emerging realities of twenty-first-century global financial markets. In large part, this chapter is analytical, focused on principles and practices rather than case studies of particular institutions in their home jurisdictions. It is arguable that financial institutions share with more conventional types of firms the same market imperatives—including the costs and benefits of insourcing as opposed to outsourcing and offshoring. However, financial institutions operate in a quite distinctive environment with particular factors driving behaviour. Articulating these imperatives is the goal of this chapter.

THE INFORMATION–INDUSTRY NEXUS

For the first fifty years of the twentieth century, it was reasonable to suppose that banks, relying on large corporations for their business, financed industrial capitalism. From the early stages of the Industrial Revolution, this 'model' had a distinctive geographical footprint that persisted in many countries through to the second half of the twentieth century (Martin 1999). Closely held corporations served by local banking institutions, which together controlled large parts of national economies, represented the dominant model of continental European capitalism (Clark and Wójcik 2007; Dore 2000). In the Anglo-American world, however, household saving was increasingly tied to workplace pension schemes, which assumed an institutional form (and function) separate from their sponsors (Clark 2000; Dixon 2012). The disconnection between bank-led industrial capitalism and third-party, savings-led financial capitalism was evident in the United Kingdom and the United States by the mid-1970s (witness the Wilson Report 1980).

For much of the twentieth century, the asset allocation policies of pension funds, insurance companies, and related institutions were formulaic and subject to government regulation. There were limits on equity and overseas investment and, in many jurisdictions, these institutions were required to hold a certain portion of their assets in domestic government bonds. These restrictions were lifted by Anglo-American governments through the 1980s, although some US states maintained restrictions for longer and, in a number of cases, continue to do so (Mitchell et al. 2000). These restrictions were also commonplace in continental Europe until the introduction of the euro, when most were eliminated. Through to the 'big bang' of 1986, UK financial institutions pursued rather rudimentary investment strategies hemmed in by regulation and accepted convention. As the constraints were lifted, and market liberalization empowered a new form of financial capitalism, these institutions took aim at the remnants of industrial capitalism.

Underwriting the deregulation of financial institutions and markets was a revolution in financial theory and practice. One thread of this revolution was the widespread adoption of modern portfolio theory (MPT) (Markowitz 1952a). In conjunction with a liberal conception of fiduciary duty, MPT facilitated a switch in risk assessment from individual investments to the investment portfolios of institutions. In a sense, the decision of whether or not to invest in a particular security (company stock or government bond) was replaced with an assessment of the risk profiles of asset classes and how those 'summed-up' to the entire portfolio. A second thread in the revolution was adoption of the efficient markets hypothesis (EMH), which encouraged the belief that traded securities were properly priced and that the risk and return profiles of securities could be meaningfully projected into the future. The neoclassical theory of finance provided a recipe book for portfolio investment (Ho and Lee 2004) and, arguably, the global financial crisis (GFC).

In effect, the premium on local knowledge was discounted. In its place, financial products were developed, representing segments or slices of asset classes with distinctive industry and geographical characteristics. Instead of trading a handful of company securities based on expert knowledge or some informational advantage, financial institutions were offered products that carried with them risk and return characteristics based on historical trends. The design of these products was, and remains, dependent on simulating their underlying properties, informed by theories of market movement and cross-correlations with other financial instruments. Instead of a premium on local knowledge, the premium has been on product design and performance, in which relationships between product providers and consumers have replaced relationships with 'insiders'. If buzz is important, it is framed as a matter of the rate of return preferences and the expectations of product purchasers.

Two other aspects of the financial market are crucial to this chapter. It is self-evident that London and New York dominate their respective financial 'hinterlands'. Although both have been nationally and internationally significant for many years (centuries in the case of London), their current hegemony is owed to three intersecting forces or market dynamics. Most obviously, both markets have benefited from the public listing of corporate and government securities (including continental Europe). As the volume of financial assets grew through workplace pension saving, the benefits of public listing were accompanied by discounting the power of major shareholders, and the rise of 'universal owners' who were content to remain in the minority and largely silent (Hawley and Williams 2007). Moreover, with rather weak and immature financial markets dominating many developing economies, London and New York became magnets for European and international portfolio managers (Clark 2002).

Notwithstanding the reliance of financial institutions on these and other, smaller markets, these same institutions have also sought to manage their relationships with geographically dispersed clients. Whether by inertia or the continuing significance of client–financial institution relationships, financial markets have acted as giant vacuum engines, using pipelines to collect assets from dispersed sources and channel them to centralized switch points in the global economy. As indicated in Chapter 2, this has been made possible by the development of market intermediaries such as custodian banks, asset managers, and third-party brokers, which locate close to financial markets in order to manage the placement, switching, and distribution process. These pipelines have been so successful, in fact, that many financial institutions have largely given up their own systems in favour of market intermediaries. This has allowed sponsors to remain 'remotely located' relative to global and national financial markets.

INSTITUTIONAL SIZE AND SCOPE

Much of the literature on the size and scope of the modern firm begins with Coase's (1937) seminal paper. Coase sought to explain how and why firms internalize tasks and functions relative to the market for services. Utilizing standard microeconomic tools (for example, average and marginal costs), he was able to show that firms grow in size to the extent that the costs associated with increasing size (including complexity) are more than offset by the benefits (including flexibility) that accrue to entrepreneur coordinators when they hold tasks and functions internal to the firm. His argument was based on a rather inchoate theory of the employment contract (cf. Hart and Moore 1999). In effect, he distinguished between what modern theorists of the firm term (internal) relational or incomplete contracts and (external) discrete or complete contracts (Macneil 1980; see also Baker et al. 2002).[1]

When augmented by reference to the separation of owners from managers, which is characteristic of modern firms (Easterbrook and Fischel 1991), transaction costs (Williamson 1975), and sunk costs (Clark and Wrigley 1997), Coase provides the beginnings of an analytical rationale for the size and scope of industrial enterprises. Nonetheless, his conception of the firm is rather idealized given the coexistence of different types of employees subject to different incentive systems inside and outside the somewhat arbitrary boundaries of modern firms. The limits of this particular perspective are obvious. For example, the claimed distinction between relational and discrete contracts seems to favour a (large) firm-centred arrangement of production and supply where, in fact, other arrangements could be just as desirable. Jensen (1993) contended that relational contracts are often self-defeating because they reinforce the inertia of entrenched managers against the ever-changing circumstances of competitive markets.

It is arguable that the Internet, through inexpensive and virtually instantaneous electronic communication networks like Twitter and Facebook, has profoundly altered the terms of trade. The comparative advantage is now found in the decentralized networks of suppliers and producers who drive down the costs of production and promote innovation (Benkler 2006). Whereas Coase emphasized the costs of finding relevant market information on potential suppliers, as well as potential market opportunities, as crucial impediments to outsourcing tasks and functions, this type of information is increasingly available at a click. The retention of production at a centralized location is less important than hitherto assumed. Grossman and Rossi-Hansberg (2008: 1978) suggest that 'revolutionary advances in transportation and communications technology have weakened the link between labour specialization and geographic concentration, making it increasingly viable to separate tasks in time and space'.

Gene Grossman and his colleagues also acknowledge that search costs are important, reflecting the analytical logic of Coase (1937) if not his assessment of what is possible in space and time. Grossman and Helpman (2005) suggested that outsourcing requires firms to find suitable partners with expertise consistent with their requirements. They need to convince them to 'customize' their production systems to be consistent with the systems of the 'home' company. They must also be responsive to the terms and conditions of agreed contracts and to changes in those contracts in response to markets. By their account, firms seek distant partners that are simultaneously committed to the firm *and* are flexible with respect to unanticipated changes in the terms of agreed relationships. Grossman and Helpman suggest that finding these types of partners may be difficult—large and deep markets (cities) are deemed preferable to small and thin ones.

Largely ignored in their analysis are issues related to the governance of the home firm and how this intersects with the governance of networks of decentralized suppliers. At one level, they suggest that the home firm's preference for flexible external networks means that the relationship between the firm and its extended networks may be best conceptualized in terms of incomplete contracts. Suppliers are functionally part of the firm and could be treated as such, even if they are located outside its formal boundaries and outside the borders of the home firm's jurisdiction. Even so, if suppliers are located in large urban markets, the home firm may attempt to control these suppliers via discrete and complete contracts rather than relational and incomplete contracts. However, the search costs involved in switching suppliers may be low, given existing knowledge of other suppliers gleaned through initial searches for current partners. In a similar manner, suppliers may well resist customizing their production systems, given the possibilities of switching to other firms that offer more advantageous conditions.[2]

The control of suppliers or partners is a significant issue and has two dimensions. In Chapter 4, we distinguish between the authority of senior managers and the mechanisms that coordinate the firm and its production systems (internal, external, and offshore). Much of the literature on the digital economy assumes that the relationships between firms, partners, and suppliers are bilateral (Pareto optimal) and often short in duration. By contrast, much of the literature on the modern firm assumes that authority is crucial for setting goals and objectives, just as the efficient management of the component parts that make up the production and sale of the final product is crucial in realizing those objectives. By this logic, authority is a necessary condition for effective coordination. In the absence of an active owner, authority may be highly contested inside and outside the firm. The allocation of 'decision rights' and how they are exercised is vital for the functional performance of firms.

Recognizing the governance costs associated with dispersed networks of suppliers, Grossman and Helpman (2005) locate authority with the home firm. They suppose that suppliers operating at a distance are controlled by complete contracts that stipulate the nature and performance of their production. Grossman and Rossi-Hansberg (2008) distinguish between suppliers according to their specific tasks and functions, believing that detailed rulebooks or sets of instructions can govern suppliers and the configuration of production. By this assessment, it is efficient to offshore tasks and functions when the home institution is able to orchestrate the coordination of tasks and functions, when there is an ease of substitution between suppliers, and when there are complementarities between suppliers and home production systems.

GOVERNANCE OF FINANCIAL INSTITUTIONS

Theories of the modern firm are, more often than not, based on entities that make and sell commodities. The analytical logic relies on tangible or physical assets. The coordination of labour and capital is a crucial task of senior managers, recognizing that production can take place at home or offshore from the firm's notional headquarters. Notwithstanding absent or silent owners, authority (decision rights) over the coordination of the firm is located with senior managers and is distributed down through the firm by virtue of an established hierarchy of roles and responsibilities. If markets are an alternative to hierarchies (Williamson 1975), the choice of markets over insourcing is presumably exercised by senior managers on behalf of their owners.

By contrast, financial institutions do not make and sell commodities. They produce a rate of return via decisions made about the appropriate mix of asset classes and the implementation or execution of investment strategies through portfolio managers (Campbell and Viceira 2002). Financial institutions rely on two intangible assets—human capital and the process of decision-making—and one tangible one, namely a data and information system. As in other types of firms, owners are either absent or silent. Although one might think that this would give senior managers a great deal of authority over the production process, because there is a premium on human capital, the exercise of authority is mediated by the need to sustain cooperation between senior managers and portfolio managers (see Chapter 4). As Rajan and Zingales (2001) note, flat hierarchies are characteristic of human-capital-intensive industries (see also Teece 2000).

Here, we suggest that the governance 'problem' of large financial institutions is framed by reference to authority and coordination (the powers and responsibilities of senior managers) and the skills and expertise (human capital) of portfolio managers. Skills are distinguished from talent in the sense that the former are owed to formal training and education relevant to responsibilities, while the latter reflects domain-specific knowledge and experience. As such, the tasks and functions of portfolio managers are specialized and distinguishable, for example, by asset class, style of investment, industry, and geographical association. Furthermore, portfolio managers run teams of similarly specialized individuals, binding team members together by reference to common performance objectives, incentive programmes, and prospective opportunities (inside and outside the institution). There is a market for talented portfolio managers and their teams (see Che and Yoo (2001) on the logic of team-based systems of production and Rosen (1981) on the market for 'super' talent).

As noted, the product produced by financial institutions can be conceptualized as the planned risk-adjusted rate of return on assets under management (AUM). This rate of return target can be seen as representative of the goals and objectives of the entire institution, or it can be distinguished or differentiated by reference to the goals and objectives of the institution's clients. Some institutions, like pension funds, have a single target rate of return. Other types of financial institutions bring together a myriad of clients each with their own target rates of return. Even so, there are significant incentives for clients and producers to pool the available AUM to reap economies of scale in the management process, the governance and oversight of investment, and in the nature and volume of transactions in financial markets. For argument's sake, we assume that our representative institution has a single rate of return target.

We assume that the target rate of return is provided to senior managers by the client. This may be an explicit mandate or it may be inferred by senior managers, given the long-term commitments of the client. Senior managers then frame the institution's investment strategy, focusing on the optimal mix of asset classes that should achieve the target rate of return over some preferred time horizon. Given the volume of AUM, tranches of assets are allocated to the various asset classes that make up the optimal investment portfolio. Very simply, assuming AUM of £100, £50 might be allocated to domestic equities, £30 to government bonds, £15 to tangible assets, and £5 held as cash. Assuming the institution has the relevant portfolio managers, this allocation provides assets to the investment teams within the institution to manage on behalf of the ultimate clients or sponsors. Senior managers view their investment teams as complimentary tasks and functions. However, portfolio managers typically view one another as rivals for the allocation of investment funds. Reputation is based, in part, on the volume of AUM.

We also assume that senior managers either allocate funds to third parties that provide asset-specific investment products (for example, active domestic equity or passive domestic equity), or they allocate funds to their own portfolio managers to 'make' products (returns) that mimic or are superior to the available products in the market. If they outsource, the institution's managers engage in searches for external providers; here, they focus on the relative performance of managers and monitor the performance of selected providers. If they 'make' their own products (insource), their performance (in terms of costs and rates of return) is, inevitably, judged against what is available in the market. A successful outsourcing institution has senior managers with skills, experience, and judgement consistent with those they hire. Likewise, successful insourcing institutions have internal portfolio managers with the talent and skills at least equal to those who might be hired in the external market.[3]

Whether it makes or buys financial products, our representative institution relies on financial markets to realize its target rate of return. Directly or indirectly, it holds the traded securities of companies, governments, other investment houses, and related synthetic products. One way or another, its investment performance depends on the flow of market information. Senior managers setting the institution's strategic asset allocation rely on data on the long-term performance of asset classes (separately and together). Senior managers seeking to determine whether to make or buy portfolio investment products rely on data on the costs and market performances of competing options. Managers seeking to hire external providers rely on data on the market performance of third-party providers. Finally, portfolio managers seeking to realize asset-specific rate of return targets rely on data on market opportunities over the short, medium, and long term.

The quality and quantity of information are thus important factors in the effective governance of these institutions. Senior managers seeking to realize the institution's rate of return objectives through its strategic plan and the coordination of portfolio managers' investments have an interest in monitoring portfolio managers' actions. In part, oversight reinforces a priori agreements about the nature and scope of investment policies, the risks associated with those policies, and how the policies of separate investment teams cohere and complement one another (Clark 2002). This may involve, for example, the daily transmission of information to senior managers on the flow of transactions, current positions against benchmarks, risk profiles, and the nature and status of outstanding positions (bets on market momentum).

By this logic, senior managers rely on information to impose their authority on investment teams and ensure that coordination is both effective and consistent over time. Failure, in terms of an oversight or the subversion of information or monitoring systems, can result in a crisis—the so-called 'rogue trader' phenomenon. If this type of failure flows on to other institutions, counterparties, and market makers, it can result in market failure. Therefore, there is a premium on the timely flow and veracity of information internal to the institution, just as there is a premium on access to information on financial markets.

THE ARCHITECTURE OF FINANCIAL INFORMATION

On the supply side of the equation, the financial services industry is concentrated in global, national, and, to a limited extent, regional nodes. Tokyo, Shanghai, London, and New York are the primary international financial nodes, overshadowing national financial centres such as Sydney, Singapore, and Frankfurt, which, in turn, cast large shadows over their respective regional centres such as Melbourne, Manchester, and Munich (Porteous 1999). Institutional consumers of financial services, by contrast, tend to locate within, or adjacent to, national and regional population centres, thus matching the locations of their primary sponsors. Whereas New York, with significant offshoots in Chicago, Los Angeles, and Miami, dominates the US financial services industry, public-sector pension funds are found in every state and in many municipalities.

The search for suppliers is a two-way process. Institutions seeking suppliers signal the market about their needs and expectations, while on the other side, potential suppliers signal institutions about their particular attributes and expertise. Conceived in these terms, markets are highly decentralized and information is widely dispersed (Spence 1977). As a result, the search process, negotiation over contracts, and the assessment of actual and potential suppliers can be a costly affair. In the finance industry, however, potential suppliers are not dispersed over time and space, but instead are concentrated in global and national financial centres with offshoots in major regional centres.[4]

Coase noted that intermediaries can make a difference to search costs, but the problems of time and space remain significant. In the financial services industry, the spatial concentration of potential suppliers is reinforced by co-located market intermediaries whose purpose it is to screen, sort, and recommend relevant suppliers to financial institutions. Intermediaries like Mercer and Willis Towers Watson have become significant for collecting data on market suppliers; they package it in parcels relevant to different types of investment services and then distribute it to institutional consumers of financial services on a timely basis (see Chapter 8). Furthermore, the largest providers of financial services seek to bypass market intermediaries by establishing relationships with the larger financial institutions, thereby absorbing the costs of market intermediation. In some smaller countries dominated by relatively few large financial institutions, intermediation has, in effect, been absorbed.[5]

There are significant economies of scale in the collection, packaging, and distribution of financial market performance data on a 24-hour/365-day basis. Companies such as Thomson Reuters and Bloomberg dominate this segment of the financial services industry, with market performance data distributed to institutional consumers on an almost real-time basis from national and global financial centres. Furthermore, they provide data in large and small bundles with display routines, analytical tools, and routines for sifting and searching data for the most relevant indicators of performance. For financial institutions that have their own internal portfolio managers, Cerulli Associates and Reuters have obviated the need to collect and manage most market data. Indeed, the existence of these types of intermediaries has made portfolio investment-at-a-distance possible in the sense that being located on the margins of Europe relative to London does not appear to carry a price (in terms of access to data that most other market participants hold).

Notice, however, that data providers on the supply side of the market do not certify the veracity of their products. Their role is to collect, package, and distribute data rather than determine whether the data can be trusted. In any event, in most developed economies, the behaviour of agents and institutions in the financial services industry is regulated by legal principles such as fiduciary duty and/or statute-based rules and regulations regarding honesty and conflicts of interest. Moreover, given the costs and consequences of a failure to observe legal requirements as well as industry norms and conventions, many institutions in the industry have their own audit and compliance departments. Alternatively, in a manner consistent with the practice of intermediation in the industry, this function may be outsourced to specialized independent service providers.

In sum, the financial services industry is awash with information. It is distributed through electronic communication networks that resemble pipelines: Bathelt and Glückler (2011) refer to the ways in which information is distributed through 'trans-local pipelines' with 'often predefined goals planned in advance'. To realize their goals and objectives, they distinguish between the unorganized and sometimes spontaneous actions of individual agents seeking one another as part of the process of gathering information (buzz), and the deliberate use of information pipelines by institutions. In the financial services industry, pipelines of information are similar in form and function to what Casson (1997) refers to as channels of communication. Most importantly, we would suggest that the virtues of these pipelines of information are to be found in the 'width of the pipes' (the volume of information that can be communicated) and the 'speed of the flows' (real-time access to spatially dispersed market information).[6]

Financial institutions typically share pipelines of information in that they use common service providers to bundle and distribute data. In Figure 3.1, we provide a schematic representation of the information flows inside and outside

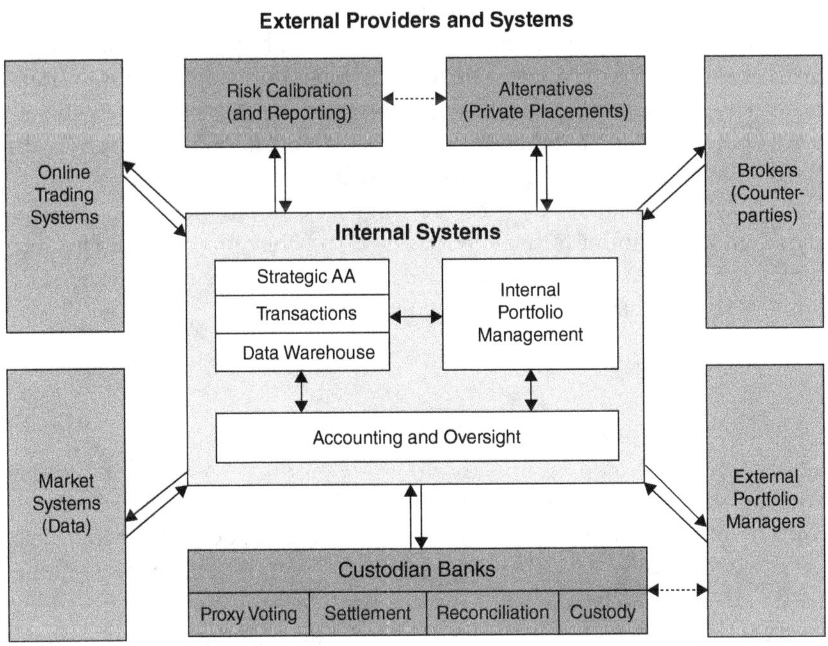

Figure 3.1. Financial institutions—pipelines of information

Source: Authors

financial institutions such as pension funds, insurance companies, and sovereign wealth funds. Unless a financial institution is extremely large, these types of entities rely on six elements. These are:

(i) external pipelines of market data (bottom left-hand side);
(ii) the pipelines of custodial banks and related service providers (bottom);
(iii) the providers of standardized reporting systems that allow financial institutions to communicate with external managers, receive their reports, and oversee their performance (bottom right-hand side);
(iv) the direct communications with brokers and online trading systems via electronic channels of communication (top right-hand side and top left-hand side);
(v) the intermediaries that specialize in risk assessment (top left); and, all the while,
(vi) the data from portfolio investment providers (top right).

In some institutions, external pipelines go through the institution to the relevant function or office. In others, the flow of information is enveloped in an enterprise-wide information system. Given the premium on imposing authority and ensuring coordination between functions, this may result in bespoke or tailor-made networks of communication that are based on industry standards, but modified for the specific circumstances of the institution. At this level, standardized pipelines of information are mediated by the heterogeneity of financial institutions in terms of their histories and geographies (for example, their relationships with sponsors, regulators, and beneficiaries) (see generally Von Hippel 2005). At another level, whether an institution or a sponsor can afford its own information systems typically depends on AUM. Smaller institutions have little option other than to piggyback on external pipelines, while relying on their administrative hierarchies as the frame of reference for electronic reporting. As such, in small funds, 'buzz' may have to compensate for rudimentary channels of electronic communication.

INVESTMENT ON THE MARGIN

Over the past fifteen to twenty years, many institutions have failed to meet their rate of return targets. Discount rates have declined over the past twenty years, systematically reducing the benefits of a balanced portfolio of equities and bonds while, in the case of defined benefit (DB) pension schemes, adding significantly to prospective liabilities. Figure 3.2 displays the monthly discount rates on thirty-year UK government bonds (gilts) since the late 1990s. The precipitous decline in discount rates from the mid-1990s onwards in many

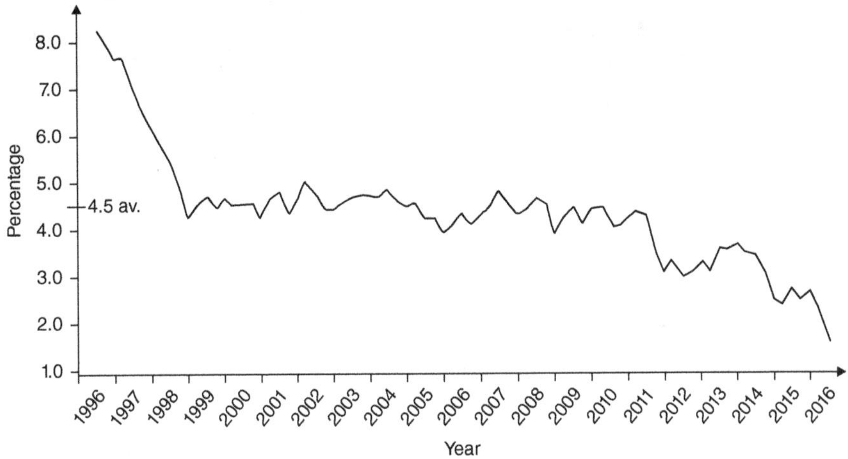

Figure 3.2. UK monthly thirty-year bond yields, 1996–2016
Source: Authors, Bloomberg

developed economies has been argued by some to reflect the benefits of globalization as well as the easing of commodity prices. Just as importantly, the US Fed has used 'easy money' policies to stabilize the US economy in the face of repeated financial crises. The effects of this policy have flowed onto other countries, notably the United Kingdom and emerging markets. One result has been the discounting of returns on savings, and the concomitant search for higher returns in traded and non-traded securities.

Anglo-American equity markets have failed to produce, over much the same period, an average rate of return much above 3 per cent (real) per year. The equity-risk premium, so important for investment strategy over the past fifty years (Dimson et al. 2002), has withered. Figure 3.3 displays the gap between assumed yearly rates of return reported for US state pension-fund systems and actual returns on a balanced portfolio of US equities and bonds.[7] Many US state government pension institutions assume rates of return in the order of 6 to 8 per cent per year. When looked at over the past ten or so years, realized US portfolio returns have been subject to considerable market volatility, with episodes of high returns followed by episodes of low returns. Equally, there is widespread recognition that the risks associated with an index-based balanced portfolio are much larger than is often appreciated. Shortfalls in target rates of return and growing liabilities threaten the viability of many different types of financial institutions, both public and private. Not surprisingly, institutions have looked for alternatives to make up the difference (see Jones 2012).

Financial institutions have sought to realize their rate of return targets by shifting asset allocations towards asset classes quite different from conventional

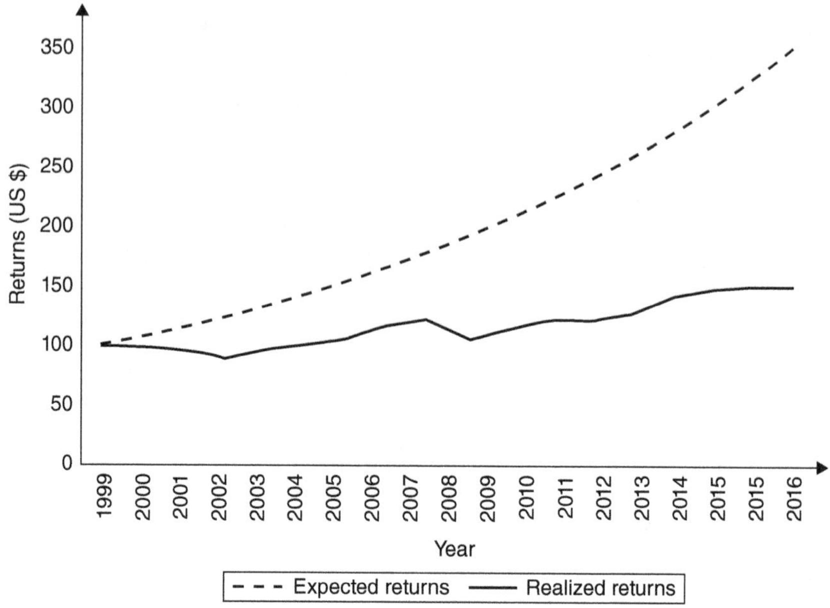

Figure 3.3. Expected and realized returns

Source: Authors

traded equities and debt. One approach has been to invest on the margin, seeking to take advantage of the growth prospects and momentum associated with emerging markets. We refer to three types of strategies towards which funds have gravitated to meet their return objectives. First, funds have sought *pipeline extensions* using established communication channels and pipelines of information to access geographies previously not included in their investment portfolios. A related strategy involves *pipelines and buzz* where institutions compensate for imperfect information systems by investing in a market presence that complements existing pipelines. Finally, some institutions have discounted pipelines in favour of *buzz*, pursuing relationship-intensive investment strategies that are not amenable to management through conventional channels of communication.[8]

Pipeline Extensions

The logic behind investing in emerging markets via pipeline extensions is entirely conventional. Working from senior managers' strategic asset allocations, financial institutions reallocate a portion of their existing AUM to portfolio managers who specialize in emerging markets either internal or external to the organization. If institutions insource, this strategy depends on the availability of relevant information pipelines, the degree to which senior managers can oversee these new responsibilities, and the level of complexity that such strategies add to the institution. Outsourcing is often an easier option, piggybacking as it does on existing network relationships with external portfolio managers. As such, the shift towards emerging markets via pipeline extensions tends not to disrupt internal commitments, while external providers rely on spatially extensive information channels without having to establish new pipelines from scratch. In these circumstances, senior managers can use discrete contracts to govern external providers, rather than negotiate with their own portfolio managers who may be entrenched in their own disciplines.

With reference to Figure 3.1, the relevant pipelines connect senior managers to external portfolio managers (and those managers to markets around the world). Senior managers typically utilize benchmarks and related measures of performance to govern external portfolio managers via these pipelines, which also connect them to global data providers. In these ways, pipelines of information reach beyond existing channels of communication through the core markets of the global financial system to peripheral markets. In a sense, this type of information architecture reinforces the pre-eminence of global financial markets as switch points through which information and financial assets flow in a mutually reinforcing manner. Financial institutions without experience or knowledge of emerging markets rely on third-party channels of communication located in global financial centres.

Pipelines and Buzz

A characteristic of both emerging markets and alternative investments is the significance of information asymmetries among market participants and providers. As a result, market pricing does not always reflect underlying value and is subject to unanticipated volatility. The standard techniques used to price risk in developed markets and thereby integrate dispersed traders via pipelines of trading information are known to be ineffective. One response, especially important for emerging markets, has been to establish off-site offices and portfolio investment teams close, or adjacent to, markets deemed important for realizing financial institutions' rate of return targets. In this manner, financial institutions may insource and offshore the framing and implementation of asset- and market-specific investment strategies. In doing so, this strategy places a premium on control. Consequently, offshore teams may have limited autonomy and remain closely connected to senior managers via proprietary or dedicated pipelines of information and communication that link the home institution with its offshore entities. This is a 'pipelines and buzz' corporate strategy.

The success of this approach depends on a number of factors. Obviously, the real-time effectiveness of the control systems and information pipelines connecting the home entity to its offshore sites is a crucial factor. More problematic, perhaps, is the issue of loyalty. That is, the degree to which off-site officers see their career prospects through the lens provided by their home institutions or in local opportunities. If senior managers control their off-site managers with reporting regimes that limit autonomy, it may be difficult to recruit and retain portfolio managers in those markets. If authority is the issue, the home institution may place its own employees at off-site markets on a secondment basis. However, this may, of course, militate against penetrating and holding the attention of the local market networks that are so important for market intelligence (buzz). The alternative is to outsource offshore activities, using either contracts to tie providers to the home institution, or partial ownership of providers to claim a share in local pipelines of information.

Buzz

Given the risks involved with investing at a distance, Western financial institutions have also sought access to private equity and hedge funds because they are often located near the core centres of the global financial system. These types of financial products are typically accessed on an outsourced basis. Whereas knowledge of the suppliers of these types of products is easily obtained through existing third-party pipelines of information, knowledge of how vendors produce their rates of return is very difficult to obtain using conventional sources. Indeed, the promise of private equity and hedge funds is often found in their proprietary systems of investment management and their access to information not otherwise available to financial institutions. In this respect, *buzz* has two dimensions and may not be shared with financial institutions *before* they enter into contractual relationships with desired vendors.

Such is the premium on higher rates of return that financial institutions may willingly give up their claim to authority and control over the management of their own internal portfolio managers. In addition, senior managers may be forced to forego contractual terms and conditions typically applied to conventional external fund managers, especially regarding the generation and distribution of information on investment strategy and related proprietary trading systems. At the same time, given that realizing strategic asset allocation goals involves assembling complementary investments, contracts with private equity and hedge fund providers are often accompanied by rulebooks that proscribe certain types of activities, including certain risks that would or could affect the institution's overall risk profile.

Rulebooks can be extensive. For example, they can limit the use of certain kinds of credit and debt instruments (privileging listed equities); they can define permissible levels of leverage and they can provide upper and lower bounds on assumed risks and fund volatility. Rulebooks can exclude certain types of stocks and securities (the object of other portfolio managers) and set time limits on positions taken on stock options. In a similar manner, they can exclude certain industries and geographies, while allocating any risks associated with currency exposures to the portfolio manager. Rulebooks can undermine the authority of the home institution by setting terms for the desired liquidity of investments. They can also set the terms for reporting on risk exposure and the performance of risk control systems, namely the mechanisms whereby breaches of rulebooks are reported to the home institution and the penalties that may be invoked in relation to such reported breaches. In some cases, given that they are less a matter of contract and more a matter of operational management, the home institution can vary the rulebooks at a moment's notice.

In these ways, the rulebooks accompanying contracts with the vendors of alternative investments are quite different from those used in commodity supply-chain management. Grossman and Helpman (2005) suggest that the rulebooks accompanying offshoring contracts set the ways in which vendors produce the products desired by the home institution. By contrast, in the financial services industry vendors have significant autonomy over how they produce desired rates of return; the limits imposed by financial institutions seek to protect the authority and the risks borne by clients.

CONCLUSIONS

Pipelines of information are important in many industries, not just global financial services (Maskell 2014). The flow of assets to global financial markets, the widespread adoption of the principles of financial theory, and the role of third parties in channelling information have, over the past two decades, reinforced confidence in formal models of governance and investment management. So significant, in fact, has been the development of third-party systems of information processing that it has been possible to talk of an 'end of geography' in financial markets (O'Brien 1992). In this vein, it has been suggested that the information architecture and systems of information flow integrating market players around the world have made the position of financial institutions much less significant in time and space than the global centres of financial trading. This argument matches observations made by economic geographers about the compression of time and space characteristic of advanced industrial economies (Harvey 1989; Warf 2006, 2011).

Coase and his followers suggest that firms tend to grow in size to compensate for the search costs involved in finding and retaining market partners.

Those concerned about the scope of large multinational firms have argued that the development of cheap and efficient systems of transportation and communication made outsourcing and offshoring possible. Specifically, Grossman and his colleagues argue that these types of search costs have been radically discounted, particularly in distant but large developing economies. One effect of the global diffusion of electronic information and processing has been the incorporation of distant sites of production into the production systems located in the core markets of Western economies. Here, again, it is argued that pipelines of information have radically discounted the virtues of buzz.

The subject of this chapter has been the information architecture of financial institutions and markets. We noted that these types of institutions are rather different from the firms commonly associated with commodity-producing industries. Whereas industrial, manufacturing, and retail firms typically claim market advantage by virtue of their tangible assets, financial institutions have few obvious tangible assets, so they rely on intangible ones such as human capital and their systems of decision-making (governance), as well as their (tangible) systems of information processing. This point is developed in subsequent chapters with regard to the governance of human capital and decision-making. In this chapter, we have focused on information processing, noting that, at one level, financial markets are simply massive information-processing machines. There is an extraordinary premium on managing information both internal and external to the institution.

It is commonly held that buzz dominates financial markets. For example, in stories told about the importance of coffee houses in seventeenth-century London, through to the importance of family and the old school tie in the years leading up to the big bang in 1986 (Dale 2004), buzz was and remains important. This is especially true for those whose careers rely on networks that bind together financial institutions with the institutions that manage and invest those assets. Nonetheless, we contend that pipelines have come to dominate buzz in part because of the sheer volume of information to be channelled and moved around institutions within and between networks of market providers. Indeed, some of the world's largest financial service providers are simultaneously sites of asset holding and switching, sites for market information and data, and sites of asset placement with portfolio managers.

Throughout, our argument is framed with reference to the authority of senior managers who set institution-wide investment and management policies. For them, information is a vital ingredient in the governance of financial institutions, for it provides portfolio managers, whether internal or external to the institution, with oversight and control. Whereas this may be conceived of in terms of coordinating complementary elements of an overall investment strategy, equally important is the control of information as a means of exerting authority over the elements that make up the realization of planned target rates of return. This is as important inside the institution as it is outside it;

portfolio managers are highly specialized and, in their own domain, often uniquely placed with respect to the skills and competence of those who oversee their activities. The flow of information over time and space inside and outside the institution can give rise to management strategies that mix and match pipelines of information with buzz.

It should be noted that the doctrines underwriting MPT and the information architecture sustaining flows of financial assets within and between global financial centres have faced very challenging circumstances over the past few decades. In the aftermath of the Asian crisis of 1997, the long-term capital management (LTCM) debacle, the technology, media, telecommunications (TMT) bubble, the subprime bubble, and now the euro crisis, financial markets have become hostile environments. Conventional models of market processes and behaviour are unreliable, even as the premium on ambitious target rates of return has significantly increased over the past decade. In this context, investment on the margins of markets has become an essential element in the investment strategies of many institutions. However, these types of environments are just as challenging as the core markets of the global financial system, albeit for different reasons. These types of markets are, quite obviously, relatively inefficient and characterized by significant information asymmetries.

In this world, buzz has reappeared as an issue of significance. However, many financial institutions are ill equipped to operate in this type of environment, especially when entry to emerging markets and adoption of the protocols that typically govern relationships with hedge funds disturb internal systems of management and the complementarities between portfolio managers. As a result, institutions have developed a variety of strategies to deal with these management conundrums. One such strategy has been to rely on global investment managers' pipelines of information, which give financial institutions an opportunity to piggyback on a third-party information infrastructure right through to the emerging markets. Another strategy has been to combine information pipelines with the collection of market-specific information and data involving (in some cases) the establishment of off-site and offshore (but internal) portfolio managers. At the limit, financial institutions have abandoned their own strategies and rely almost entirely on external portfolio managers who claim proprietary advantage in terms of their information processing over the bulge-bracket investment houses.

Here, we suggest that outsourcing and offshoring result in very different contractual systems and governance regimes compared with industrial, manufacturing, and retail networks (Grossman and Helpman 2005). Commodity supply chains and detailed rulebooks establishing how tasks and functions are produced relative to the home firm are seemingly complementary. In the global financial services industry, though, rulebooks tend to disallow certain activities, limit risk exposures, and seek to impose authority over performance and reporting. These rulebooks do not seek to determine how third parties produce rates of return; rulebooks are designed to allow considerable discretion for those charged with realizing agreed targets. As such, they are used to control the activities of external portfolio managers, which may harm the positions of institutional clients.

NOTES

1. The finance industry relies on analytical frames of reference for organizing market information. Whether imposed by theoretical principles, accepted models of measuring and pricing risk, or by evident patterns in the pricing of traded securities, the formal representation of market information is believed to guard against impulsive market behaviour, including herding, opportunism, and being caught up in speculative bubbles. Compare Ho and Lee (2004) with Hilton (2003).
2. Baker et al. (2001: 212) define relational contracts as 'self-enforcing agreements in repeated games'. They also suggest that relational contracts are 'informal agreements and unwritten codes of conduct that powerfully affect the behaviours of individuals within firms. There are often informal quid pro quos between co-workers, as well as unwritten understandings between bosses and subordinates about task assignment, promotion, and termination decisions' (Baker et al. 2002: 39). This approach resonates with Bathelt and Glückler's (2011: 6–7) relational economic geography, even if their approach is more programmatic and methodological than it is specific to a particular type of institution.
3. It is widely assumed that complete contracts are framed according to legal norms. By comparison, relational contracts are assumed framed against social norms and conventions including reciprocity, cooperation, and trust (Bowles 2004: 264–5). Whether either of these types of agreements comes to court is hardly ever considered. Notice, London provides third-party arbitration mechanisms for the resolution of disagreements over discrete contracts. Financial services and legal services are complementary industries (Beaverstock et al. 1999). These points are developed in Chapters 6 and 7.
4. Storper and Venables (2004: 354–5) emphasize face-to-face contact. They believe it is 'essential to the transmission of complex, tacit knowledge'. See also Gertler (2003). Faulconbridge (2006) points out that the communication of tacit knowledge can be an organized social practice and have a spatial reach that goes far beyond the local to the global.
5. Wójcik (2011: 145) observes that proximity between traders is very important when the issue is 'latency—the speed with which an order can reach the matching engine of the exchange, be executed, and the confirmation of its execution return to the computer from which it was sent'. It may pay high-frequency traders and certain types of hedge funds (algorithmic traders) to locate close to one another, linked by dedicated infrastructure systems. In these situations, trading at a distance through electronic pipelines may incur higher risks and a discount on returns.
6. The ways in which information is parcelled and distributed by third-party providers can frame expectations and hence market behaviour. A similar point is made

by MacKenzie (2006) when discussing the significance of the Black–Scholes model of risk pricing.

7. The data for this chart were compiled using Datastream. The expected returns line was calculated using the 126 funds in the Public Fund Survey and averaging their reported 'expected returns'. This came to roughly 7.9 per cent, which was then applied to the $100 and compounded over time. The realized line was generated by applying the realized returns from equity markets (the average of S&P 500; FTSE 100; DAX; NYA; and W5000) and fixed income markets (the average of US Bank Prime Loan—Middle Rate; US Corp Bonds; Moody's Seasoned AAA; BOFA ML US DOM MSTR—TOT RETURN IND; LIBOR; US Treasury Const Mat 1 Year—Middle Rate; US CORP BONDS MOODYS SEASONED BAA (W)—MIDDLE RATE; and UBS AU COMPOSITE BOND 1+YEARS—TOT RETURN IND) and then applying those returns to the $100 portfolio, with a 60–40 breakdown, and compounding over time.
8. In effect, this characterization matches that introduced by Clark and O'Connor (1997) where *pipeline extensions* match transparent financial products, *pipelines and buzz* match translucent products, and *buzz* matches opaque products.

4

Production of Investment Returns

Research in finance and investment management often takes as given the topography of finance—financial centres as sites for the production of financial services and financial markets as the means by which financial assets are placed and investment returns produced (Ho and Lee 2004). As noted in Chapter 3, through much of the twentieth century, financial centres and financial markets were co-located. The production and distribution of financial services were located with financial markets, thus reinforcing the shadows cast by London, New York, and Tokyo over their hinterlands. O'Brien (1992) and O'Hara (1995) contended that being able to trade at a distance from financial markets via electronic networks would spell the end of geography. Yet, large and small investment houses continue to cluster in financial centres even if their investment strategies are realized through global financial markets (Storper and Venables 2004). Even financial products can reflect their sites of production (see Hong et al. (2005) on the neighbourhood effect apparent in mutual fund products).

In Clark and Thrift's (2005) study of currency trading in a major financial institution, it was shown that the *management* of currency trading is an essential ingredient in producing returns, given the risks associated with trading currencies around the globe and between financial markets on a 24/7 basis. More broadly, financial institutions domiciled in the West have sought to extend their investment strategies to emerging financial markets to reap the benefits of long-term growth in Africa, Asia, and Latin America. In part, this reflects the search for a premium on assets under management (AUM). It also reflects a response to the adverse consequences of relative economic stagnation in the West (El-Erian 2008). For these reasons, being located in or near a 'core' financial centre is now insufficient to make good on institutions' return aspirations. Here, this issue is framed by reference to the power and authority of senior managers to adapt to these new realities. To illustrate, it is assumed there are two types of financial institutions (asset owners), large and small, with either growing or declining AUM.

We begin with Coase's (1937) theory of the firm, along with those who have been following his lead. These include Easterbrook and Fischel (1991) and Hart and Holmström (2010), as well as the related literature in economic geography by Maskell (2001), Taylor and Asheim (2001), and Scott (2008). Williamson (1975), who focuses on the coordination of the production of goods and services through 'hierarchies and markets', has inspired a significant body of research. Here, we focus our analytical lens on the significance of human capital or talent within financial institutions for the production of investment returns. There is a growing body of research on the importance of human capital for the production of value, which leads some analysts to suggest that we have entered a new era of 'cognitive capitalism' (Scott 2008). Human capital is assumed to have two key components—skill and expertise, both of which are domain-specific and largely non-substitutable.[1]

There have been few studies published on the production of investment returns (but see Demsetz 1968). There are, however, many theories that are supposed to guide investment professionals in the production of returns, including modern portfolio theory (MPT) and risk diversification (Ho and Lee 2004; Litterman et al. 2004). These rulebooks are, more often than not, highly quantitative. They reflect the transformation of the investment management industry from one dominated by intuition and privileged access to information (buzz), to one dominated by mathematical and statistical risk and return pricing systems, executed by professionals employed by financial institutions (Amin and Thrift 1992). The widespread adoption of the Black–Scholes theorem by market participants on a global basis in the lead-up to the global financial crisis (GFC) is indicative of the institutionalization of investment management (MacKenzie 2006). Producing returns depends on managing systems, motivating employees, and facilitating coordination within and between institutions in relation to market risk and uncertainty.

Investment institutions face many challenges when managing talented professionals who command a scarcity premium in financial centres. Although neglected through the 'golden era' of Western financial markets, the GFC revealed the importance of effective investment management. Senior managers are the key to timely institutional coordination and the exercise of judgement in response to unanticipated shifts in market performance. This is what senior managers do, or could do, if they have the power and authority to do so. We show that financial institutions often contest senior managers' power and authority. Relying on talented individuals to produce investment returns tends to discount the capacity of senior managers to put the institution's interest ahead of other claims. This is manifest in different ways in large and small institutions, in growing and declining circumstances, and when investing in spatially extensive financial markets.

COASE, CONTRACT, AND LOCATION

Coase's (1937) theory of the firm can read as a precursor to Demsetz's (1968) theory of transaction costs, Williamson's (1975) hierarchies and markets, Krugman's (1991) increasing returns to scale and the virtues of agglomeration economies, and Bathelt and Glückler's (2011) relational theory of organizations, market economies, and geography. At a stretch, Coase can be allied to recent developments in the economic theory of the firm that focus on issues of fairness and motivation (see Hart and Moore 2008). Coase emphasized the authority and powers of entrepreneurs, but also noted that there are limits to the exercise of such powers, given community norms and conventions; he cited common law expectations about the obligations of 'masters' and 'servants'.[2] He was also concerned to demonstrate that the assumptions underpinning his analytical framework were 'tractable' and 'realistic'.

At the heart of his theory of the firm was the entrepreneur-coordinator—a person who, by virtue of owning the firm and exerting the authority set out in the relevant firm-wide employment contract, 'directs production' and the 'coordination of the various factors of production' (Coase 1937: 388). In Coase's account, power comes with the ownership of property. The authority to command others is legitimated by contract. Key to his model of the firm, Coase assumed that one type of employment contract would be sufficient to cover a firm's employees. He also assumed that employment contracts would be written in such a way as to provide the entrepreneur-coordinator with wide discretion over the management of the tasks and functions that make up the production process. Any limits to this discretion were shared between local firms, rather than being idiosyncratic. Coase suggested that the incompleteness of labour contracts has the virtue of enabling the variation of employees' tasks and functions without incurring the costs of renegotiation.

Coase provided an explanation of how and why firms grow in size, of when market arrangements become viable, and of the costs of complexity. He also provided a rationale for the spatial configuration of the firm, suggesting that the costs of organizing production increase as the spatial extent of those activities expands beyond the site of production. In part, he suggested that the broader the spatial field of the firm, the more diverse or dissimilar are its activities, and hence the higher the costs of coordination and the prospect of making mistakes. He suggested that firms would grow in size at a particular place to the extent that technology allows for the concentration of the factors of production and innovation, which, in combination, allows firms to serve spatially extensive markets.

Five assumptions underpinned his analysis. First, labour is a homogeneous factor of production. Second, labour is plentiful, both within the company and in the local market. Third, labour can be switched at will between the tasks and functions that make up the production process. Presumably, then, productivity is the product of an entrepreneur's power and authority. Fourth, the production of manufactured commodities depends on the combination of labour (undifferentiated), capital (machinery), and raw materials (resources)—motivation is not an issue. Finally, each firm is an island unto itself. He deemed the production of commodities not contingent on cooperation with other firms (local or distant); for Coase, markets simply provided options for self-organization. He assumed that if the entrepreneur contracted external providers, those relationships were Pareto optimal (see Bolton and Dewatripont 2005).

In what follows, each assumption is contested with reference to the financial services industry. In the first instance, the entrepreneur-coordinator is replaced with senior managers who do not have the powers of a company owner. Her control over the production process is dependent on her location in the corporate hierarchy. It is assumed that the tasks and functions of certain classes of labour are distinct and separable. This means that, in certain cases, both sides of the employment relationship seek function-related labour contracts. Senior managers use the segmentation of the workforce to enhance their authority, while employees seek a premium on their roles and responsibilities that is more or less consistent with their notional 'price' in the external market. It is also assumed that, over the short run, there is limited supply of certain skills and expertise in the market. Managers can be held hostage by those upon whom they rely to produce the firm's returns. As a result, switching labour between tasks and functions can be problematic.

Rosen (1986) was one of the first theorists to recognize the limited supply of highly skilled professionals. He was particularly interested in how talented individuals used tournaments to represent the process that enabled certain individuals to play the market to reap enormous profits and thus claim a premium on their skills and expertise. More generally, Lucas (2009) emphasized the importance of human capital in modern economies and of how those who have a claim on ideas can earn a premium in the economy. Overlapping the Chicago tradition, Florida's (2002a, 2002b) work on the nature of talent, and the process whereby certain localities become havens for highly talented individuals, are key contributions to understanding the economic structure of urban labour markets. Similarly, A. J. Scott's (2008) argument that the increasing importance of cognitive reasoning in modern economies is embedded in the hegemony of metropolitan economies has deepened our understanding of the topology of talent.

Nonetheless, there are a number of puzzles in Coase's model of the firm. Why assume that an entrepreneur-coordinator starting out as a small firm would internalize the production process? Coase's answer, it seems, depended on the benefits obtained when using a single contract to govern the various tasks and functions needed to produce the final product. Implied as well is a presumption that an entrepreneur's power and authority *within* the firm are unconstrained; if entrepreneurs were to rely on external contractors, the norms and conventions of bilateral contracting would constrain their power and authority. By contrast, contemporary evidence suggests that small and medium enterprises in commodity-producing industries tend to outsource many of their tasks and functions to local suppliers and that they only internalize activities when the latter grow to a size sufficient to take advantage of the economies of scale associated with producing within a company rather than between companies.

What exactly do the factors of production work upon to produce commodities for sale? Coase's answer was raw materials or resources. How was that possible? His answer was that rail transport had made the spatial concentration of production viable. Notice, thirty years or so later, urban economists sought to explain how and why US cities and regions had become highly specialized in terms of their industry profiles by virtue of access to resources, the costs and benefits of specific transport technologies, and the spillover benefits of co-location within industries (see Thompson (1965) on US urban growth and decline). Over time, the real costs of raw materials and resources have declined relative to labour costs, which is partly because of the increasing efficiency of capital equipment in processing raw materials. With advances in communication and transport, many companies and industries have taken on a global form, leaving behind their original geographical footprints (Beugelsdijk et al. 2010; Dicken 2011; Grossman and Helpman 2005).

Two implications follow from this brief assessment of Coase's theory of the firm. First, to the extent that skills and expertise are important in realizing the value of the many tasks and functions that make up a firm's production process, managers may lack the power to impose order on the production process and can face situations in which the market for talent compromises their authority. Embedding this prospect in the theory of the firm would seem to be an essential ingredient in making a 'modern' theory of the firm. Second, untheorized and left aside is the issue of what managers do when the factors of production do not work on raw materials to produce products. These issues are important in understanding the performance of financial institutions.

FINANCIAL INSTITUTIONS: BUILDING BLOCKS

Here are three building blocks that underpin our exposition of how financial institutions produce investment returns in the context of spatially extensive financial markets. Throughout the book, we seek to situate our analysis by reference to industry circumstances—factors that influence strategy and decision-making. Reference is also made to Coase as a way of clarifying what is particular about the industry. Inevitably, our logic is schematic in that diversity is eschewed in favour of an initial, simple, model.

Ecology of Finance

There are many types of organizations in financial markets representing the functional scope of intermediation characteristics of the financial services industry. Attempts have been made to map intermediation, from the smallest and simplest service providers through to the largest financial institutions that, through their production of investment returns, can determine the scope of intermediation in local and global markets. Assume that asset owners either produce investment returns internally, or outsource this function to asset managers, or some combination of both. We should remind the reader, though, to suggest that pension funds and the like are asset 'owners' is an assumption of convenience. As indicated in Chapter 1, in that they are subject to fiduciary principles and practices, pension funds normally represent the interests of beneficiaries. In this respect, these institutions are asset 'owners' because the ultimate owners—beneficiaries—are either silent or uninvolved.

The raw material used to produce investment returns consists of the stock of financial assets held by the asset owner, or in the case of the AUM by portfolio managers (whether internal or external to the organization). The stock of financial assets is hardly ever fixed: it can be augmented (or diluted as the case may be) by contributions (benefits), inflation (deflation), investment returns (losses), leverage (losses), and acquisitions (disestablishment). Typically, the institution (and/or its sponsor) collects the contributions from and distributes the benefits to the participants or beneficiaries. Stocks and flows are almost always transferred electronically. Beneficiaries may be geographically concentrated, as is the case of public pension plans, spatially distributed to match the geographical scope of a corporate sponsor, or found nationwide as is the case of many insurance companies. Importantly, there are significant economies of scale in the management of financial assets. Small pension funds face considerable challenges in being cost efficient.[3]

If marked 'to market', the value of the assets that owners and managers hold will vary from minute to minute as the financial markets rise and fall. In this regard, financial markets are *both* the medium and the means through which financial institutions produce investment returns. Financial markets can be public or private. The precise form of a financial market is less important for the moment than the functions it performs in bringing investors together with investment opportunities (Dixon 2012). There are significant opportunity costs in leaving assets unplaced; it is important that the stocks and flows of assets are managed in a timely and effective manner.

Managers and Workers

Formally, boards decide on strategic issues such as asset allocation and investment strategy. They delegate to senior managers the responsibility of realizing the institution's goals and objectives, including the target rate of return. In turn, senior managers realize the institution's goals and objectives through the relevant departments and sections that make up the institution, with the proviso that these tasks and functions could be produced internally or externally, or some combination of both. Notice, however, that boards may intrude upon the delegated responsibilities of senior managers, and senior managers may dispute board decisions, particularly those that compromise their ability to produce investment returns.

Producing the target rate of return relies on the human capital and decision-making procedures of the institution and its employees. The tasks and functions of the institution can be rank ordered, beginning with those that require generic skills and expertise, through to those that require domain-specific skills and expertise. Even tasks and functions that require generic skills and little expertise are likely to benefit from employees who have sector-related experience. This kind of experience can be found in other banking and non-banking organizations. At the other end of the spectrum, domain-specific skills and expertise are likely to be in short supply. These are the product of tertiary education; knowledge and understanding of the theory and practice of asset management; and judgement consistent with the segment or segments of financial markets relevant to their responsibilities (see Demsetz (1968) on the importance of judgement in financial markets).

At one end of the spectrum, some employees (Type I) rely on generic skills and expertise to perform their tasks and functions. They are offered a standard contract consistent with industry norms and conventions. At the other end of the spectrum, some employees (Type II) have domain-specific skills and expertise and are offered individualized contracts subject to market competition for other similarly placed employees. At the limit, there may be as many contracts as there are types of employees, creating constraints on the ability of senior managers to switch labour between tasks and functions. Nonetheless, those employees closer to Type II than Type I could demand a Type II-class contract for reasons of equitability and fairness, producing a cascade of contractual terms and conditions down through the institution.

Coordination

In the absence of an entrepreneur-coordinator, senior managers' claims to manage are contested in two ways. We would like to suggest that, for all the effort devoted to creating a template or formal recipe justifying the division of power and authority, competition for power can fracture the relationship between boards and managers. Just as important, managers can face significant difficulties handling employees who command a premium in the market. One response may be to introduce an overarching purpose to the organization that trumps internal contests for power and privilege. A related response might be to introduce a 'model' contract to the organization, which includes common terms of reference for judging performance and remuneration. The weighting of these 'terms' could vary according to the significance of different types of tasks and functions required to realize the institution's overarching purpose.

Many theorists of the firm doubt whether 'collective goals' are ever meaningful, noting the apparent 'gap' between formal authority, and authority in practice (see Aghion and Tirole 1997). Indeed, leading theorists of the firm have contended that organizations are, more often than not, characterized by unresolved conflict (Cyert and March 1963). This assumption is threaded through the literature, being found in many guises (see Easterbrook and Fischel 1991). One response is to use a form of contract that matches specific tasks and functions with a view to segmenting the production process in ways that enhance the power and authority of senior managers. If tasks and functions can be provided externally as well as internally, a divide-and-conquer (DAC) strategy can be sustained—with an implied threat that failure to cooperate will result in outsourcing the relevant function (see Marglin 1974). Segmentation and task-related contracts can facilitate DAC strategies, thereby enhancing control over the production process, albeit subject to bargaining. Notice that realization of the benefits of DAC depends on the authority of senior managers and the flexibility of the contract. If implementing DAC strategies requires the approval of the board, and if bargained agreements are inflexible, senior managers may find themselves impotent.

A second option would be to enrol portfolio managers into a fund-wide management system with a view to sharing responsibility for the production of investment objectives across the institution. In doing so, a horizontal process of incorporation (HPI) for realizing stated goals and objectives, including the institution's broader purpose, would augment the hierarchy of tasks and functions. Here, senior managers and portfolio managers have two distinct but complementary responsibilities. Senior managers are responsible to the higher tiers of the organization, which is often the institution's board. In the second instance, they are also responsible for enhancing cooperation across the institution. Portfolio managers have to realize their asset-specific goals and objectives *and* must be willing to compromise on their immediate interests (the status and significance of their investment teams) in relation to the objectives of the institution. Realizing a stable and reciprocal relationship between different elements of the institution is, arguably, the *raison d'être* of senior managers (Pitelis and Teece 2009). DAC strategies are simpler, but limited compared with what a successful HPI strategy could achieve.

Figure 4.1 provides a 2x2 matrix that links senior managers' strategy with the nature of labour contracts offered to an institution's employees. There are two extreme cases—instance D, where a DAC strategy is reinforced by labour

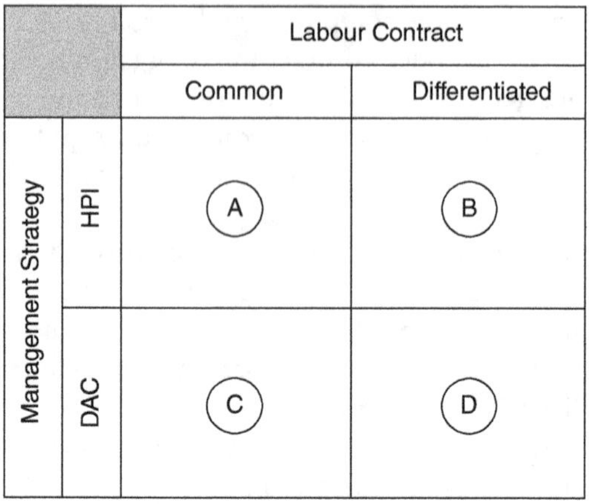

Figure 4.1. Management strategies by the nature of labour contracts

Note: Where 'common' refers to a company-wide labour contract; 'differentiated' refers to contracts by task and function; DAC is a 'divide-and-conquer' strategy of management; and HPI is a strategy of horizontal incorporation

Source: Authors

contracts differentiated by skill and expertise, and instance A, where HPI is reinforced with a common labour contract across the institution augmented, perhaps, with different weightings on the shared components of compensation according to the scarcity value of specific skills and expertise. This could, of course, degenerate into instance B, where the benefits of HPI are discounted by labour contracts that give preference to certain types of employees. It is less obvious that a DAC strategy would be accompanied by a common labour contract (instance C), except in circumstances where it is imposed by the home jurisdiction's norms and conventions. In these cases, financial institutions could spatially segment their workforces so that certain types of employees are kept at home, while other types are moved offshore to jurisdictions that enhance senior managers' overall authority.

PRODUCING INVESTMENT RETURNS

Like Gertler (2001) and Glasmeier (2000), our concern here is with the production process of financial returns in context; it is not our intention to produce theorems applicable to all organizations, industries, and places. To set the scene, we assume that there are two types of financial institutions—large and small—located at, or close to, a financial centre. It is also assumed that both types of institutions seek a long-term investment return of at least 2 per cent (net) on invested assets over and above the rate of inflation. For argument's sake, this is a rather modest rate of return target chosen to allow us to focus on key issues related to the management of financial institutions.

Stocks and Flows

The stock of AUM is comprised of five separate flows—the inflow of contributions; the outflow of paid benefits; the costs associated with investment management; the returns due to investment management; and interest paid on assets otherwise not committed. Since our institution has a real rate of return target, AUM can grow in nominal terms but decline in real terms (especially if subject to increasing costs associated with compliance and regulation). Contributions and paid benefits are predictable, if considered over a three- to five-year period. One should notice, however, that if benefit entitlements include automatic inflation adjustment, the benefits could be less predictable than the contributions. The costs associated with investment management are somewhat predictable and subject to contract. Investment returns are unpredictable, being subject to the performance of financial markets and the mix of asset classes that make up an institution's strategic asset allocation.[4]

Let us assume that our representative financial institution employs an external custodian to manage the flow of assets—the collection and disbursement of financial assets to the tasks and functions of the institution, including the production of investment returns. An institution with a small volume of AUM is likely to be a price taker in the market and to incur higher costs per unit of AUM than an institution with a large volume of AUM.[5] Large institutions are able to bargain for lower charges. Likewise, the bundling of services can allow large institutions to claim significant discounts from service providers on the overall costs of investment management. Notice that contracts for financial services tend to be open-ended. While there are start and end dates to contracts with a specific tranche of assets, contracts are often repeatedly turned over, with adjustments made when there are minor changes in the stock of assets the provider manages.

Small and Large Institutions

In Coase's (1937) world, small enterprises provide the services required to produce the company's product. By contrast, most small financial institutions contract out virtually all the services needed to produce investment returns. The set-up costs associated with internally providing the tasks and functions necessary to produce returns are significant and sunk, for the services are so specialized that their provision cannot be spread across the institution's activities. Specialist external service providers are able to discount the costs of provision by pooling clients' assets, thereby maximizing the benefits of task-specific contracts in ways that small institutions cannot achieve. Given the costs of maintaining a register of financial flows, small institutions are at a cost disadvantage compared with large institutions.

A large institution has various options, including determining which tasks and functions to produce internally, and which to purchase from the market for financial services (see Chapter 5). Evidence from the mutual fund industry suggests that insourcing has two distinct benefits. First, while outsourcing may appear to be cost-efficient, governing the relationship between the institution and its provider can incur unanticipated costs due to the rigidity of contracts and the inability of the institution to derive benefit from the market for services. Second, it would appear that the incentives driving external providers are more often 'internal' to the provider than in the relationship between the institution and the provider (Chen et al. 2004). By implication, and consistent with Coase, insourcing can facilitate the rapid redeployment of AUM. We should notice, however, that a *mix-and-switch* sourcing strategy can be in senior managers' interest if they are unable to realize the benefits associated with strategies of horizontal incorporation (HPI). While mix-and-switch strategies tend to empower managers relative to both internal and external portfolio managers, this may be inconsistent with an institution's overall goal of producing investment returns.

There are, nonetheless, two reasons why managers may combine insourcing with outsourcing on a selective basis. Managers can use outsourcing as a way of learning about new providers and/or new asset classes on the margin of the institution's strategic asset allocation; managers can also use contracts with specialist external providers as a first step towards acquiring those groups. As suggested in Chapter 7, outsourcing can facilitate the search for opportunities and learning about innovations not available within the organization.

Flexibility and Adaptation

Being flexible and adaptive to market risk and uncertainty is an essential ingredient in realizing longer-term investment return targets. A well-known hedge fund manager put it as follows: 'for the investor to thrive in [today's financial markets], he or she must think creatively and be adaptable to the changing modes of acuity. You must be able to imagine different realistic states of the world and think as both the mathematician and the artist' (Cole 2012: 14). Whereas conventional models of investment strategy focus on parcelling up and allocating the stock of financial assets to asset classes and their portfolio managers, there is a premium on flexibility that treats asset allocation as a dynamic process rather than a fixed formula (Lo 2012). In other words, it is crucial to be able to allocate and reallocate AUM between asset classes and portfolio managers in anticipation of, and in response to, market movements.

There are dangers in flexibility and adaptation: institutions may be over-responsive to perceived and actual shifts in financial markets. As recognized in the behavioural literature, being over-responsive is correlated with overconfidence (Aikman et al. 2014). Nonetheless, this model of financial markets implies that management capabilities and resources should be proportional to the volume of AUM, to the costs and benefits of time-dependent strategic asset allocation, and to the opportunities available on the margin of markets for sheltering from adverse shifts in market sentiment. If an institution is to be effective in this kind of world, managers need sufficient power and authority, both inside the organization and in relation to external providers, to reorder commitments to portfolio managers. Being a large institution with a complex array of internal and external commitments may be a disadvantage when compared with smaller organizations that, notwithstanding their limited capabilities and resources, are fleeter of foot and less entrenched in past commitments.

As we know, some flows are more predictable than others. As such, a constant rate of change is normally integrated within the organization. The more interesting cases are when changes in inflows and outflows are unexpected (see Lamont 1992). Consider the implications of the following cases for our two institutions, large and small (represented in Figure 4.2).

- Case 1: net inflow of assets; a marginal change to the existing stock of financial assets.
- Case 2: net outflow of assets; a marginal change to the existing stock of financial assets.
- Case 3: net inflow of assets; a significant change relative to the existing stock of financial assets.
- Case 4: net outflow of assets; a significant change relative to the existing stock of financial assets.

In Cases 1 and 2, the most likely response of portfolio managers is incremental adaptation, adding to or subtracting from the stock of financial assets allocated to them.[6] This type of response reinforces the status quo and requires little from managers in terms of authoritative decision-making. In a large institution, with a complement of internal portfolio managers, incremental adaptation is, more often than not, an administrative procedure. However, contracts with external providers may be asymmetrical in the sense that asset managers may be willing to accept modest inflows of assets to manage, but may be unwilling to give up, even on the margin, small volumes of AUM. Compensation for external asset managers typically includes a provision weighted in favour of larger rather than smaller volumes of AUM.

Two implications follow. First, to the extent that a large institution has a mix of internal and external portfolio managers, internal managers may disproportionately bear the consequences of marginal declines in AUM. Second, a small institution relying on external portfolio managers may have to rewrite contracts with providers to accommodate even marginal declines in AUM.

Case 3 (net inflow of assets; a significant change relative to the existing stock of financial assets) represents an important opportunity for managers in large and small institutions to revise both their investment policies and their procedures vis-à-vis asset allocation, and to adapt to actual and perceived changes in financial markets. Consider the case of a large institution: with a complement of internal portfolio managers, incremental adaptation is unlikely to absorb a significant inflow of assets. In any event, claiming a large share of the inflow of assets would mean that portfolio managers are willing to build and expand their investment teams. Not all portfolio managers have this type of flexibility: some smaller asset classes, such as private equity, can have few additional opportunities and may require long-term commitment to build capacity. By contrast, global equity portfolios may be more able to absorb additional assets, given that 'timing' depends on the state of play in global markets.

Here there are two possibilities. First, managers may use the opportunity to establish new asset classes within the organization, thereby broadening the organization's scope in areas perceived to benefit the production of investment returns. Second, managers may use the opportunity to build alliances with other related institutions, thereby broadening their knowledge of the market and sustaining their authority to innovate and adapt to longer-term trends.

In this world, smaller institutions may have the capacity to internalize a select set of asset classes that could underwrite the production of investment returns. This would empower an institution's managers in two different ways. First, the capacity to internalize an asset class, or set of asset classes, would give senior managers more power and authority over existing external providers. The terms and conditions of investment management agreements (IMAs) could be adapted in favour of the senior managers of a small but growing institution, thereby reflecting the unceasing competition in the global financial services industry for AUM. Second, the opportunity to build internal asset management capacity could provide managers with opportunities for career advancement. Success in such a venture could enable a senior manager to move on to much larger organizations. Careers are made by these opportunities.

By contrast, Case 4 (net outflow of assets; a significant change relative to the existing stock of financial assets) carries with it the seeds of destruction. Incremental adaptation cannot accommodate a significant and long-term decline in AUM. For a large organization, with an existing complement of internal portfolio managers, this can mean reducing the scope of the organization by closing whole asset classes and outsourcing any residual commitment to those classes to external providers. In doing so, senior managers may seek to distinguish between the core activities of the institution and those that are secondary when considered over the long term. In this respect, as the scope of the institution is reduced, its capacity to adapt internally to shifts and changes in global financial markets is also likely to decline. Adaptation could be found, however, in external providers.

One response may be to scale back the institution's investment return ambitions to match its reduced capabilities and resources. Another response may be to reduce the number of asset classes that make up the institution's investment strategy, thus sharpening distinctions between asset classes and, as far as possible, reducing cross-correlations between them. The first response makes few demands on managers' powers and authority. The second, however, places a premium on managers' judgement and knowledge and, consequently, can strengthen their power and authority within the institution. As a corollary, realizing the potential of a more focused and more aggressive investment strategy can mean empowering managers to pursue an active mix-and-switch sourcing strategy that is more comparable to a DAC than an HPI strategy. Boards dominated by an ethos of risk aversion are likely to favour the first response to declining volumes of AUM rather than the second.

For small institutions already reliant on external providers as opposed to internal asset managers, declining AUM means reallocating assets among external suppliers as contracts come due for renewal. Here, however, are three likely outcomes. First, small institutions are likely to become more reliant on external advisers, including asset consultants, thus foregoing opportunities to frame and execute fund-specific investment strategies. Second, small institutions with significant declines in AUM may be excluded from opportunities that innovative external asset managers provide. With limited available funds, and an inability to join clubs of like-minded investors willing to make a commitment of funds to new opportunities, small institutions are likely to be relegated to external managers willing and able to accommodate these types of investments. Third, it may become increasingly difficult for the boards of such funds to attract talented individuals as managers and/or advisers.

Figure 4.2 provides a 2x2 matrix summarizing the discussion about the interaction between the size of a financial institution and changes in the flow of assets to the institution. We shall consider two particular scenarios, Case 2 and Case 4, both of which deal with a change in the net inflow of assets that are marginal or significant to the institution. As noted, a marginal increase in the flow of assets to a small institution (instance A) is unlikely to make an appreciable difference to senior managers' asset allocation strategies. However, even a marginal increase in the flow of assets to a large institution (instance B) could be used to make a significant difference to the nature and

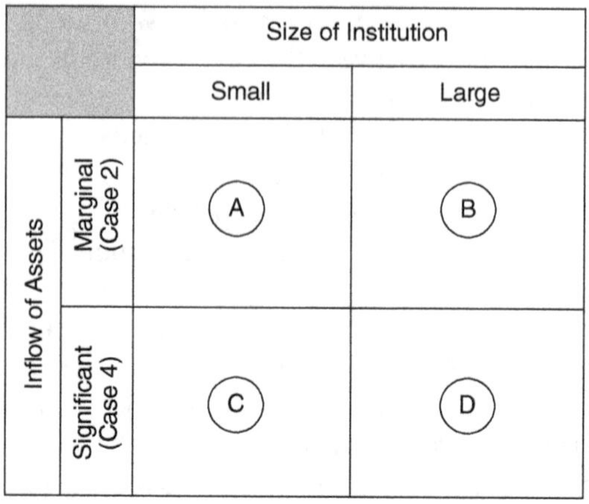

Figure 4.2. Size of a financial institution and the inflows of assets

Note: A large institution can reap the economies of scale evident in the financial services industry whereas a small institution cannot. A significant inflow of assets allows an institution the opportunity to make appreciable changes to its asset allocation in the short to medium terms, whereas a marginal change (inflows) can have differential impacts on a large institution compared to a small institution.

Source: Authors

scope of its investment strategies. A significant increase in the flow of assets to a small institution could, however, allow it to bring certain investment functions in-house, and thus broaden the scope of its activities (instance C). Likewise, a significant increase in the flow of assets to a large institution could allow it to establish new investment programmes, even offshore investment offices (instance D). In the latter case, growth may be a mixed blessing for senior managers: the scope of their responsibilities could increase dramatically but without a commensurate increase in their power and authority.

GLOBAL FINANCIAL CENTRES AND MARKETS

We assumed that our representative institutions (large and small) were co-located with a global financial centre. For example, we could refer to British financial institutions located in or close to the network of financial services that pivot on the City of London, such as Canary Wharf. This logic could be applied to US financial institutions located on the East Coast (New York City), the Midwest (Chicago), the southeast (Miami), and the West Coast. The US case is, perhaps, more geographically complex than the British one, since there is a well-developed hierarchy of financial centres focused on New York. However, even in the British case, London serves as the coordinating site for

Dublin and Edinburgh, and casts a shadow over continental European financial centres, including Amsterdam, Frankfurt, and Stockholm (Wójcik 2011).

The Base Case: Co-location

Co-location means being a near neighbour or in the immediate vicinity of a financial centre that brings together financial institutions with trading functions, a broad array of financial services, and the market for investment management. As Bathelt and Glückler (2011) and Storper and Venables (2004) have shown, co-location can bestow many advantages, including cost-effective access to untraded information and knowledge. Co-location can also discount the search costs involved in identifying, assessing, and contracting service providers. Furthermore, because service providers know that potential clients search first in their adjacent financial centre, they will locate there to take advantage of the formal and informal networks that bind together financial institutions and the remarkable range of intermediaries that make up the global financial services industry. Note that co-location facilitates the matching process, but does not necessarily constrain it, especially if the services sought are in short supply in the market.

In theory, co-location empowers the senior managers of financial institutions. Immediate access to market information and knowledge can provide managers with the insights necessary to discount the claims of portfolio managers for preferential treatment. Even so, small institutions with static or declining AUM can be marginalized; given the economies of scale inherent in the asset management industry, service providers discriminate against small institutions in favour of large institutions that can underwrite their business models. In a similar manner, a small institution with static or declining AUM will find it difficult to hire and retain skilled professionals, given opportunities on the buy side and sell side of the financial services industry. Small institutions with growing AUM may by default become the proving ground for skilled professionals with career aspirations best realized in bulge-bracket asset management houses. Whereas a mix-and-switch strategy might appear to empower senior managers, it may be the only feasible option given a vibrant market for financial skills.

The Base Case (Redux): Co-location on the Margin

Many public-sector financial institutions are located in cities that serve as administrative sites for local and state governments, some distance from the neighbouring financial centre. Equally importantly, the leading national financial centres of some countries play a secondary role to the relevant global financial centre (such as Amsterdam in relation to London, or Toronto in relation to New York). Large insurance companies that rely on geographically dispersed clients can locate in the shadow of a local financial centre that itself references a global financial centre (like Winterthur in relation to Zürich in relation to London). Similarly, large corporations with significant financial operations may be embedded in certain peripheral sites because of their past activities, but nonetheless interact with service providers in global financial centres.

Managers in small financial institutions with growing AUM often establish ongoing relationships with external consultants who have a significant presence in the relevant national and global financial centres. Small financial institutions with declining AUM find it difficult to maintain these relationships, so they become increasingly isolated from the service industry on which they rely. By contrast, the managers of large financial institutions may find a marginal location empowering in the sense that some financial institutions might exert too dominant an influence over others operating in the local jurisdiction. This can have two mutually reinforcing effects: (i) sustaining managers' attempts to build an institutional culture separate from, and at a distance from, the financial services industry; and (ii) providing senior managers with the authority to shape the functional structure of the organization in favour of its overarching goals and objectives. As such, senior managers may shift from a DAC to an HPI strategy that relies on insourcing the production of investment returns.

This is likely to be successful until senior managers are no longer prepared to pay the price of attracting the highest performing portfolio managers in certain asset classes. It may benefit an institution's managers to be simultaneously on the margin *and* close to a national and global financial centre, so that they can recruit talented portfolio managers and/or outsource functions that would otherwise undermine their power and authority in the organization. Notwithstanding the segmentation of the financial services labour market into finely distinguished tasks and functions with appropriate contracts and compensation systems, large financial institutions find it difficult to contain the ratcheting-up effects of compensation and entitlements that come with employing portfolio managers whose compensation and entitlements consist of self-referencing market terms and conditions.

The Intermediate Case: Global Market Integration

As suggested, there is a well-established spatial hierarchy of financial markets—a handful of global financial markets dominate, filtering down to national and, in some cases, regional ones (Engelen and Glasmacher 2013). Throughout the twentieth century, London markets were forced to share dominance with New York and, to some extent, Chicago and Tokyo. More recently, there has been considerable competition for dominance in the East Asian time zone, pitting Singapore, Sydney, Shanghai, and Hong Kong against one another and against the Tokyo market. Nonetheless, electronic communication systems have made possible the creation of an integrated global financial market that is subject to the trading systems and behaviour of financial institutions on a 24/7 basis and to the regulation of financial markets (O'Brien 1992; Wójcik 2011).

Large and small investment institutions located on the margin of national and global financial centres can be represented in these markets. For a small financial institution, a mix-and-switch investment management strategy can be used to access equity portfolios, whether national or international in geographical scope, index-based, or thematic in composition, and actively or passively managed. In many cases, the specific characteristics of these equity products are less important than their risk and return characteristics, which can be compared with and contrasted against industry benchmarks using common metrics over time. There would appear to be little difference between a national and an international equity portfolio in terms of ease of access: market integration allows small institutions to access the rest of the world through existing networks of local intermediaries and service providers. If there are limits to this type of mix-and-switch strategy, these limits are to be found in the internal flexibility of the institution with respect to the decision protocols used to frame and implement its investment strategy.

Large institutions seeking access to international equities to complement their domestic equity exposure can, in the first instance, use a mix-and-switch strategy, just like a small institution. If it is experiencing increasing volumes of AUM, a large institution can quickly build up a significant stake in an international equities portfolio managed by an external provider. Over a three- to five-year time horizon, its international equities portfolio could affect the institution's overall investment performance. However, if it is experiencing decreasing volumes of AUM, any switch to an international equities portfolio will require disinvestment in other investment classes managed by internal and external portfolio managers. This could be a slow process, made more problematic by discounts on management costs offered by external providers seeking to maintain their mandates in the context of the institution's overall reconfiguration of its investment portfolio. In this case, external providers may offer a mix-and-switch strategy that allows for the transfer of a portion of assets already under management from one asset class to another within the investment manager.

Most problematic would be the reallocation of AUM from internal portfolio managers (domestic equities) to external providers (international equities). As AUM internal to the institution declines, and as significant tranches of assets are switched from internal to external portfolio managers, the rationale for insourcing over outsourcing may itself be discounted. Costs are likely to rise; skilled portfolio managers are likely to leave; and the ethos of the institution may be subject to dispute within the firm through to the governing board. One response of senior managers under such pressure may be to permit internal portfolio managers (domestic equities) to establish a trading and investment function devoted to international equities. Inevitably, establishing this type of function may require hiring a small complement of employees to take responsibility for this function. Another response by managers under pressure may be to find virtue in the status quo.

The Limit Case: Realizing Value in Emerging Markets

To treat global equities products in the same way as domestic equities ones in mix-and-switch investment strategies implies assuming that the pricing of market securities is efficient at home *and* away. Even if market pricing is more efficient in Western markets than in emerging ones, the effectiveness of this type of investment strategy depends on being able to attribute an appropriate risk profile and concomitant return expectations to emerging markets. The pricing of traded securities in emerging markets is relatively opaque—and 'position' in such a market is a crucial ingredient in risk pricing (Wójcik 2013).

If global equities are subject to mispricing, and if access to Asia's economic growth prospects is fundamental to realizing their investment objectives, large and small financial institutions from the West must find ways of investing in emerging markets. They could have a presence on the ground with a view to acquiring local information and knowledge that is consistent with their investment objectives. Small financial institutions, even those with growing AUM, are likely to find this a huge challenge. Many of these institutions benefit from being close or adjacent to a global or national financial centre in their home jurisdictions. Being at a distance from markets such as Hong Kong, Singapore, and Shanghai means that senior managers of small institutions simply cannot afford the expense of a protracted search for intermediaries, vendors, or direct investment opportunities in these markets. Not surprisingly, they rely on asset consultants with a global reach based in their home markets to provide insight and advice on distant opportunities.

Recognizing the risks that come with such a strategy, recognizing the possibility that asset consultants may be unable to discriminate effectively among vendors offering long-term superior returns, and recognizing that senior managers in small institutions are likely to be risk averse (especially regarding their career objectives), small institutions are unlikely to allocate a large volume of assets to these opportunities. Should these investments fail, the overall performance of the institution would be compromised. For small institutions with declining AUM, the search costs associated with finding investment opportunities in emerging markets, combined with the caution of senior managers, are such that this type of institution is likely to fall back on the global equities portfolios that vendors from their home jurisdictions offer. Being unable to extend their geographical reach to emerging markets, these types of institutions could see their relative performance falter and decline.

Large institutions with growing AUM, by contrast, have a great deal of flexibility when searching for vendors in distant markets. They can choose vendors, especially senior managers, who best suit the interests of the institution; and they can pursue investment strategies that seek higher risk-adjusted returns, while ameliorating the possible career risks of poor performance among the senior managers. With a large tranche of assets to be allocated to emerging markets, and with the prospect of further commitments of assets over the longer term, equitable relationships can be established with asset consultants and placement agents at a distance. Furthermore, these types of institutions are able to consider the virtues or otherwise of establishing their own investment offices in distant markets, as opposed to developing joint ventures, partnerships, and/or collaborative relationships with third-party portfolio managers based in those distant markets. Each option carries advantages and disadvantages. In all cases, their effectiveness depends on the power and authority of senior managers to negotiate, monitor, and intervene where necessary in these relationships.

It has been noted elsewhere that establishing an offshore investment office within an institution, but at a distance from its management centre, can pose significant challenges (Dixon and Monk 2014). If established with limited resources and a narrow mandate consistent with identifying investment opportunities and appropriate vendors, this type of office could empower senior managers at home by giving them access to otherwise unavailable information and knowledge, either at the board level or among portfolio managers inside and outside the institution. If it failed in relation to the placement of AUM in emerging markets, it could be closed without any harm done to senior managers' reputations. However, if it were established with considerable resources and an investment mandate for framing and implementing investment strategies in emerging markets, it could become a rival organization to existing internal and external portfolio managers. Being at a distance from senior management, it might take on local characteristics instead of maintaining a commitment to the ethos of the home institution. Under these circumstances, it could accumulate power and authority sufficient to challenge home-based senior managers.

The options are likely to be more limited for large institutions with declining AUM. Given the difficulties of reallocating AUM among existing portfolio managers, establishing a new investment offshore office with a significant tranche of assets would require boards to underwrite the power and authority of senior managers. A more likely strategy would be to join other related institutions with a view to discounting the costs of establishing a presence in emerging markets. If successful, this type of institution could build up a significant offshore presence, even if it takes time and is unlikely to affect the overall investment performance of the institution. As such, it is better seen as an option on the future rather than a fully fledged investment programme. Note that in both cases, it is assumed that communication technologies and spatially extensive networks of intermediaries are more than adequate to the task of integrating decision-making at home with distant locations (see also Beaverstock 2004).

IMPLICATIONS AND CONCLUSIONS

This chapter began with Coase's (1937) model of the firm as reliant on the power and authority of the entrepreneur-coordinator to direct the production process. In his account, the entrepreneur-coordinator was responsible for assembling the inputs or raw materials used in the production process, directing the labour needed to produce output, and choosing the mix of internal and external suppliers consistent with growing the business. For Coase, the overarching legal framework determined the power and authority of the entrepreneur-coordinator: property rights established their control over raw materials and machinery, while contract law provided them with the authority to direct labour in the production process. With respect to the role of 'bosses', the connection between Coase (1937) and Marglin (1974) is more significant than often appreciated.

This chapter also demonstrated the distinctive attributes of financial institutions, especially vis-à-vis the power and authority of senior managers. Three key issues drive the analysis. First, in the absence of active 'owners', the power of senior managers is contingent on their relationships with the governing board of an institution, and with the skilled professionals responsible for the production of investment returns by asset class. These relationships are often formalized in contract and in models of management that seek to impose coherence on the institution. Second, the segmentation of the workforce is more a reflection of the premium on domain-specific skill and expertise found in financial markets than something that is imposed on unwilling workers. Both sides of the labour contract have an interest in distinguishing tasks and functions; this allows managers to exercise authority on specific issues while also allowing portfolio managers to seek advantage in contractual negotiations by reference to the market for scarce skills and expertise.

Third, this chapter demonstrated that the production of investment returns depends on allocating the flow of financial assets to portfolio managers, who then invest those assets in public or private financial markets. Returns flow back to the financial institution via positions taken in financial markets by portfolio managers, and are then distributed to beneficiaries. Nevertheless, there is a premium on asset-specific skills and expertise. In fact, this particular issue has two related dimensions. The financial institution's overall investment performance depends on the investment strategies that senior managers formulate and implement through portfolio managers. Crucially, the institution's location vis-à-vis financial markets can have significant consequences for realizing investment return objectives. References to co-location, location on the margin, global financial market integration, and emerging markets illustrated this point. Whereas Coase's managers were assumed to have control over the entire production process, the production of investment returns depends, in part, on the structure and performance of financial markets.

It is not surprising, therefore, that financial institutions, especially their portfolio managers and traders, are tempted to corner the market. In some markets, insider trading is endemic; in others, major institutions are able to move market sentiment to their advantage. Furthermore, some markets lack the transparency and discipline necessary to allow financial institutions located elsewhere to play an active and effective role. To illustrate these arguments, we drew a somewhat arbitrary distinction between 'small' and 'large' financial institutions to capture the apparent differences between institutions by size as regards their capabilities and resources in producing investment returns. We also distinguished between institutions according to whether they were growing or declining—that is, whether they were experiencing net inflows of assets or net outflows of AUM. We showed that being large with growing AUM, as opposed to being large with declining AUM, can affect the nature and scope of senior managers' options when investing locally and when investing in emerging markets.

We noted that being located on the margin of established markets in the West need not be a significant impediment to realizing planned investment returns. Even small financial institutions with limited capabilities and resources located on the margin of global financial centres can gain access to desired financial products—albeit through intermediaries such as asset consultants. Reliance on external providers can, through a mix-and-switch strategy, provide small institutions with the flexibility to vary the geographical composition and reach of their asset allocation programme. Flexibility is enhanced if the inflow of assets does not require the institution to reallocate existing commitments towards emerging markets. However, small institutions subject to a net outflow of assets can find it difficult to move assets from conventional asset classes to emerging market products in a way that can make an appreciable difference to the production of investment returns.

At best, small institutions have access to product providers willing to accept relatively small tranches of assets—most likely those offering little more than 'average' returns (against relevant benchmarks). At worst, small institutions are likely to be frozen out of emerging markets because they lack the flexibility to realign their asset management strategies. By contrast, large institutions, whether growing or declining in terms of the inflow and outflow of financial assets, can place significant tranches of assets in emerging markets—either through intermediaries or directly with providers who have substantial activities in those markets. Indeed, large institutions with significant inflows of financial assets can establish their own offices in these markets, thus bypassing intermediaries and asset managers. Here, as in small institutions, the power and authority of senior managers to innovate is a key ingredient in determining whether large institutions can realize the potential opportunities that come with size. In fact, large institutions experiencing a declining volume of assets could lack the flexibility to make swift and effective changes in the geographical composition of their asset allocation strategies.

Explanations of home bias in the allocation of financial assets tend to rely on behavioural predispositions and/or arguments to the effect that local investing is more cost-effective than global investing (Huberman 2001). This chapter has provided an explanation of home bias that relies on the underlying circumstances of funds, and the realization that the power and authority of senior managers to switch asset allocation may be so contested that the institution remains in place, rather than expanding its investment horizons to encompass the globe.

NOTES

1. Human capital, talent, and expertise are used to represent, first, the quality of labour; second, the capacity for innovation; and third, the occupation-specific realization of the value of labour (see Florida and Mellander 2014). Recent treatments emphasize the spatial concentration of human capital and the attendant consequences for urban employment and income (Glaeser et al. 2009).
2. According to Coase (1937: 393), 'a firm, therefore, consists of the system of relationships which comes into existence when the direction of resources is dependent on an entrepreneur'.
3. Industry respondents observe that financial institutions need at least five billion US dollars' worth of AUM if they are to acquire and maintain bespoke operating systems. Otherwise, they must rely on external providers and take-as-offered operating systems that are generic or (more likely) reflect the priorities of external providers. We should note that being 'small' could include local and provincial public-sector pension funds with far larger volumes of AUM, given the cost constraints that their political masters impose.
4. Consistent with the logic of the chapter, this account of financial stocks and flows references asset owners rather than asset managers. Vayanos and Woolley (2013) provide a model of the causes and consequences of flows between asset managers, which explains the incidence and significance of financial bubbles and busts in

financial markets. While there is, no doubt, a role for behavioural issues in driving senior managers' behaviour in response to changes in stocks and flows, this issue is left for another occasion.

5. Economies of scale are to be found in functions such as administration, electronic infrastructure, distribution, and compliance. There is evidence from the mutual fund industry to the effect that portfolio managers require a certain minimum volume of AUM to be effective investors, although this varies by asset class, liquidity requirements, and the scope of related investment products (Chen et al. 2004).
6. A more sophisticated response would be to accumulate the marginal increase in inflows of assets in a cash account, supplemented by planned rebalancing between asset classes, and then place these assets into 'new' positions that complement the existing ones. Here, there is a trade-off between market opportunities foregone and the prospect of reaping a return in the future from a new position and the altered asset allocation. Significant delays can incur significant opportunity costs, particularly in volatile markets.

5

Scope of Financial Institutions

As suggested in Chapter 4, financial institutions, like any other firm, must organize the production process to realize their a priori objectives. This can involve deploying their own resources to produce financial products or deciding what services to purchase from the market. The issue of insourcing versus outsourcing dominates much of the literature about the nature and scope of the firm (Hart and Holmström 2010). It resonates with related research in economic geography and management studies on the functional and geographical scope of firms in specific industries and political jurisdictions (see D'Agostino et al. 2013; Lowe and Wrigley 2010). In this chapter, we develop the model introduced in Chapter 4 to explain the scope of the tasks and functions of financial institutions.

The scope of financial institutions is analysed in terms of the choices managers face *given* the distinctive industry and national environments in which they are located. Conceptualizing choice in this manner follows recent arguments to the effect that context frames corporate structure and behaviour (Dicken and Malmberg 2001). These arguments are based on analytical frameworks that emphasize the relational elements of economy, geography, and society (Bathelt and Glückler 2011). To understand the nature of decision-making, we emphasize both the significance of assets under management (AUM) and what count as firm-specific strategic assets. As we have indicated, financial institutions have few tangible or fixed assets; they rely on human capital, governance procedures, and the information-processing systems that support human capital and decision-making. In accounting for the scope of financial institutions, we refer to the related literature in economic geography and to the significance it attributes to the relationships that sustain the effectiveness of financial institutions (see Torrance 2009).

In the next section, 'Theory of the Firm', we return to Coase's (1937) seminal paper on the firm, and the related literature on insourcing, outsourcing, and offshoring. We follow this with a discussion of recent developments that have prompted a shift in focus from 'firms as sets of transactions' to 'firms as sets of contracts'. To set the context of the analysis, we lay emphasis on the environment a representative financial institution faces, provide a rationale for the organization's decision-making, and identify the relevant assets and resources used in the production of financial returns, as well as the significance of risk and uncertainty in realizing planned outcomes. This is followed by two related sections devoted to the insourcing versus outsourcing issue and the issue of onshoring versus offshoring. The latter is best understood in relation to the former. We note that the offshoring of financial institutions is an evolving and contested issue (internal and external to these institutions).

THEORY OF THE FIRM

For Coase (1937), the question was obvious: why do entrepreneurs insource tasks and functions that could be obtained in the market? Before providing an answer to the question, Coase opened with a statement on methodology emphasizing the need for a 'tractable' and 'realistic' perspective centred on the role of the 'entrepreneur-coordinator'. We share his interest in a 'tractable' and 'realistic' perspective that focuses on the distinctive attributes of financial institutions. Coase's analysis resonates with the experience of many corporate entities, especially on the importance of senior managers as coordinators when the 'principal' (owner) is either too abstract or too remote to be relevant (Stout 2012). In many jurisdictions, financial institutions act on behalf of 'silent' beneficiaries subject to legal standards of behaviour such as fiduciary duty (Woods 2011). Building on Chapter 4, we also assume that those who claim status from their skills and expertise often contest the authority and control that senior managers claim.

Coase contended that 'the main reason why it is profitable to establish a firm would seem to be that there is a cost of using the price mechanism' (Coase 1937: 390). This claim is explained in a number of ways. First, and most obviously, there are costs associated with price discovery—determining the best market price for a set of services distinguished by their quality and quantity is challenging and, if intermediaries supply information, expensive. His argument resonates with more recent treatments of search costs and market signalling as exemplified by Spence (1977) and Grossman et al. (1977). Coase suggested that the costs of negotiating and agreeing separate contracts for services are significant, especially if there are many contracts reflecting diverse and unrelated activities. Hence, for Coase, the virtues of insourcing were twofold. In the first case, the firm need offer only one contract or a limited set of contracts across its various types of employees (tasks and functions) and, second, contracts need not be as complete as they would have to be for market providers, allowing the entrepreneur flexibility to vary performance criteria and terms over time.

Firms benefit from 'the system of relationships which comes into existence when the direction of resources is dependent on an entrepreneur' (Coase 1937: 393). Coase explained why firms tend to be larger when the costs of insourcing are lower than the costs of outsourcing and when the rate of increase in those costs remains equal to or less than the costs of transacting in the market. This suggests that firms will be larger, as opposed to smaller, when the costs of mistakes due to increasing institutional complexity remain lower than the payoffs to be obtained from sourcing in the market. Finally, he contended that firms will be larger, rather than smaller, when the prices of internal factors of production are lower than the market prices. Importantly, he recognized that there may be decreasing returns to scale: at some point, it will pay the entrepreneur to outsource rather than insource services. By his account, there are three strategic variables with respect to managing the firm—the relative costs of services, the costs of mispricing services, and the complexity of the firm.

Coase also noted that 'it seems improbable that a firm would emerge without the existence of uncertainty' (Coase 1937: 392). He disputed Knight's (1921) contention that the existence of risk and uncertainty is the crucial factor driving the establishment of firms and, especially, their size. Nonetheless, it is apparent that the entrepreneur stands to gain from insourcing if markets are subject to significant information asymmetries that introduce risk and uncertainty when pricing inputs to production. There is a balance to be struck between the search costs involved in determining market prices on the one hand, and the costs associated with mispricing internal inputs to the production process on the other. Equally, there is a premium on being able to vary production with some frequency relative to the market for services in response to unanticipated changes in market conditions for final products. Throughout, he assumed that entrepreneurs have the authority to vary inputs to the production process in ways that can realize optimal solutions to unanticipated changes in market conditions.

Importantly, he suggested that the costs of coordination, whether internally or by market, will determine the spatial scope of the firm, and that those costs will increase with the spatial dispersion of transactions. To the extent that the spatial concentration of production can limit the costs of coordination, firms will grow at centralized sites and dominate spatially adjoining consumer markets. He suggested that communication technologies, such as the telephone and telegraph, were crucial for reducing the cost of organizing the firm over time and space (Coase 1937). To make his point, he invoked von Thünen to explain why and how there may be geographical patterns in the size and location of firms. Recent commentators suggest that use of von Thünen was not, and is not, entirely plausible (Dicken and Malmberg 2001). Nonetheless, he recognized that industries and jurisdictions often have distinctive patterns of transaction and pricing practices, which would mean that vertical integration in one industry and jurisdiction might not be the favoured solution for that same industry in another jurisdiction.

Grossman and Helpman (2005) approach the problem of outsourcing in a similar manner. Like Coase, they suggested that offshoring is made possible by the geographical scope and efficiency of communication and logistic technologies and that these technologies, in recent years, have become remarkably cost-effective (see also Coe et al. 2008). Elaborating, Grossman and Rossi-Hansberg (2008: 1981) go on to suggest that 'the cost of offshoring a task may reflect how difficult it is to describe using rules-based logic, how important it is that the task be delivered personally, (and) how difficult it is to transmit or transport the output of the activity'. In effect, they assumed that there is a relationship between the simplicity of tasks and functions and the costs of coordination over time and space. The decision to go offshore is taken when tasks and functions can be conceived and executed according to well-defined and non-negotiable terms and conditions, and when communication technologies allow for the efficient and unambiguous transmission of instructions.[1]

In many respects, Coase *as well as* Grossman and Helpman were concerned with the complexity of the production process. Coase's conception of complexity was, however, rather vague and lacking in substance. He hinted at organizational inefficiency and limits on coordinators' responsiveness to the market because of the confusion of overlapping tasks and functions. Even so, he assumed that coordinators have the authority to impose solutions on problems of complexity. In Chapter 4, we suggested that senior managers of financial institutions do not always have this authority because their 'assets' are found (embodied) in their employees' skills and expertise. Furthermore, given the ever-present risks and uncertainties associated with financial markets, senior managers must rely on human capital and the ways in which decision-making is governed inside and outside the institution to realize planned outcomes. Complexity must be negotiated, not resolved by the exercise of authority. By Jensen's (1993) assessment, complexity may reinforce the 'rents' claimed by powerful and entrenched interests.

GOVERNANCE, CONTRACT, AND THE FIRM

Notwithstanding the importance of Coase for theories of the firm (see Taylor and Asheim 2001), and his importance for the transactions-based conception of the modern firm (Scott 1986), his focus on the 'entrepreneur-coordinator' was problematic. It could be argued, of course, that managers and the management process, if suitably incentivized, can represent the entrepreneur-coordinator. However, to do so would ignore one of the most important features of modern firms, namely that they are hierarchies of authority characterized by different types of employment contracts, according to different levels of responsibility, tasks, and functions (Williamson 1975). In this respect, the governance of the firm is of fundamental importance if managers are to realize their objectives. In fact, there is a large and ever-growing literature on agency problems within firms (Pratt and Zeckhauser 1985; Schoenberger 1997).

To accommodate this issue, the theory of the firm has moved away from the nature and structure of transactions inside and outside the firm to contracts (Hart 1995).[2] For some theorists, the employment contract is simply a device for coordinating the firm. For others, it is the means of conceptualizing the modern firm (see Easterbrook and Fischel (1991) on the firm as a nexus of contracts). Yet other theorists contend that contracts are the best means of governing a firm, for they use the agreed objectives of the firm to reconcile the interests of managers and workers (Jensen 2000). As such, contract theory claims centre stage when discussing the theory of the firm. It stands for a range of issues, including the authority of managers, the responsibilities of workers, their respective rewards for committing to the objectives of the firm, and expectations surrounding their job tenure in relation to competing opportunities in the market. Given the nature of contracts, it may be very difficult to specify fully the terms of engagement, and their execution against prospective and unanticipated events (Hart and Moore 1999).

Following Hart and others, we assume that within the firm, employment contracts are 'incomplete' and 'relational'. Given the transaction costs of complete contracts, it would seem that employees are first hired according to their 'fit' with prescribed tasks, functions, and appropriate standards of compensation and then, as they gain experience and their tasks and functions evolve in response to the environment, the terms and conditions of employment are informally adapted to changing circumstances. As is well appreciated, these types of firms typically rely on well-defined tasks, functions, and formal mechanisms of evaluation. However, internal labour markets often take precedence over external markets of services when seeking to respond quickly and effectively to changing circumstances. Continuity of contract facilitates on-the-job learning as well as the exploitation of firm-specific tacit knowledge (Gertler 2003). In this respect, employment contracts are not only incomplete, but also relational in that they facilitate ongoing relationships between co-workers, managers, and workers (Baker et al. 2002; Bathelt and Glückler 2011).

By contrast, it is often assumed that contracts with external suppliers are, as near as possible, complete and discrete. One reason why managers like to enter into contracts with external providers is to avoid making a long-term commitment to suppliers. In this respect, it is assumed that contracts with external suppliers are contingent on performance and can be terminated 'at will' (with compensation). Compared with internal contracts, the market for services (tasks and functions) gives managers an opportunity to realize their goals and objectives without making a commitment to the future. Likewise, to dampen the escalation of internal commitment and impose discipline on the expectations of their own employees, managers may vary the mix of internal and external suppliers. As such, there may be an efficiency gain in balancing (internal) relational and (external) discrete contracts as managers seek to enforce their authority over the production process. In this manner, outsourcing depends, in part, as Grossman and Helpman (2005) suggest, on the simplicity of contractually agreed tasks and functions.

The distinction between discrete and relational contracts is idealized.[3] Even if governed by discrete contracts, suppliers may come to rely on the firm for the flow of contracts, so thus tie themselves to it. Equally, recognizing the discrete nature of the contract, some suppliers may evade their responsibilities vis-à-vis the quantity, quality, and delivery of agreed tasks and functions (Hart and Moore 2008). In this respect, the costs of ensuring compliance with discrete contracts may rise—especially if firms come to rely on certain market suppliers for component parts of their production systems. When suppliers are required to invest in capital stock and logistic systems to match the internal configuration of the firm, their reliance on discrete contracts may become a threat to their long-term survival. By this logic, both the firm and its suppliers may become enmeshed in knots of contracts that, in effect, carry implicit commitments akin to relational contracts (Monk 2008). Fealty to sunk costs on both sides of the relationship (firm and suppliers) may amplify reliance (Williamson 1975).

In Figure 5.1, we summarize this discussion, providing two sourcing options (internal and external) for the firm in two contractual regimes governing the relationship between the firm and the providers of tasks and functions. Instance A and instance D (top left box and bottom right box) provide the standard ways in which the nature of the contract represents insourcing and outsourcing. However, outsourcing governed by discrete contracts may evolve in such a way that instance C comes to play a significant role in the governance of firms' supply relationships. Equally, firms may attempt to bifurcate the contractual regimes governing internal relationships to distinguish between employees with crucial skills and knowledge of the production process and those who have rather simple, replicable, and well-defined tasks and functions. To the extent that managers can maintain this type of distinction internal to the firm, instance C may well mimic the conditions obtaining in the market for related tasks and functions (instance D) rather than relational contracts. Job tenure may be limited, wages subject to market conditions, and firm-specific training non-existent.

Offshoring can be seen as synonymous with outsourcing in that once the decision is made to seek suppliers of tasks and functions outside the firm, it is a question of location nearby (instance B) or far away (instance D). In

		Sourcing Policy	
		In	Out
Type of Contract	Relational	A	B
	Discrete	C	D

Figure 5.1. Contractual regimes
Source: Authors

		Sourcing Policy	
		In	Out
Location Policy	Home	A	B
	Away	C	D

Figure 5.2. Sourcing options
Source: Authors

Figure 5.2, the models of Grossman and Helpman and the field research of economic geographers loom large, especially over the degree to which firms rely on advanced communication technologies, rule-based tasks and functions, and standardized production systems and technologies to manage their supply networks. This issue is often cast in terms of suppliers located in less developed economies (instance D) transforming the pattern of trade from whole products to the component parts of products assembled in the home location (instance A). The process of offshoring relies on the coexistence of very different norms and conventions governing the workplace so that, by virtue of distance and jurisdiction, the firm can maintain its desired contractual arrangements. This suggests that managers may seek distant locations with profoundly different cultures and standards of living. These types of differences are also found within developed economies, for example in the differences between advanced metropolitan regions and semi-rural or less-developed areas (instance B).

Much of the literature tackles the issue of offshoring by reference to the relationship between the firm's command centre and its distant sites of production. It is entirely possible that the production and delivery of firms' outputs will require insourcing at home and away, in the sense that products may be comprised of components that are assembled and distributed around the world via the officers that represent the firm. In this respect, companies in some industries may be multi-locational and require coordination between managers at the same level of the firm, as well as coordination between the firm's different tiers. This conception is developed in more detail in the following section, 'The Institution and its Industry'. Here, it is assumed that outsourcing usually carries with it a rather different contractual framework from that obtained for insourcing. It remains to be seen whether insourcing at home and insourcing away involve a shared contractual framework that is distinctively different from that of external suppliers.

THE INSTITUTION AND ITS INDUSTRY

Focusing on the contractual norms that match stylized conceptions of insourcing, outsourcing, and offshoring provides the basic building blocks for understanding a firm's structure and governance. Nevertheless, the relevance and expression of these principles depends on the economic environment or context in which the firm and its industry functions. In this section, we provide a more detailed account of the distinctive attributes of financial institutions as they pertain to the structure and governance of a firm. In doing so, specific cases are eschewed in favour of a schematic or stylized representation of the essential features of financial institutions.

To be specific, we make a distinction between the process of collecting and lodging AUM with our institution and the investment process itself. For example, if our representative financial institution inherits (or is provided by tender) the stock of AUM (ignoring gross flows for the moment), the size of the institution is assumed to be given, but the scope of its activities is yet to be determined. This is an important point of clarification. More often than not, firm size and the scope of activities are treated as synonymous. Importantly, our institution also relies on global financial markets to produce investment returns. Just as managers seek information from the market for financial services, the investment performance of the institution is dependent on the collection, analysis, and deployment of market-sensitive information. In other words, information is the lifeblood of the organization, affecting its form and functional performance.

For simplicity, we assume that our representative financial institution seeks to maximize the risk-adjusted rate of return either on its own behalf or on behalf of clients who neither express their preferences nor are able to self-organize to affect the institution's investment strategies and policies. We assume that because the net return to beneficiaries is crucial in underwriting a firm's reputation as a desirable investment organization, the costs of producing the risk-adjusted rate of return are significant. On the output side of the equation, it is assumed that the notional product that the institution produces is the risk-adjusted rate of return; this income stream is produced by investing the available assets via (1) the manager's strategic asset allocation framework, and (2) asset-specific (specialized) portfolio investment teams.[4] Most importantly, our institution is a planning and decision-making entity that seeks to realize its objectives in the context of market risk and uncertainty. Managers are responsible for supervising the performance and decision-making of the institution's portfolio investment teams.

Here, two important distinctions affect the structure of the institution and relationships between investment teams. We assume that strategic asset allocation is the responsibility of senior managers informed, no doubt, by the institution's target risk-adjusted rate of return and its available resources. There are, as well, specialist tools available for framing and implementing strategic asset allocation, including diagnostic ones aimed at determining institution-wide and portfolio-specific risk exposure. In this respect, portfolio investment teams are subsidiary to the institution's overarching goals and are, themselves, governed a priori by determined performance targets and risk budgets. At one level, portfolio investment teams are complementary activities in that the overarching strategic asset allocation 'formula' provides a means of coordinating portfolio investment teams (Clark 2002). At another level, however, portfolio investment teams are competitors for institutional resources and, especially, AUM. The challenge is to provide incentives consistent with a priori performance objectives, while ensuring that activities remain consistent with the overarching interests of the institution.

Whereas much of the research on the firm has, as its object, firms that rely on fixed or tangible assets, our institution relies on three assets that are quite unlike plant and equipment. Performance depends on the institution's human capital and the governance of the institution—these are assets in the sense that human capital provides the intellectual resources to set strategic asset allocation and drive the performance of portfolio investment teams. It is important to note that human capital can be thought of as comprised of two elements—skill and expertise. Here, it is assumed that common sense is no substitute for domain-specific knowledge and experience (Wagner 2002). Skill refers to the ability of portfolio investment managers to anticipate and respond to the flux and flow of markets, utilizing so-called subjective as well as objective cues to inform decision-making in timely and effective ways. Expertise is, of course, related: it refers to the use of judgement in situations where decision-making protocols and routines do not provide a ready recipe for action.[5] Governance can be divided into two elements—namely that coordination across the various tasks and functions is essential for realizing the risk-adjusted rate of return; and authority is vital for deciding on the investment strategy and how it will be realized. Coordination is based on procedures of management, whereas authority involves taking decisions on the institution's goals and objectives.

To summarize, Figure 5.3 sets out how human capital and governance intersect and overlap to frame the institution. Each pair of elements provides an action 'space': highly talented individuals characterized by significant levels of skills and expertise are shown as instance A (portfolio managers and their teams); those who sustain the coordination of the institution while assuming significant levels of responsibility for its overall performance and structure are shown as instance B (senior managers). Notice that Figure 5.3 provides space for other related tasks and functions. For example, instance C indicates that some skill and authority are important for job performance

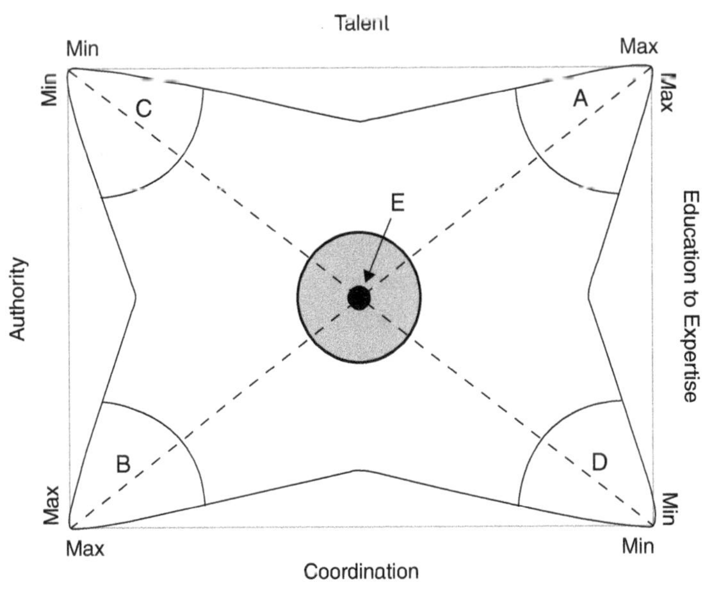

Figure 5.3. Intangible assets
Source: Authors

(as in human resource management) and instance D indicates that some skill and expertise, as well as a role in institutional coordination, are important in job performance (as in information technology (IT) provision). Being a four-sided box, it is assumed that other tasks and functions are not located at the corners of the box.

Underpinning this framework is a third asset, namely the information infrastructure that informs managers responsible for governance and the portfolio investment teams responsible for performance. As indicated in Chapter 3, market providers such as Thomson Reuters and Bloomberg dominate the distribution of financial information. However, our institution also seeks market information that is not so commodified in the hope of gaining an advantage over its competitors, whether by identifying underlying trends or disjunctions or by testing competing expectations of market performance. Equally important is the processing of information internal to the institution, so that those responsible for investment strategy and for coordinating the elements that make up the institution's investment strategy know as much about risk exposure and market position as those who conceive and execute investment strategies. At one level, the information infrastructure provides enough information to manage the whole institution; at another level, the information infrastructure provides managers with the information through which to exercise authority.

TASKS AND FUNCTIONS

Here, we analyse the configuration of our idealized financial institution in relation to its size and scope. We assume that it seeks to maximize the risk-adjusted rate of return, first through its strategic asset allocation framework and second through the performance of its specialized portfolio investment teams. It does so with reference to the costs of producing its desired risk-adjusted rate of return and its strategic assets. It is also assumed that our institution has its complement of managers—those responsible for setting the goals of the institution and deciding on its tasks and functions.

Insourcing

Assuming that our institution has a modest sum of AUM, the rate of return objective of the institution's managers may fail to match the assets of the institution—because of its size, it may lack the requisite human capital, governance procedures, and infrastructure necessary to realize its ambitions in a cost-effective manner. Whereas conventional treatments of the firm assume that, in its embryonic form, managers do almost everything internal to the firm, in this case it would seem that almost everything is done outside the boundaries of the institution. At this level, there is a premium on the governance capacity of managers with respect to external providers; coordination and oversight of those providers are crucial if the institution is to realize its objectives. However, it is important to notice that they are likely to depend on the reporting systems of external providers. In effect, our institution relies on the human capital and economies of scale of external providers in the market for financial services.

As the institution grows in terms of its AUM, managers are able to bring an increasing number of functions into it. If our institution retains an ambitious rate of return target, the functions brought into it are likely to be those that can be managed and executed in a cost-efficient manner. By this logic, insourcing depends on three factors. These are, first, being able to allocate resources to a select number of functions that can meet, or better, the costs of buying the same tasks and functions in the market for financial services. Second, insourcing also depends on being able to recruit the requisite human capital to realize the performance objectives of those functions in relation to the overarching strategic asset allocation framework. Finally, insourcing depends on a governance budget consistent with those functions, complemented by an appropriate system of information infrastructure for facilitating institution-wide oversight and control. Investment in human capital and infrastructure is consistent with ensuring the long-term sustainability of insourcing policies.

At some level, AUM will be sufficient to insource the tasks and functions needed to realize the institution's objectives. We assume that managers choose to insource to reap the benefits of being a firm rather than a network of market providers. These benefits include the standardization of contracts, insulation from short-term volatility in the market pricing of services, and, given market risk and uncertainty, the flexibility of incomplete or relational contracts. For the financial services industry at large, these benefits are apparent and significant. Given their reliance on human capital, the managers of these institutions use the relational nature of the contract to insulate themselves from market competition for skilled and talented labour on the fund management side of the business. Equally important, relational contracts can give senior managers breathing space to develop investment strategies that are different from those of their competitors. For example, some of the largest funds have made long-term commitments to portfolio managers with expertise in direct investments, infrastructure, and alternatives—who therefore carry a market premium. In doing so, however, institutions may find it impossible to hold to a single, standardized contract.[6]

One response to the heterogeneity of tasks and functions has been to overlay each type of contract with a set of incentives and benefits that link compensation to the performance of the individual, the team, and the institution. Market-facing tasks and functions may claim a premium on short-term incentives linked to performance, whereas governance tasks and functions may claim a premium on longer-term incentives linked to realizing the institution's overarching target rate of return. Further, relatively complete (discrete) employment contracts cover market-facing tasks and functions, whereas executives may be offered open-ended contracts with incentive payments that stretch out over time—possibly one, three, or even seven years. Portfolio managers employed on short-term contracts may be subject to exacting standards of performance and the threat of termination at will. If insulated from short-term changes in the market pricing of talent, they may be strategic when playing off internal rewards against market opportunities.

Outsourcing

Notwithstanding the benefits of insourcing, managers face a tripartite governance problem. This is to do with the difficulties of balancing the long-term benefits of insourcing against the short-term ones of outsourcing; systematically under- or overinvesting in the infrastructure needed to oversee the provision of services; and the possibility that the complex nature and scope of insourced services will result in bureaucratic inertia and/or confusion. Here, there are several options. For example, the institution could use a 'shadow' market to price the production and exchange of services internal to it. Another option would be for senior managers to establish units dedicated to facilitating the efficient coordination of complementary activities located at the 'centre' of the institution (as represented by instance E in Figure 5.3). A third, albeit related, option would be to facilitate coordination by introducing a compensation regime that promotes cooperation and the sharing of responsibility in the realization of the institution's objectives.

Outsourcing can be seen as yet another solution to these problems. Coase and those following in his footsteps argued that the availability of information on the cost and relative performance of market providers determines the scope of outsourcing. By this account, sorting through competing service providers to find the most efficient one means repeatedly having to pay transaction costs as new market opportunities arise. In any case, this type of information is readily available in the financial services industry. Furthermore, service providers touting for business often provide the information directly. However, whereas the costs of service provision are readily at hand, for some types of services (notably those involving portfolio investment management), performance is only known on an *ex post* basis. Our institution's managers face the possibility that, however effective they are in selecting the most cost-efficient service providers, shortfalls in performance may prompt unplanned searches for providers who promise better relative performance.

Here, there are two possible management strategies. First, rather than switching between market providers because of short-term variations in costs and performance, the preferred option may be to issue long-term contracts based on absolute cost and performance. Second, managers may choose to hold more than two or three market providers for the same tasks and functions (this will impose discipline on each provider), while using information about market suppliers to inform any future search for related service providers.

At issue is the rationale for choosing which tasks and functions to outsource and which to keep in-house. Here, again, there are two possible options. Managers may find it more cost-effective to outsource those that add to the complexity of governing the institution, but retain those that are complementary and that share existing human capital and information infrastructure systems. For the same reason, outsourcing tasks and functions that require more specialized or different human resources and supervisory systems may aid governance. In other words, complementarity simplifies governance (Clark 2002). External providers also require management and supervision. Notwithstanding transaction costs, discrete contracts can be a way of imposing discipline on these providers in ways not possible within the institution.

Tasks and functions may be outsourced because they lack centrality to the objectives of the institution. Here, however, is a paradox. At one level, one could argue that the institution's most important tasks and functions should remain in-house, subject to internal governance procedures. At another level, however, recognizing the risks associated with bureaucratic inertia and entrenchment, one might outsource the most important tasks and functions to give managers the option of radically restructuring and redesigning their execution in the future. Whereas insourcing can provide firms with greater flexibility by virtue of the nature of incomplete contracts, it is entirely possible that ongoing commitment to internal teams becomes an escalation in commitment—where insourcing becomes self-defeating (Levin 2002: 1088). This may be why some of the largest financial institutions tend to hold to routine tasks and functions, leaving the innovative and difficult to manage ones in the marketplace subject to discrete contracts (see Chapter 10).

GEOGRAPHICAL REACH: OFFSHORING

Recent treatments of offshoring have tended to assume that the firm is located at the heart of Western consumer markets, with the option of sourcing inputs to the production process from the margins of the global economy (Grossman and Rossi-Hansberg 2008). By contrast, the global financial services industry can be seen as hierarchical, pivoting on just a handful of global financial centres that are linked through national and regional financial centres to the consumers of financial products (Wójcik 2011). In the global financial services industry, 'consumers' are decentralized, whereas 'producers' are highly centralized.

We have noted that insourcing and outsourcing are management options, mediated by the institution's rate of return target, strategic assets, and AUM. We also noted that insourcing and outsourcing may have distinctive geographical footprints, just as offshoring may be inside and outside the institution. In this section, we look more closely at the imperatives behind offshoring, treating insourcing and outsourcing as expressions of this phenomenon. As in Chapter 4, we assume that there are two types of financial institutions, small and large. The former have insufficient AUM to do much more than govern a network of external suppliers in accordance with their rate of return targets. Large institutions, by contrast, are assumed to have the option to insource and outsource. For the sake of exposition, we set out both the options and the constraints; we also provide a summary of current offshoring strategies in the financial industry and emerging hybrid strategies and trends. Given the recent global financial crisis (GFC) and the euro crisis, there is a constant search for winning strategies.

In Figure 5.4, we provide a 2x2 box summarizing the options facing institutions, given their size (AUM) and location. Size represents the governance capacity or potential of the institution—in effect, the bottom left-hand corner of Figure 5.3 joins the coordination and authority functions of our institution's managers. With a core location, a small financial institution at the centre of the global financial services industry is likely to reap the benefits of relatively low search and transaction costs. Being at the centre of the global financial

		Assets under Management	
		Small	Large
Market Location	Core	A	B
	Periphery	C	D

Figure 5.4. Strategic scope

Source: Authors

services industry, even a small institution is able to access relatively sophisticated financial products that have 'global' reach. Nonetheless, the minimum size of investment required by major investment houses may limit access to these types of products; the institution's capacity to hire and retain specialized portfolio managers and executives with well-developed industry networks may also limit access. Relational contracts may be essential for maintaining their human capital.

Small institutions in peripheral market locations, by contrast, face relatively high search and transaction costs. These types of institutions must rely on third-party information providers whether through electronic mediums or through consulting and advisory companies specializing in industry-wide information (Chapter 8). While the electronic medium is often highly efficient, it is widely recognized that the type of information distributed across the landscape to provincial centres without any apparent loss of immediacy provides little in the way of market advantage. Furthermore, having a peripheral location in relation to a major financial centre is likely to incur a discount on returns (Wójcik 2011). Consulting and advisory companies are particularly effective in packaging information. Nonetheless, the effective use of this information depends a great deal on the skills and expertise of managers; otherwise, they may come to rely on consulting companies for strategic investment policy as well as the choice of portfolio managers. By default, the preferred management strategy may be to outsource, even offshore, crucial functions related to fund governance (authority and control).

Large institutions located in core financial markets may benefit from low search and transaction costs. Furthermore, being of sufficient size to choose whether to insource or outsource, managers may be able to design and configure the institution in accordance with the relative benefits of insourcing versus outsourcing by specific tasks and functions. If this is one of their roles and responsibilities, to give effect to these types of strategies may require executives to have long-term relational contracts that lock their career and compensation prospects into the performance of the institution. At the other end of the spectrum, however, a large and vibrant market for financial services may make it very difficult for executives to retain talented staff on anything other than short-term, discrete contracts. In this environment, tournaments for staff may dominate the market for financial services, forcing managers to choose between the tasks and functions they can hold internally and those that can only be obtained externally. Exercising this choice is likely to involve consideration of the costs of coordination, as well as task and function complementarities.

By this logic, large institutions located in core financial markets have permeable boundaries and contingent relationships internal and external to the institution. By contrast, large institutions located in peripheral sites relative to core financial markets face considerable challenges. Unlike small institutions, they have the governance capacity to be an effective presence, even at a distance, in global financial centres. Furthermore, they may benefit from a steady stream of product providers willing to incur the transaction costs involved in providing market insights and information at the institution's headquarters. Just as importantly, a peripheral location may enable the institution to hold onto its skilled portfolio managers without incurring the same level of compensation costs characteristic of similar institutions located in core financial markets. However, there is a significant trade-off between insourcing and outsourcing: it may be difficult to hold the most skilled and talented employees responsible for executing specialized tasks and functions that carry a market premium. Managers may be forced to outsource and even offshore these functions.

Large institutions in peripheral locations may, in fact, be tempted to establish branch offices or wholly owned subsidiaries in core markets. This is an offshoring strategy internal to the institution; it is a means of economizing on search and transaction costs, for it channels market information and insights through the information infrastructure systems owned and operated by the institution. Here, there is a premium on 'governance at a distance'—the internal coordination and management of separate entities in a manner consistent with the overarching goals and objectives of the institution. At one level, this type of strategy insources but offshores tasks and functions to overcome the costs of a peripheral location. At another level, however, this strategy has its own tensions and dilemmas—for example, whether to carry over to separate entities the same governance systems and employment contracts characteristic of the home location. Equally problematic, the privileged location of these separate entities may provide them with the informal 'authority' to circumvent the institution's strategic investment policies.[7] Ultimately, the scope of this type of offshore strategy may be circumscribed by 'home' managers concerned to maintain a coherent and integrated governance regime (and culture) across the institution.

IMPLICATIONS AND CONCLUSIONS

In this chapter, we have sketched the principles, or building blocks, for understanding the functional and geographical scope of financial institutions. Our analysis eschews the details of specific institutions and their particular jurisdictions, suggesting that our conceptual building blocks are important in their own right and bind the experiences of similar institutions around the world. Of course, there is a trade-off between conceptual abstraction and the practical details of time and place—here we have chosen the former over the latter in the interests of clarity. Elsewhere, we have provided detailed case studies of the structure and management of sovereign wealth funds, which is one particular kind of investment institution (see Clark et al. 2013).

Beginning with Coase (1937), we also drew on more recent research that emphasizes the problematic nature of authority within firms, and the nature and structure of contracts within and outside firms. In doing so, we exploit recent interest in the geographical reach of the modern firm and how managers deal with the costs of space and time. Grossman and Rossi-Hansberg's (2008) model of offshoring relies on communication technologies to mediate the transaction costs involved in contracting at a distance. While significant for our analytical framework, it is also apparent that the focus of many scholars of the theory of the firm is on institutions that literally make things, exchange commodities, and sell them in the global marketplace. Our theoretical framework distinguishes between firms that make things (as in commodities) and financial institutions that produce investment returns that are disembodied from the commodity production and distribution systems that girdle the world.

A crucial point of departure for the chapter was the objective function of our representative financial institution—the maximization of the risk-adjusted rate of return. We explain how this is conceived and how its various elements drive the 'production' of the financial 'product'. Importantly, we distinguish our idealized financial institution from conventional firms by the nature and scope of its strategic but intangible assets. Unlike conventional industrial firms, financial institutions have little in the way of fixed assets: they rely on human capital, governance procedures and policies, and systems of information infrastructure that allow for oversight of their operations and access to the global financial system (Clark and Urwin 2008a). It is debatable whether these assets are actually assets in the sense that, like plant and equipment, they could be sold to the highest bidder. In many respects, these assets are sunk costs: they represent significant investments that, to competitors, may be seen as comparative advantages in realizing investment goals.

Based on these distinctions, we explain the nature of the governance problem in large and small financial institutions. Likewise, we explain how and why those that produce financial returns have distinctive claims for compensation and advantage in their own right. On this basis, utilizing our characterization of the assets of financial institutions, we explain the logic behind insourcing and outsourcing and, ultimately, the geographical reach of financial institutions. Whereas the logic behind insourcing and outsourcing may be familiar, we suggest that extending the geographical reach of financial institutions is intimately related to their location in the global hierarchy of financial centres. Indeed, quite unlike conventional models of the firm, which treat the market for services as ubiquitous, in our formulation it matters a great deal where financial institutions are located relative to national and global financial centres.

It is widely believed that there are decreasing returns to scale, in the sense that the increasing complexity of a firm's tasks and functions may become costly relative to the market for services and thereby prompt managers to switch to outsourcing. We also emphasize the coordination problems associated with large financial institutions, suggesting that managers may seek to mediate these costs by introducing internal or shadow markets for services produced by the institution. Managers may also establish coordination platforms and virtual sites of functional integration designed to rationalize service provision and use. These types of management strategies focus on the complementarities between tasks and functions. Outsourcing, or even offshoring, by contrast, should be understood as driven by the lack of complementarities between certain tasks and functions. This argument reflects a related point made by Clark (2002) about how and why certain financial tasks and functions are concentrated in single sites of production, characteristic of bulge-bracket global investment houses.

Finally, it should be acknowledged that our models of management assume that managers are well intentioned and have, as their overriding interest, the welfare of beneficiaries. While useful for the purposes of conceptual clarity and analysis, this assumption may not withstand scrutiny in certain cases. Indeed, industry commentators acknowledge that there are many instances of entrenched executives relying on insourcing to drive the scope of the institution and ultimately the compensation of managers. This would seem to be an ever-present threat to the effective governance of these institutions. Not surprisingly, one way of mediating this possibility is to link the objective function of the institution (maximizing returns) explicitly to the welfare of its ultimate beneficiaries and customers. Whether this is a successful strategy would seem to depend on the degree to which internal cultures of value can be distinguished from the interests of talented individuals in reaping a premium in the global market for financial services. This issue is significant for financial regulators around the world.

NOTES

1. See also Aoyama and Ratick (2007) on the importance of trust and control when it comes to assessing whether the promised benefits of outsourcing can, in fact, be realized.
2. In a related vein, Maskell (2001: 329–44) disputed the importance attributed to transactions inside and outside the firm, arguing that any such distinction rests on an assumption that there is something special about markets compared with firms. He goes on to indicate that 'thinking of all organisations as groups of explicit or implicit contracts among owners of factors of production represents a fundamental advance'.

In what follows, we amplify this argument using a somewhat different typology of contracts relevant to financial institutions.

3. MacNeil (1980: 10–11) described discrete contracts as 'primitive' compared with relational ones in that the latter bind together interdependent economies with high levels of specialization and exchange. Others, however, see discrete contracts as consistent with economic efficiency, for they offer the contracting parties an option to abrogate commitments if need be. As such, discrete contracts are consistent with philosophical conceptions of liberal democracy, in which individual preference and choice trumps social commitment.
4. It is widely observed that high levels of intimacy, personal commitment, and mutual benefit characterize some of the most successful portfolio investment teams. They motivate one another, they monitor one another's commitment, and they reinforce their shared identity against the authority of the institution's managers (Teece 2000). It is not surprising that when other institutions poach 'star traders', they take their team members with them.
5. Harvey (2012: 200) summarizes the notion of skill in terms of 'practice makes perfect'. He, like Yates and Angott (2012), distinguishes skill from judgement, suggesting that the latter is more than the deployment of a practical routine; it involves making decisions based on the use of probabilistic reasoning. We prefer to use the term 'expertise' in that it includes judgement along with other types of reasoning that allow agents to go beyond accepted modes of decision-making.
6. Differential compensation with this type of institution is often more difficult when a public body or agency sponsors it. Therefore, the advantages of insourcing may not be realized because of the lack of flexibility of senior managers with respect to standards of contract and remuneration. By this account, outsourcing may be more desirable, especially if the terms of external contract and engagement demand little in the way of reporting requirements.
7. In these ways, offshore offices that carry with them a team-based ethic or sensibility may see themselves as rather separate from the sponsoring institution's goals and objectives. As with many portfolio investment teams, the premium on internal coherence and common commitment may reinforce a sense of separate-and-different, which differences between jurisdictions in compensation practices, reward systems, and career prospects amplify.

6

Investment Management Contracts

In this chapter, we focus on contractual relations between financial institutions and their service providers, emphasizing the form and functions of agreements with investment management providers. We explain how and why these contracts are quite different from those that bind together firms and suppliers in commodity-producing industries. Many contracts for investment management services can be terminated at will. Nonetheless, they are used because they provide frameworks for governing relationships in the context of risk and uncertainty rather than simply as instruments for managing the supply of services. We also explain how and why the jurisdiction in which these contracts are written matters to parties on both sides of the market. This is especially significant for the United Kingdom and Europe, but also for other regions. Jurisdiction selection is explained by reference to financial institutions' need for procedural fairness. In some instances, the suppliers' interest in discounting their accountability to clients can explain the choice of jurisdiction.

There is an extensive literature on offshore financial centres, especially those that shelter the financial services industry from tax liabilities (Wójcik 2013). Although this is an important consideration (Wainwright 2011), these offshore centres also have significant roles in the governance of contractual relationships with the financial services industry. Explicating how and why this is the case is one contribution of the chapter. Here we articulate the conceptual building blocks needed to understand the role of contracts in the investment management industry. Our analytical strategy recognizes that risk and uncertainty are pervasive aspects of financial markets and are arguably deeply embedded in the contractual relationships that bring financial institutions and their suppliers together. Likewise, we suggest that the geography of contract is important, with jurisdictions such as the United Kingdom serving as the bridging point between geographically dispersed financial institutions and centralized market providers.

In the next section, 'The Nature of Contract', we begin with the standard model of contract, noting its underlying principles and the differences between discrete and relational contracts. The real world of financial markets and the financial services industry complicate this logic because risk and uncertainty temper expectations of the diligence of service providers in realizing agreed objectives. To illustrate, we compare the nature and performance of contracts in commodity-producing industries against those in the financial services industry. Taking the argument a step further, we suggest that many financial institutions treat contract as a desirable thing in itself *and* as a framework for governing relationships over time and space. In these ways, contract plays a complex and not entirely consistent role in the financial services industry. This is illustrated by reference to the demand and supply of contract by jurisdiction, suggesting that the choice of jurisdiction is a significant aspect of the European and global financial services industry. Based on this research, we would suggest that the ideal of contract is a chimera where the practice of contract involves the exercise of power (Shiffrin 2007). As indicated here, the choice of jurisdiction in relation to the exercise of contract can be intimately related to the relative powers of the contracting parties.

Before proceeding, it is important to comment briefly on the exposition of our argument and the limits of our research. As noted in Chapter 1, our discussion of contractual frameworks is necessarily abstract because private contracts are proprietary documents. These documents are subject to confidentially clauses designed to limit third-party disclosure of the form, terms, and conditions of agreed contracts. In a number of instances, we have encountered situations where disclosure of contractual terms and conditions has been strictly limited, even *within* organizations, between functions. It is not surprising, therefore, that most studies of contract in the social sciences, including economics, sociology, and management studies, do not disclose the sites of fieldwork, the nature and content of the documents analysed, or the parties involved.[1]

THE NATURE OF CONTRACT

Bolton and Dewatripont (2005) and Posner (2003) begin their expositions of bilateral contracts with two self-interested parties who have more to gain from forging a transaction and carrying it through than acting separately. Bolton and Dewatripont assume that both parties are means-and-ends rational and seek to maximize their respective interests. Explaining the significance of contract, Bolton and Dewatripont suggest that risk and uncertainty can complicate the realization of planned transactions between well-intentioned individuals. Less analytically, Posner demonstrates that the time involved between making a commitment and realizing its completion can provide parties with opportunities to engage in gamesmanship. This type of behaviour may harm one or both of those involved or, worse, undercut the willingness of others to make similar commitments.

Whereas individuals can get by on a 'cash-and-carry basis', Posner contends that society as a whole benefits from the 'good-faith performance' of past commitments. Indeed, the modern economy, based as it is on the division of labour and the specialization of tasks and functions, trade and exchange, and networks of collaboration, is only possible if commitments to the future are honoured (even in their breach). Posner (2003: 94–5) argues that 'the fundamental function of contract law … is to deter people from behaving opportunistically towards their contracting parties in order to encourage the optimal timing of economic activity and (the same point) obviate costly self-protective measures'. In a related statement, Bolton and Dewatripont (2005: 3) note that their exposition presupposes the existence of 'a well-functioning legal system'. They assume that 'contracting parties do not need to worry about whether the courts are able or willing to enforce the terms of the (agreed) contract precisely'. Posner is not nearly as sanguine.

Bilateral contracts have certain characteristics. The parties undertaking them are assumed to do so from unencumbered positions, which allow them to negotiate the best deal without concern for the past. It is also assumed that the costs of contracting are small relative to the benefits, not just in absolute terms (for every contract) but also relatively (comparing one contract to another). If circumstances change to make the original terms and conditions unduly onerous on one or both parties, it is assumed that there are mechanisms available to renegotiate them. This may include compensation for parties that relied on the original terms and conditions. The efficiency of bilateral contracts depends on the clarity of the terms and conditions, especially over what counts as the appropriate measures of performance of both parties to the contract. Bilateral contracts are assumed 'complete' in that on termination there are no residual claims to be adjudicated or interests to be reconciled.

For Bolton and Dewatripont and Posner, the virtues of contract can only be realized if there are independent bodies to adjudicate between the competing claims of self-interested parties. This is not meant to imply that every contract is subject to the force of law. Rather, the *existence* of a system of adjudication, mediation, and enforcement provides both parties with incentives to carry through their commitments. To the extent that the legal system is an effective and reliable adjudicator of contractual disputes, parties to contracts seeking to avoid the costs of adjudication are likely to self-regulate their behaviour in ways consistent with societal expectations. As Posner observes, a contract is more often than not a legal document that has its origins not only in the intentions of the parties concerned, but also in the legal apparatus of the state. In this respect, bilateral contracts are instruments for facilitating the efficient realization of transactions between parties.

Whereas much contract theory presupposes that the object of analysis is a bilateral contract, attention has shifted towards relational contracts, which are, by definition, incomplete in three ways. First, they may extend in time without a specified or required date of termination. Second, their terms and conditions may be subject to revision and renegotiation over time as circumstances change and as parties seek to rebalance separate and mutual benefits *within* the contract. Third, they may be a means of economizing on the search costs associated with finding other parties who may or may not provide complementary services. In this respect, bilateral contracts can become relational—a means of governing economic and financial relationships rather than instruments based on a priori defined costs and benefits that open and close at certain dates and times.

Discrete contracts provide a start and termination date, as well as an explicit accounting of the costs and benefits to be shared between the contracting parties. If underwritten by social norms and conventions, such as the moral obligations associated with making a promise, there need be no ambiguity over realizing their expected benefits, and the role of law in ensuring that those expectations are, as much as possible, met. Relational contracts are more complex and multifaceted. Without a specific termination date, there are periodic reviews of the costs and benefits of remaining with the contract, balancing progress to date in meeting desired objectives against the costs of breaking it and the search costs associated with finding other contractual partners. By contrast, relational contracts are judged successful to the extent to which they cope with and enable parties to adapt to changing circumstances.

FINANCIAL INSTITUTIONS AND FINANCIAL MARKETS

Whereas much discussion about contract in law and economics eschews contextual variables, economic geographers emphasize the interaction between principles and context, suggesting that observed outcomes are best understood at the intersection between these elements of theory and practice (Bathelt and Glückler 2011). It is notable that cognitive science makes a similar move when explaining observed behaviour: the environment in which people make decisions mediates cognitive predisposition and provides for wide variation in plausible behaviour (Clark 2013). Five factors are crucial to understanding the nature and scope of contracting in financial institutions and markets.

Agents, Principals, and Fiduciaries

The financial institutions that are the objects of our research are beneficial in that they act on behalf of absent owners or silent principals. Attempts have been made to engage principals in the hope that it will encourage them to get involved and directly express their interests. However, most principals are neophytes when it comes to understanding and giving voice to their long-term financial interests. Corporate officers and trustees act in their stead, subject to common law and statutory requirements on the exercise of authority and responsibility. As such, they typically delegate responsibility to others, whether inside or outside the institution, to realize the investment objectives of the institution and hence the interests of beneficiaries. These agents are accorded deference for their domain-specific skills and expertise (see Chapters 4 and 5).

In large part, fiduciaries join the interests of beneficiaries with the skills and expertise of agents. Typically, they report to beneficiaries on an annual basis on the status of their entitlements, the financial standing of the institution, and the circumstances affecting their current and expected welfare. Agents report on their performance to fiduciaries on a more regular basis (perhaps monthly, often quarterly, and certainly annually). Performance criteria are normally established by contract; more often than not, performance criteria are part of the norms and conventions of the financial services industry and include, for example, appropriate third-party measures of relative performance against industry benchmarks. In many cases, fiduciaries employ other agents to certify the integrity and quality of reported performance measures. To provide reference points against which to evaluate stated performance, fiduciaries may also employ agents to collect performance data from a wide range of industry providers.

Geographical Structure of the Industry

Financial institutions owe the location of their headquarters, if not their sites of operation, to whatever entity (or entities) is their 'sponsor'. Their corporate officers and trustees are typically located at some distance from major financial centres and the handful of global financial markets that dominate international financial stocks and flows. By contrast, most agents co-locate in national financial centres and have a significant presence in global financial markets (Storper and Venables 2004). Electronic networks sustain the routine communication between (dispersed) financial institutions and their (centralized) agents, as well as the collection and distribution of financial assets to the myriad of agents located in major financial centres.

Multinational firms dominate the financial services industry at the global level. Economies of scale and scope reinforce the complementarities between tasks and functions to enable the provision of products and services with appropriate market-facing characteristics (Clark 2002). In London and New York, small providers operating on the margins of service provision and amenable to innovation and development (such as hedge funds) co-locate with the large ones. In the major continental European centres, large banking institutions—often the national 'champions'—tend to dominate the provision of financial services. Their size and significance is such that intermediation is limited, with many tasks and functions held internally rather than outsourced. This has implications for the site and process of contracting (Gilson et al. 2013). London and New York are hosts to a remarkable depth and range of financial service providers, offering products, services, and organizational forms not otherwise available in national financial centres.

Products Sought and Produced

Manufacturing industries produce material goods. Financial institutions deliver products and services: they contract investment managers to produce a target rate of return on assets invested. This rate may be specific to an asset class, a certain (industry or geographic) segment of an asset class, or to the style or strategy of the investment. The target rate of return may be accompanied by limits imposed on risk exposure and the holdings of certain securities within agreed asset classes. Typically, investment managers report performance against either an absolute or a relative return target measured against industry norms and benchmarks. Investment managers require a minimum volume of assets, base fees on assets under management (AUM), and shy away from performance-related compensation (aside from certain classes of alternative investments).

In Chapter 4, we explained the financial production process in relation to the investment organization's resources and assets. These include the talent and skills of portfolio managers, the process of decision-making, and the information infrastructure that supports judgement, authority, and action. Typically, contracts between financial institutions and investment managers are open-ended in that investment managers are expected to invest according to some measure of performance until the client indicates a wish to change strategy and/or terminate the agreement. In part, this is because the target rate of return is set either against expected liabilities, or some notion of future welfare (extending ten, twenty, even fifty years into the future). The transaction costs involved in assessing performance, deciding to change managers, and hiring replacement managers (or reallocating AUM to existing managers) are significant for both small and large financial institutions.

By convention, both parties can terminate these contracts at a month's notice. However, some investment managers, particularly in illiquid asset classes like infrastructure, require clients to commit assets over the long term, utilizing lock-in provisions and penalty clauses for early termination to deter financial institutions from switching assets between managers should performance fall short of expectations. In many cases, target rates of return allow for a specified range of returns around a benchmark. To the extent that target rates of return are set with respect to industry benchmarks, the interests of financial institutions and investment managers may diverge when, for example, managers meet their benchmarked target rates of return in a declining market. In any event, many 'manage' returns in a way that maintains good relations with their clients—even if that means adapting or dramatically shifting their investment activities and transactions to meet return targets at specific dates.

Product and Financial Markets

Investment managers in national and global financial markets produce returns, but there is considerable variety in the structure, performance, and management of financial markets around the world (Wójcik 2011). Furthermore, it is evident that there is a hierarchy of financial markets. This means that regional markets tend to follow national markets, and national markets either lead or follow global markets, depending on their place in the 24-hour trading clock (Clark and Thrift 2005). Some markets are more efficient in terms of price formation and disclosure than others. Drawing on our discussion, there are four issues immediately relevant to the process of contracting:

- First, developed markets oscillate between periods of relative calm, when expectations tend to be met and encourage further trading, and moments of turmoil and disruption, when expectations are often not met; this might either encourage higher levels of turnover, or move investors to sit out market turmoil in the hope of re-entering when expectations are more settled.
- Second, financial markets are non-stationary in the sense that momentum carries forward market participants, their expectations, and their plans for the future. Because market participants adapt their expectations against observed and expected conditions, markets hardly ever go backwards and, more often than not, go forwards (Lo 2012). As such, risk models that approximate current market conditions are vulnerable enough to unanticipated shifts in market conditions and expectations to become self-defeating.
- Third, the repeated process of producing the rate of return does not necessarily lead to an ever-closer approximation of the target. The production process depends on anticipating market movements and others' reactions to more or less commonly observed information. Unanticipated shifts in market sentiment and behaviour as well as exogenous shocks are common (Shleifer 2000). Noise can radically affect the skills and expertise

of managers who were better than average in previous periods (compare Clark 2015 with Levitt et al. 2012).

- Fourth, herding is a reasonable defensive strategy if the target rate of return is benchmarked against market performance; following market sentiment is a way of approximating clients' expectations—even if this type of behaviour reinforces systemic shocks.

Investor Strategy and Skill

We distinguish two kinds of investing: one is deliberate and based on skills and expertise with respect to target rates of return, while the other is essentially gambling on the path of market sentiment. Unfortunately for clients, it is difficult to differentiate the two, especially if there appears to be some randomness in the period-to-period sequence of returns reported to clients. Investment managers may reap the benefits of having a certain stock of skills and expertise, and decision protocols that map onto current market momentum. However, past success can promote an illusion of skill, ignoring the underlying properties of financial markets (Kahneman 2011). In this respect, clients may incorrectly attribute skill and expertise to investment managers, thereby reinforcing commitment by increasing their allocation of AUM. When events turn against investment managers, it may be difficult to identify the causes of shortfalls in performance.

CONTRACT: FORM, FUNCTIONS, AND PERFORMANCE

For some theorists, historical differences between the institutions and markets of different nations are enough to distinguish between the Anglo-American, continental European, East Asian, and Latin American types (see the literature spawned by Hall and Soskice (2001) on the 'varieties of capitalism'). For others, form is less significant than substance in that the former is deemed a 'shell' given life by the specifics or issues that take it into the world of practice (Kennedy 1976). For yet others, differences in institutional form are less significant than their functionality when nation-states and major corporations respond to global financial imperatives (see Clark and Wójcik 2007; Dixon 2012). In this section, we argue that contractual form is very important and valued as a thing in itself. So too are the functions of contract and how it is governed. Both are important in understanding the performance of contractual relationships between financial institutions and agents and the choice of jurisdiction in which to locate contract.

Form

According to Summers (2006: 80), a 'form-oriented mode of analysis' should focus on the units of a legal system, emphasizing their purposes, constituent features, and organizational structure. A unit can be distinguished in terms of its resources and its boundaries. He noted that units must be seen in relation to 'the legal system as a whole'. Crucially, he suggested that legal procedures, rules, and regulations usually come after the formation of legal systems and units. Anglo-American legal systems are widely acknowledged to combine vestiges of English common law, of which contract law is a constituent element, and statutes that represent the scope and significance of the regulatory state through the twentieth century (Calabresi 1982). For centuries, English courts regulated the nature and scope of private contracts on a case-by-case basis. Through the twentieth century, contract law was formalized in statute in terms of its scope and its necessary ingredients.

Contract embodies certain intrinsically valuable features. Riles (2011) observed that when the US government rescued American International Group (AIG) in the depths of the global financial crisis (GFC), the one thing deemed sacrosanct was the rule of law, or maintaining the integrity and enforceability of contracts. The significance of contract could be attributed to its functionality. However, the point that Riles made is that whereas one can measure and gauge functionality in terms of contractual efficacy, the significance that policymakers attribute to contract as an institution means that policies that might discount the value of contractual commitments are simply not considered. She also observed that, despite the majority of financial transactions and agency agreements originating in far-off jurisdictions, the global financial services industry places a far higher value on UK (England and Wales) and US contract law than on the contract law of other jurisdictions.[2]

Being a constituent element or unit in Anglo-American legal systems, contract is expressed in validated documents. Financial contracts come in a variety of shapes and sizes as befitting the specific interests and circumstances of the parties to them. However, it is apparent that the financial services industry and its associated professional bodies have encouraged the adoption of standard contractual models and templates. Standardization simplifies negotiation and agreement, encourages the formation of shared expectations and commitments, and economizes on transaction costs. It also facilitates agency relationships with external providers and ultimately deepens the market for financial services. Furthermore, standardization gives legal advisers and the consultants who manage the process of evaluating agents a ready-made independent basis for assessing the proffered contractual terms and conditions. There is a market for standardization with various providers competing for dominance (Gilson et al. 2013).

Functions

Posner (2003: 94–5) summarized the functions of contract as follows: '(1) to prevent opportunism, (2) to interpolate efficient terms, (3) to prevent avoidable mistakes in the contracting process, (4) to allocate risk to the superior risk bearer, and (5) to reduce the costs of resolving contract disputes'. These functions have a behavioural element, a procedural benefit, and an overarching economic benefit relevant to the parties concerned, as well as to society as a whole (for example, to allocate risk to the parties best able to bear it).

In the financial services industry, standard investment management agreements (IMAs) cover a wide variety of asset classes and are intended to prevent opportunism and reduce the costs of resolving contractual disputes. We should note, however, that investment managers rarely bear the costs directly of poor investment performance; poor performance can, however, prompt clients to terminate their IMAs. In this context, the narrative accompanying contract is used to define what the agreement covers, the terms it uses, and the procedures whereby it is implemented (start date, notice of termination, and expectations on continuity). Contract is a means of performing an agreement between parties. Contracts for financial services can be extensive in scope and quite demanding in terms of the expertise needed to understand each clause. The standard UK IMA is between sixty and seventy pages in length and requires side letters to clarify points subject to interpretation. Some principals and agents, however, are content with short, simple, and relatively open IMAs, leaving the meaning and interpretation of the agreement to the parties concerned on an ongoing basis. In this respect, contracts serve as frameworks for relationships with service providers that stretch over time and space.

IMAs normally specify the fees involved in managing allocated assets, varying by asset class and style of investment. However, these agreements are less precise when it comes to specifying the 'service' provided by investment managers and the criteria to be used when determining whether performance has met agreed targets. As noted, risk and uncertainty are ever-present features of global financial markets. In this regard, contracts can be seen as instruments designed to forestall overreaction to unexpected events in financial markets, thereby promoting a longer-term view of the significance of individual events in relation to market volatility. Notwithstanding the fact that most IMAs allow for termination at will, the transaction costs involved in exercising those rights are significant, especially if switching between providers becomes a customary response to short-term events. Even so, it is widely assumed that clients switch between providers more often than is justified by trends in manager and market performance (Kay 2012).

Performance

By convention, contract is 'performed' in the financial services industry in three different ways. First, clients are sent quarterly reports on investment performance that reference the appropriate benchmarks and risk protocols. Second, repeated visits to the client by the fund manager provide an opportunity to justify investment performance and prospects. Third, the fund manager may solicit representatives of clients to attend conferences that set out new research and investment programmes. Here, fund managers seek to bypass other agents like investment consultants. The default option is continuity of the relationship. Breakpoints in the relationship appear when there is evidence of systematic negative (relative) performance over time, or where there are indications that the fund manager's narrative on the chosen investment strategy, its conception and implementation, and its place in the world relative to other fund managers lacks coherence or plausibility.

Fundamentally, contracts help service providers sustain their businesses. With increasing returns to scale, continuity of client commitment is a necessary, albeit insufficient, condition for success, especially given that company-specific compensation is often tied to the volume of AUM and that portfolio managers benefit from liquidity when seeking to manage returns against benchmarks. Large short-term inflows and outflows of assets can not only rapidly increase processing costs but also disrupt the risk and return strategies across the entire spectrum of a financial institution's asset classes. Under such circumstances, many investment managers have an interest in writing IMAs in such a way as to dampen client switching while, if necessary, giving their portfolio managers time to recover their short-term positions against the relevant benchmarks. Contract is performed in a manner consistent with the separate as well as shared interests of clients and managers.

CHOICE OF JURISDICTION

In this section, we bring the discussion of contractual form, function, and performance to bear on the choice of jurisdiction. We show that the choice of jurisdiction can play an important role in governing contractual relationships. We concentrate on three strategic options—*in situ* or default contracting; contracting in London; or contracting in offshore jurisdictions.

In Situ or Default Contracting

Ethnographies of financial institutions note that market participants take the structure of the industry for granted (Abolafia 1996; O'Barr and Conley 1992;

Riles 2011). In a similar fashion, economic theorists take the existence of well-functioning legal systems for granted (Bolton and Dewatripont 2005). One indication of the significance of the commonplace in the global financial services industry is the ready acceptance of standardized IMAs. As noted, these agreements find favour on both sides of the market and are often legitimated by agents with an interest in certifying their status. These agreements are not 'official' in the sense of being mandated by government but originate with industry associations, professional bodies, and consulting companies. Given the importance of a small number of multinational law firms in the global financial services industry, it is not surprising that similar IMAs are to be found around the world, including the United Kingdom and Europe, North America, Australia, and Hong Kong (Beaverstock 2004).[3]

Standard IMAs reference the asset class or classes and the investment style of the mandate; they also summarize the objectives of the mandate and the fees charged by the manager. If a target rate of return is identified, it is set within the context of a relevant benchmark, an acceptable band around that benchmark, and the time period over which performance is to be judged. Accompanying these schedules are documents on issues such as custody, securities lending, and risks. Also included are statements about how redemptions might be made, the notice period required in exercising redemption, and caveats on redemptions, such as when exogenous shocks disrupt markets. Parties to these contracts agree not to disclose terms and conditions without the express permission of the other party. As for disputes about performance, IMAs typically set out a dispute resolution process that can include the investment manager's head of compliance and industry-based dispute resolution systems (national and international).

However, care should be taken not to exaggerate the significance of standardized IMAs. In some corners of the investment services market, notably hedge funds, clients confront complex contracts that lack the transparency and disclosure typical of standard IMAs. This leaves them with a choice of either having to accept these types of contracts or incurring the transaction costs involved in negotiating the proffered terms and conditions line by line and provision by provision. For many clients who rely on fee-for-service external legal advisers, the transaction costs involved can be a significant constraint on the willingness of parties to negotiate. As a result, these providers may produce a type of 'standardized' contract that does not carry the approval of the relevant industry associations and professional bodies, but nonetheless is 'accepted' industry practice. The willingness of clients to accept these types of contracts in niche segments of the market is often legitimated by claims of superior financial performance.

Contracting in London

There are many accounts of London's domination of the European financial services industry (for example, Clark 2002; Faulconbridge et al. 2007). London provides a deep market for the services needed to function in global financial markets; it casts a significant shadow over Europe's financial centres. As Gilson et al. (2013) anticipated, London provides off-the-shelf standardized contracts for a wide range of financial services. Standardized contracts often come with the approval of relevant industry associations and professional bodies, the advice of consultants and law firms, and the tacit approval of the UK financial regulator (notwithstanding the exceptions noted). When coming to London to purchase financial services, including investment management, European financial institutions rely on the experience and expertise of London-based institutions. Reliance is reinforced by low transaction costs and claims of accepted convention legitimated by practice, both of which are often not available at home.[4]

By writing contracts in London, or by writing contracts that require settlement in London, purchasers of financial services rely on the form and functions of UK law. Whereas it is easy enough to understand the functionality of the legal system, the formal properties of UK law are desirable in their own right. In part, this is because of the independence of the UK judiciary and the equitable status attributed to claimants in the legal system. Its reputation for adjudicating disputes on the merits of the issues provides claimants with confidence that their interests will be respected, even if they should not win.[5] Furthermore, close consultative arrangements between the City of London, Bank of England, and financial regulators ensure that events or cases that would render adjudication problematic are used to fine-tune the relevant supervisory processes (McCormick 2010). Finance, law, and geography are bound together in ways that sustain the status of London in the global financial services industry in much the same way that Delaware dominates the US market for corporate governance (see Gilson et al. 2013).

It should be emphasized, however, that few contractual disputes find their way to the ombudsman or to alternative dispute resolution processes. There are three possible explanations for this. First, the parties that use the standard IMA believe that provisions for governing contractual relationships are fair and equitable. Second, the transparent nature of the judicial system carries with it the prospect of reputational damage should investment managers violate the norms and conventions associated with the implementation and execution of such agreements. Third, the widespread reliance on London as the site through which to contract financial service providers is such that it provides clients with the opportunity to legitimate decision-making—even if mistakes are made in the governance of those contractual relationships.

Contracting in Offshore Jurisdictions

In the section 'Contracting in London', we explained why financial institutions from continental Europe and beyond find London a desirable jurisdiction in which to write contracts with global financial service providers. It is apparent, however, that UK and European financial institutions also write contracts in jurisdictions beyond the immediate reach of the courts of England and Wales. For example, Dublin and Luxembourg are financial centres that specialize in certain types of financial services that provide tax-related advantages for both principals and agents. In this section, we are less concerned with European tax havens than offshore jurisdictions such as the Cayman Islands (Wainwright 2011; Wójcik 2013). Far-off jurisdictions give financial service providers like hedge funds opportunities to write contracts with distinctive governance characteristics.[6]

One difference between UK IMAs and the contracts offered in offshore locations is simplicity. Investors are typically offered an application form to purchase shares in a notionally self-governing fund *administered* by agents located in those jurisdictions, but *managed* by agents located in London. Application forms include provisions for the legal status of applicants, according fund administrators the opportunity to exclude certain institutional investors likely to demand greater transparency and accountability. According to the size of the investment, applicants are offered different classes of shares, some of which have voting rights. In many cases, the goals and objectives of the fund are broad and emphasize the style of investment. There may be little detail on the expected exposure to certain asset classes, target rates of return, risk budgets, and relevant benchmarks against which to judge performance. In some cases, clients have the right to sell their shares back to the fund (subject to terms and conditions). In other cases, clients must agree to long-term lock-in provisions and the commitment of further assets over specified periods whatever the performance of the manager.

In many cases, applicants are informed that the fund administrator and its agents have discretion over all matters pertaining to the fund's administration, management, and investment strategies. In some cases, applicants are given a fund Prospectus and a notice that the fund's Articles of Association are available upon request. If applicants purchase voting shares, they may be permitted to attend the annual general meeting of the fund held in the offshore jurisdiction. However, the power to appoint directors, set the agenda for annual general meetings, and purchase services from other agents typically resides with the fund administrator. The fund, its custodian, legal adviser, auditor, and investment manager are notionally separate legal entities. Yet, when deciding whether to invest in the fund, financial institutions interested in doing so normally receive presentations from the London-based investment manager. Whether by management and/or ownership, the offshore fund and its London-based investment service providers are intimately related (Wainwright 2011).[7]

This type of contract could be cast as relational in that it binds the parties together over the long term. In a formal sense, it has a governance structure that permits the representation of client interests. Whether or not clients hold voting shares and exercise their powers through the Articles of Association normally depends on whether they are willing and able to meet the threshold of investment required to claim voting rights, and wish to exercise those rights. The costs involved in exercising voting rights in offshore jurisdictions are significant, given that these types of investment vehicles are normally small components in most institutions' overall investment strategies. Consequently, it is not surprising that these contracts default to being purchasing agreements with little in the way of effective governance procedures. Here, form is an empty shell. Its functionality in terms of promised returns is the primary variable in deciding whether to enter into such a relationship.

THE MAP OF CONTRACT

In this chapter, we brought together the form and functions of contracts that bind asset owners to asset managers, noting that form (the laws of England and Wales) and function (the governance of the relationships between organizations) matter. At one level, the standard IMA has many properties consistent with a bilateral contract. It provides both parties with the opportunity to terminate any contract for investment services at will, with very little advance notice. The standard IMA also provides considerable detail in terms of the costs of services, the relevant benchmarks against which to evaluate performance, and reasonable boundaries on the asset classes and instruments deemed consistent with the investment mandate.

However, we have argued that the standard IMA is actually a relational rather than a discrete contract and, as such, is used to govern the relationship between parties. In this respect, the standard IMA dampens opportunism, limits overreaction to short-term events, and provides investment managers with a timeframe through which to demonstrate skill and expertise. If, as Kahneman (2011) contends, investment management promotes an illusion of skill, treating bilateral contracts as relational allows asset owners a chance to judge service providers against competing options. Knowing this to be the case, investment managers seek to dampen short-term volatility in returns, while guarding against trends in longer-term performance that fall short of the relevant benchmarks. By this logic, parties to IMAs understand the game played on both sides of the agreement and willingly accept its rules. Continuity of contract is often explained in terms of inertia (a behavioural predisposition). Here, we explain it by reference to the advantages of maintaining relationships, market risk, and uncertainty.

By this assessment, both sides of the market have an interest in converging on a standard or accepted form of contract. This is made possible by industry groups and professions with a stake in facilitating or deepening the market for financial services; in the absence of a widely accepted form of contract, institutions would more than likely try to avoid the transaction costs involved in designing, negotiating, and executing bespoke agreements. As indicated in Chapter 4, the largest institutions would probably substitute contracts for financial services with employment contracts for the personnel they use to produce these services inside the organization. Intermediation is made possible by the standardization of contract and, most importantly, the ready acceptance of one jurisdiction as the reference point for industry standards. The supply of, and demand for, UK contract law is a crucial ingredient in explaining the European map of the financial services industry and the geographical patterns of intermediation.

We have also sought to show that contract can vary between jurisdictions; for example, offshore financial centres can offer governance regimes that are quite different from those that dominate the investment management industry of the United Kingdom and Europe. Financial institutions willingly accept a form of investment contract that effectively denies them an active voice in its governance. This type of contract *appears* to be relational in that it binds the parties together over the long term with, in some cases, limits on withdrawal and mandatory periods of lock-in. Yet, notwithstanding the formalities associated with the governance of this type of arrangement, few investors have powers consistent with the effective governance of this type of arrangement. In effect, this type of arrangement is more consistent with a bilateral contract than with a relational one. Parties to these types of arrangements know the differences between standard IMAs and the types of agreements found in these offshore jurisdictions.

Even if investors have rights over the governance of these types of arrangements, they are very difficult to activate and carry through on a consistent basis. Why, then, do investors agree to terms that seem to violate the notional advantages of relational contracts? Here, there are three explanations. First, investors may come to believe that the standard IMA is a means of capturing clients rather than an equitable self-governing instrument. Investment management companies find refuge in these types of agreements as mechanisms through which to manage client expectations. This is especially important when asset owners have neither the time nor the resources actively to engage investment managers on issues that directly benefit their interests. Second, because in any event the industry as a whole may validate the standard IMA, rewriting these agreements can be a very expensive proposition without any certainty of producing cost-effective, superior rates of return.

There is a third, less obvious explanation. The existence of alternatives to the standard IMA and related expectations about its governance and execution are often strategic elements in asset owners' ongoing search for influence over the costs and benefits of contracting with the global financial services industry. In many investment portfolios, offshore providers running with asymmetric bilateral investment management contracts are relatively small components of institutions' investment programmes. Therefore, for example, the types of investment strategies that hedge funds based in offshore jurisdictions pursue are often different from those provided by the global investment houses that utilize the standard IMA across asset classes. A subtle and often-unacknowledged connection exists between the investment strategies of entities that require clients to sign up to asymmetric bilateral contracts and those that provide standard investment services. Asset owners use the existence of alternative investment managers based in offshore jurisdictions to impose discipline on larger providers in the global financial services industry.

IMPLICATIONS AND CONCLUSIONS

How financial institutions are managed, how their geographical scope is sustained, and how they are governed in relation to the network of service providers within and across markets are vital topics in our research programme. Here, we have extended the analytical framework established in earlier chapters to the nature and governance of contractual relationships in the industry, with particular reference to the place of London in the European market for financial services. In part, this chapter is about the design and functional performance of different types of contractual forms (bilateral and relational contracts). It is also about the special place of offshore jurisdictions in the market for financial services relative to continental Europe and London. Wójcik (2013) suggests that these offshore jurisdictions provide 'action spaces' for financial leverage and arbitrage. In this chapter, we have also pinpointed offshore jurisdictions as strategic elements in the governance of the contractual relations between asset owners and asset managers.

At one level, our conception of contract is quite conventional: it is how financial institutions govern their relationships with the financial services industry. It is argued that the form of contract is an important element in framing the relationships between these parties and has a number of important dimensions, including its place in the institutional framework of the state. As such, the form of contract, its design and documentation, and the proper ways in which these instruments are executed, are all reliant on the legal edifice.

We also show that contract has a number of important functions, including binding parties together over time and space in the context of financial market risk and uncertainty. Contract governs opportunism and the possibility that agents may exploit asset owners because the latter are unable to discriminate systematically between managers who are 'lucky' as opposed to 'skilled' in realizing rate of return objectives. To illustrate the ways in which these types of contracts are performed, we focused on three different strategies: *in situ* contracting, contracting in London, and contracting in offshore centres.

Our 'geography of contract' is rather different from the standard models that emphasize the role of contract as the means of realizing intended transactions. It is also different from more recent theoretical treatments that emphasize bilateral over relational contracts (Bolton and Dewatripont 2005). In our analysis, the sharp differences sometimes attributed to bilateral and relational contracts are less important than how they perform as governing devices designed to sustain relationships. By emphasizing governance, we have discounted contract as the embodiment of moral obligation or commitment, a thread of argument evident among legal scholars (Fried 1981; Kimel 2005). Nonetheless, it is apparent that the nature and performance of financial contracts are embedded in social and political formations (nation-states). Here, we have argued that form alone is insufficient to explain the use of contract as a means of governing commercial relationships over time and space (Dixon 2012; cf. La Porta et al. 1998; Thakor 1996).

Two implications follow from our analysis. One has to do with the ongoing debate about the significance of London for the global financial services industry. In some quarters, London casts an unwelcome shadow over continental Europe, subjugating domestic financial institutions into what some commentators disparage as casino capitalism (Sinn 2010). On the other side of the Atlantic, commentators rail against the continuing importance of London for international financial transactions. By our account, London thrives because of the density of market intermediaries found in the city (compared with the major financial centres of continental Europe) and the fact that these services are available in a jurisdiction that offers accepted contractual terms and conditions, underpinned by a judicial apparatus that promises adjudication on its merits if need be. That there are so few cases brought to court about the performance of contracts for financial services suggests that the form, functions, and performance of these contracts is thoroughly internalized into customary practice.

Our analysis of contracts in the investment management industry also pinpointed significant shortcomings in customary practice. The standard IMA carries with it certain advantages and disadvantages; it is a means of economizing on transaction costs, for it relies on familiarity and broad acceptance to gloss over the fact that it can be a mechanism for holding hostage clients with neither the resources nor the sophistication to rewrite contracts in their interests. Being a mechanism for governing relationships, the standard IMA tends to reinforce past commitment in circumstances where expert judgement may reasonably call for a reassessment of terms and conditions in the light of the performance of suppliers. On the other side of the market, providers offer simplified contracts that require levels of deference and delegation that clients would otherwise reject if suggested by major multinational service providers. That these rather different, even competing, forms of contract coexist in London, and are available to local, European, and international clients, suggests that customary practice is contested (albeit obliquely).

Between capture and coexistence is the strategic use of contract by clients to manage their service providers. To do so may involve, for example, discounting standard IMAs and forsaking the simplified contracts of offshore providers in favour of bespoke ones that explicitly serve the interests of clients, rather than clinging to the assumption that the parties to financial contracts are notionally equal 'partners' in the process of investment management. Here, of course, financial institutions may face significant barriers in realizing their ambitions to manage contract strategically. Few institutions have the resources necessary to design bespoke contracts, and even fewer have enough resources to oversee their implementation and compliance.

NOTES

1. For an exception, see Argyres et al. (2007), who report on a case study of the evolution of contract-making in the US information technology (IT) industry between an unidentified company and its service providers (also not identified). Their study has the virtue of making time an explicit consideration in a wider theoretical treatment of the design and development of private contracts.
2. There are various legal regimes around the world, based on quite different principles and historical traditions. La Porta et al. (1998) argue that English common-law regimes are more consistent with the imperatives driving global financial markets than many other types of regimes (notably continental European traditions). By their account, the global financial services industry gravitates to jurisdictions that rely on English common law, avoiding (when given a choice) other more restrictive or inflexible regimes. Our argument is consistent with this thesis, although we do not assume that the map of legal regimes is necessarily determinate of the nature and scope of global financial markets (see Clark and Wójcik 2007).
3. See also Faulconbridge's (2008) work on the structure and management of multinational law firms. He suggests that the interchange of legal professionals within and between these global companies aids the diffusion of templates and their sequential revision and recalibration to fit changing circumstances.

4. Asset owners often seek advice from legal advisers on the industry status of various types of contracts, relying on the norms and conventions in the industry to justify acceptance of terms or conditions that would be thought unacceptable in other jurisdictions or industries. This practice is consistent with the history of contract law and the deference shown to the terms and conditions of contracts willingly undertaken by parties to private contracts (see Eisenberg 1998).
5. There have been few UK instances of a contractual dispute over investment management coming to open court. The most celebrated case is Unilever Superannuation Trustees Ltd v Mercury Asset Management (*c.*2000), which was settled just prior to the start of proceedings. A recent case (2012) involved a UK fund manager and a group of its clients. The latter charged the former with changing the composition of its investment product beyond that allowed by the contract. The court held in favour of the fund manager. This case is exceptional, and may have harmed the reputation of the fund manager more than the claimed variation in investment strategy damaged the substantive interests of the plaintiffs. See Certain Ltd Partners in Henderson PFI Secondary Fund II LLP (A Firm) v Henderson PFI Secondary Fund II LP (A Firm) [2012] EWHC 3259 (Comm).
6. Clients are often unaware of the tax benefits that accrue to financial service companies (especially their principals) domiciled in offshore jurisdictions. Associated with these arrangements are back-office processing and compliance operations, the costs of which (local wages, office space charges, and telecommunication fees) are much lower than in London and New York. These benefits are often emphasized in 'beauty-parades'.
7. Investment managers may be better able to shelter their fund-related earnings from UK and US tax authorities in offshore jurisdictions if they use local rules and regulations pertaining to the treatment of such earnings. This can benefit the principals of such funds and spill over to employees via the payment of bonuses. This type of arrangement may be less attractive to large, diversified investment managers where ownership is diffuse.

7

Public-sector Contracting for Investment Services

A significant slice of the US financial services industry, representing more than \$2.5 trillion in assets under management (AUM), is dedicated to state and local public employee retirement systems (PERS) (Novy-Marx and Rauh 2009). These schemes cover approximately 18 million members, make payments to 8 million beneficiaries, and likely directly affect the current and expected welfare of more than 20 million dependants (Munnell 2012). When the indirect effects of public pension and health-care benefits are taken into account, state and local PERS effectively underwrite the long-term economic welfare of many US communities. Even so, US state and local PERS face challenging issues, in part reflecting the adverse consequences of the global financial crisis (GFC) for all investors and, in part, the increasing indebtedness of state and local governments—the sponsors of public-sector pension schemes. The bankruptcy of Detroit is representative of systemic financial problems at all levels of government.

The funding and performance of state and local PERS are important topics of research and public policy in their own right (Giertz and Papke 2007; Yang and Mitchell 2007). Because proffered pensions are typically defined benefit (DB) as opposed to defined contribution (DC), concern has been raised about the financial integrity of PERS (Beshears et al. 2011; Brown and Wilcox 2009; Glaeser and Ponzetto 2013). Concern has also been raised about the ineffectiveness of public accounting standards used to report scheme funding levels and liabilities (D'Arcy et al. 1999; Munnell et al. 2011). Furthermore, unlike their private-sector counterparts, which are subject to the federal Employee Retirement Income Security Act of 1974 (ERISA), it is arguable that the jurisdiction-specific nature of state and local retirement schemes provides opportunities for rent-seeking at odds with the best interests of both the beneficiaries of the plan and of taxpayers (Andonov et al. 2016; Lowenstein 2008; Mitchell et al. 2000).

It is tempting to treat US state and local pension systems as an integrated whole, as we do when conceptualizing and analysing financial institutions, markets, and regulation (Friedman and Kraus 2011). Whereas US private pensions—whatever their home jurisdiction—are subject to federal regulation, state and local public pension schemes are not. The patchwork of laws and regulations arguably reflects a bygone era of US federalism, which paid homage to state powers and the virtues of local arrangements consistent with local 'non-commercial' interests (Schapiro 2005).[1] Not surprisingly, there are wide variations in state and local governance and management practices on PERS (Monk 2009). Even so, critics contend that the procedures many state and local pension systems use to purchase financial services, including pre-contract screening devices such as state-mandated requests for proposals (RFPs), impose significant transaction costs on service providers bidding for contracts. Missing in this debate is research on the form and substantive content of RFPs among US state and local PERS; these devices frame the contractual process and set terms and conditions that affect the contracting for investment management services.

Making sense of the form and content of RFPs and investment contracts is challenging. While state and local governments may disclose the basic terms of service contracts, it is difficult to gain access to RFPs and the contracts themselves (as intimated in Chapter 6). We are able, in some instances, to report on PERS model RFPs and investment management agreements (IMAs). However, most RFPs and contracts are proprietary documents. Legal penalties apply should confidentiality be violated. The fact that PERS contracts are often subject to partisan commentary and debate reinforces caution about public disclosure. Interviews with senior managers of US public-sector pension institutions covering a range of topics and stretching over more than a decade have sustained our research on the governance and management of PERS (Clark 2008; Hagerman et al. 2006). As such, this chapter is an exercise in analysis and documentation grounded in knowledge of service agreements and contracts gleaned from fieldwork, freedom of information (FOI) requests, and intensive searches of state and local PERS websites.[2]

US state and local pension funds are embedded in social and political situations not of their making. At one level, this is a truism: institutions do not exist in a world of their own; they are made, if not as mirror images of their sponsors' interests, then certainly as expressions of the confluence of social forces that conceive of them as solutions to apparent problems (Granovetter 1985; Stewart 2011). As a consequence, institutions can be more or less effective in realizing their assigned tasks and functions (Roe 2006). Pension funds are also embedded in the global financial markets (as indicated in Chapter 6). In this chapter, we argue that the local dominates the global in the sense that the sponsors' procurement rules and regulations dominate the contractual process. This is unusual by international standards. We demonstrate that 'embeddedness' gives rise to a remarkable diversity in contractual norms and conventions—among states, within states, and within major metropolitan areas. We also argue that the effect of embeddedness has been to sterilize contractual agreements with providers.

In the next section, 'State and Local Pension Institutions', we provide a brief overview of the US state and local PERS sector, noting its economic significance and distinctive institutional ecology. This leads to a discussion of the stasis of this sector compared with the institutional dynamics of financial services and financial markets. Subsequent sections are devoted to the structure and content of RFPs, the models of contract apparent on the client side of the market, and lessons to be learned from a close reading of Illinois state and local Chicago IMAs. The long-term viability of Illinois state and local pension schemes are in doubt because of chronic underfunding and the collapse in discount rates occasioned by the GFC and quantitative easing by the US Federal Reserve (GAO 2012). In the penultimate section of the chapter, we briefly comment on the ill-fated proposal to establish the Oregon Investment Corporation (OIC). Had the legislation been passed, it would have given OIC the powers to bypass many of the public procurement rules and regulations that currently inhibit contractual relationships with external providers.

STATE AND LOCAL PENSION INSTITUTIONS

Relying on US census data, Munnell (2012) noted that there are approximately 3,418 state and local government retirement schemes. Most of these provide benefits to police and firefighters and are very small in terms of the number of members and the volume of financial assets (Munnell et al. 2013). By contrast, 107 state and 19 local pension schemes service 88 per cent of the total number of enrolled members and 83 per cent of all the financial assets. In some cases, these state-based schemes are 'universal' in the sense that they cover all state employees. In other cases, there are separate state-based plans for government employees and teachers. In others still, as in Massachusetts (Hagerman et al. 2006), the state-based schemes consist of multi-employer investment platforms that pool and invest the contributions of various state and local pension plans.

The vast majority of state and local government employees participate in DB plans that offer automatic cost-of-living adjustments. DB plans promise a retirement benefit based on final income and years of service (Clark and Monk 2008). DC plans provide a benefit based on the accumulated investment returns on contributions net of costs.[3] Munnell (2012) showed that in 1975 public and private employees had similarly high rates of DB pension-plan coverage. By 2010, 97 per cent of state and local government employees were covered by a DB plan, whereas only 26 per cent of private employees were covered by such plans.[4]

These differences have only widened in the intervening years. State and local government retirement plans are designed, like most pension plans in the Anglo-American world, to be funded in the sense that the value of invested assets should match expected future liabilities (D'Arcy et al. 1999).

The size of plans varies within states, between states, and across regions. In large part, these differences are driven by population, the size of major cities, and, more generally, a political commitment to the quality of public services. There are many small- and medium-sized funds, some large funds, and a small group of mega public-sector funds with more than a million participants and hundreds of billions of US dollars in assets. Mega funds include the California PERS, the New York State and Local fund, the Ohio PERS, Texas Teachers, the Florida Retirement System, and California Teachers. These systems are large by global standards (Clark and Monk 2011). At the other end of the spectrum, the City of Austin, the Denver School system, the Maine Local system, the Phoenix PERS, and Vermont State Employees have each about 15,000 members and less than $2 billion in AUM.

Many states have two large funds, typically separating state and local employees from teachers. There are also states with more than two funds. For example, Illinois has five large funds—Illinois Municipal (386,000 members), Illinois PERS (127,000 members), Illinois Teachers (365,000 members), Illinois Universities (190,000 members), and Chicago Teachers (60,000 members). The size of an institution is important, since it affects the nature and sophistication of the resources available to give effect to its goals and objectives. This 'fact of life' underpins our research on best-practice pension-fund governance (Clark and Urwin 2008a). There are also significant economies of scale in processing information—a necessary condition for mobilizing fund-specific assets such as the skills and expertise of employees (Amin and Cohendet 2004). Given the significance of financial risk and uncertainty for realizing pension-fund objectives, effective governance is a vital ingredient in fund performance.[5]

To facilitate the process of negotiating and agreeing service contracts, the industry has developed a set of model contracts that are designed to meet the normal expectations of clients and thereby economize on legal fees and the costs of negotiation. These IMAs have two obvious virtues. Smaller funds gain access to the products and services of the major players without incurring significant transaction costs, thereby obtaining a wider variety of investment products than would otherwise be available to these institutions. To the extent that model contracts are recognized as equitable and effective, small and large pension funds can use these devices to limit claims for special consideration by local or favoured service providers. Of course, model IMAs are subject to client-specific adaptation and negotiation (especially if large funds have their own staff capable of fine-tuning agreements). Even so, many pension plans have adopted standard IMAs without negotiation or amendment.

PENSION FUNDS: FORM AND FUNCTIONS

Successive pieces of US federal and state legislation have attempted to clarify and rationalize the proper form of a pension fund in relation to its beneficial purposes. Inevitably, legislation has often sought to solve past problems rather than anticipate the future (for example, the US ERISA, which the Studebaker debacle prompted). It is important to note that these institutions are not subject to competition for the right to provide pension income to beneficiaries. Instead, they have exclusive responsibility for collecting, managing, and investing pension contributions in accordance with terms and conditions found in statute, ordinances, and collective bargaining. Many have been in operation for more than fifty years and carry pension entitlements for at least another fifty years. By any account, these are remarkably long-lived institutions underwritten by their sponsor communities.

Governance and Management

A board of trustees comprised of political appointees and representatives of the employer, employee, and retiree, normally oversee US public-sector pension plans. In some cases, the state treasurer is the designated chair of trustees, managing a board that can include representatives from the governor's office. Given the electoral cycle, there can be considerable turnover in board membership, especially among the political appointees. Indeed, partisan political debate can envelop board members as state and local officials jostle for attention in the lead-up to elections. In large multi-employer public-sector funds, boards can have as many as twenty members. These funds carry a variety of interests that can complicate board deliberation when it comes to the formulation and implementation of investment strategy.

Boards typically employ the chief executive officer (CEO) and chief investment officer; they then delegate functions pertaining to the administration, management, and operation of the institution to this executive cadre. Delegation may be accompanied by itemized responsibilities. In the absence of such mandates, customary practice frames executives' roles and responsibilities subject to board approval (in general and on specific issues). In many cases, boards are quite heterogeneous with respect to members' skills and expertise in matters pertaining to the management of the fund. By convention, delegation is accompanied by deference to the skills and expertise of fund executives and employees. However, there can be close personal connections between board members, state and local political elites, and senior executives. These institutions are both sponsored by the community and can be held hostage to local interests in ways not so obvious in private-sector financial institutions.

Norms and Conventions

Public-sector pension plans are subject to reporting requirements on participants' expected benefits, funding levels, and funding assumptions. These requirements vary by jurisdiction, although local pension plans normally must abide by state rules and regulations. Importantly, reporting standards and requirements are rather opaque, leaving considerable discretion in reporting to funds and their sponsors, compared with the more exacting requirements found in the private sector through the Financial Accounting Standards Board (Andonov et al. 2012). Some commentators argue that the accounting standards used in the public sector disguise the nature and scope of plan liabilities in state and local pension plans (Brown and Wilcox 2009). Novy-Marx and Rauh (2009) suggested that state and local pension plans were underfunded (in 2008) by as much as $3.23 trillion.[6] Whereas US private-sector DB plans are underwritten by the Pension Benefit Guaranty Corporation (PBGC), state and local public-sector pension plans are 'underwritten' by local taxpayers (Lowenstein 2008).

Pension-plan investment is subject to the norms and conventions associated with finance theory (Merton and Bodie 2005). Modern portfolio theory (MPT), the efficient market hypothesis, and the norms associated with risk pricing (for example, the Black–Scholes theorem) inform Anglo-American pension-fund investment, including US public-sector pension plans. As noted in Chapter 6, public-sector plans are significant consumers of the products and services that the global financial services industry offers. For example, many public funds invest in index-based global equity portfolios. In large part, modern interpretations of fiduciary duty hold sway. So, for example, large diversified portfolios of securities are deemed consistent with the roles and responsibilities of plan trustees. Notwithstanding public commentary on the issue, few public-sector plans actively lobby corporate managers or campaign on behalf of the common good (for an exception, see Hebb and Wójcik 2005).

State and local pension funds share a form and many functions consistent with similar types of organizations found in the Anglo-American world. It is an organizational form that has been replicated around the world, finding expression, for example, in national pension reserve funds (Clark and Monk 2011). Having a shared purpose and similar functions, state and local plans are both more than and less than a universal institution. Embedded as they are in the community, their legitimacy relies on reciprocity, interdependence, and alliance formation (see Grabher (1993: 8–10) on 'loose coupling' among local elites). Being embedded in the community can mean having to compromise on the means chosen to realize plan goals (Bunderson and Reagans 2011). Recognizing the possible costs of loose coupling, plan sponsors and funds may formulate complex procurement procedures so as 'to protect against unethical behaviour including bribery and corruption' (Texas Municipal Retirement System, Investment Policy Statement, Section XIII, December 2012: 18).

CONTRACTUAL RELATIONSHIPS

As discussed in Chapter 6, pension plans produce the services they need either internally by employing the requisite staff, or externally through purchasing the services they need from the market via service contracts. This is the 'make-or-buy option'. However, in public-sector pension plans, the choice of insourcing versus outsourcing can be quite problematic because of the public scrutiny of fund salaries and benefits, and the application of standard procurement policies to the purchase of diverse financial services. Given their monopoly over the provision of pension benefits, it is not surprising that there are relatively few instances of organizational innovation in the sector. Alliances, networks, hybrid organizations, or joint ventures with other public plans are rare (see generally Helfat et al. 2007).

Employment Contracts

The standard US pension-plan employment contract matches that of its governmental sponsor or sponsors. As in most bureaucracies, employment contracts are job-specific, with wages and benefits set in accordance with occupation-related schedules and the compensation practices found in the government sponsor. After a probation period, employees are typically provided with continuing contracts subject to standards of conduct in public life. It is widely recognized that PERS salaries and benefits are not competitive with those found in the marketplace for similar types of jobs. There has been public commentary on proposed legislation in Oregon regarding the benefits of establishing an independent agency responsible for managing public-sector pension assets and liabilities (see Keith Larson's statement to the Senate Finance and Revenue Committee of 13 March 2013). Whereas much of the financial sector has been subject to mergers, acquisitions, restructuring, and periods of mass layoffs (and hiring), employment contracts in the public pension-fund sector are characterized by continuity, albeit without lucrative incentives and bonuses.

The offices of public-sector pension plans are often located in second-tier cities, along with those of their government sponsor or sponsors. By being located some distance from the market for financial services, the skilled employees of public pension plans may effectively give up opportunities to switch jobs and so benefit from the escalation of income that often comes with market density (Dixon and Monk 2014). Recognizing the problems related to the recruitment and retention of highly skilled employees, one response by public-sector pension plans has been to outsource the provision of those skills. Recognizing that some types of advanced financial services command an unassailable market premium, another response by public-sector pension plans has been to pursue a hub-and-spokes organizational strategy. Located at the core of the institution are planning and management responsibilities, sustained by commercial agreements with market intermediaries to supply related and complementary services consistent with realizing the goals and objectives of the organization.[7]

Pre-contract Screening

In much of the financial industry, clients conduct 'beauty parades' orchestrated by third-party consultants who evaluate vendors against the mandate and the related terms and conditions. In large funds, internal managers often perform this function, for they have the information and knowledge necessary to discriminate between competing service providers. In the public sphere, mandates are typically advertised in trade publications and on institutions' websites. Companies wishing to be considered are required to respond in accordance with official RFPs. These documents normally include the terms and conditions required by the relevant state and local governments (fund sponsors). In some cases, government agencies vet the vendors to determine their eligibility against a priori criteria and lists of preferred providers.

The standard RFP details the process whereby bids are to be made, the estimated value of the contract, the expected start and finish dates, the nature of the mandate (asset class and style of investment), and what is required in terms of an explicit commitment to state and local policies and procedures. Normally, this is a confidential process. Bidders may neither communicate with other possible providers nor directly contact the institution and its officers. Linked to the standard RFP are related documents of policies and procedures. In many respects, these are rulebooks that set out detailed definitions, selection procedures, required commitments and information, and the mechanisms by which competing bids are assessed and the winner notified. The screening process often excludes the opportunity for negotiation over, or variation in, the advertised terms and conditions.

Commercial Contracts

There are significant transaction costs associated with writing commercial contracts for financial services. In public-sector pension funds, the process of contracting for external services is highly formalized and often includes the boards of trustees. In part, their involvement is a means of educating trustees about the goals and objectives of the fund as well as the nature and scope of opportunities in the marketplace. In any event, trustees often insist on being involved because the choice of provider is an important decision for any pension fund. Binding procedures are a way of discounting the claims of certain external vendors for special consideration, while legitimating the choice of service providers to the public at large. In these ways, the use of RFPs to structure the bid process, combined with standardized and non-negotiable contracts, treat investment services as any other product or service purchased by public agencies. In many cases, few allowances are made for the contingent manner in which financial returns are produced.

CONTRACTS AND TEMPLATES

Having chosen preferred providers by asset class and investment product, deal-specific negotiation can expose public-sector pension funds to a number of challenges. Lacking the expertise of providers, funds can be taken advantage of when agreeing to terms and conditions in deal-specific negotiations. In addition, board members and senior executives can claim roles in the negotiation process, adding costs and/or complexity to the desired agreement. In any event, the high turnover on boards due to the electoral cycles of state and local governments means that some of the most important board members may be ignorant of crucial issues. Given that opportunism is an ever-present threat to the integrity of contracting (Williamson 1999), it is not surprising that *precaution* via mandated procedures and terms and conditions is the ruling ethos of the sector.

Content of RFPs

In this context, government sponsors of public pension funds and/or the funds themselves tend to converge on one or a number of default options that, in effect, replace deal-specific negotiation with off-the-shelf solutions. As noted, many state and local pension funds utilize RFPs as a mechanism for pre-screening the commercial providers of financial services. In these cases, RFPs are required by state and local governments, and are overseen by state attorneys' offices and the like. The disadvantages of screening devices are well known: the detail required of potential service providers when bidding for contracts is not always consistent with the imperatives driving financial markets. One response has been for industry bodies, such as the Investment

Management Consultants Association (IMCA), to produce model RFPs for investment services applicable to state and local PERS.

The first part of the IMCA model RFP provides a summary of the required services, the necessary qualifications of consultants, and instructions on how to submit proposals, including a four-page statement on confidentiality. Thereafter, respondents are required to answer nine questions on 'firm strength and stability', twelve on the 'investment process', and thirteen (covering three sub-sections) on 'service' provision, including performance reporting and fees. The second part (comprising twelve pages) provides a detailed exposition of the organization's investment objectives, policies, and guidelines, including statements on delegated authority, investment strategy, asset allocation, and asset classes. The Kentucky Teachers' RFP for investment consulting services has a similar structure, many of the same items and questions, and a standard statement on terms and conditions (comprising eighteen single-spaced pages). As a consequence, the Kentucky Teachers' model contract for consulting services is simply a set of statements on the consultant's obligations (six single-spaced pages). The Nevada PERS contract for investment advice, on the other hand, is only one-and-a-half pages long.

As for investment management services, an Internet search was initiated to identify state and local PERS that disclose RFPs to the public. In addition, a series of requests for information were lodged with state institutions, seeking the release of information on RFPs and model contracts. The Los Angeles County PERS provided a set of three RFPs—one for custodial services, one for active emerging markets equity, and one for real estate equity. The two equity RFPs had almost identical structures and contents, running over twenty-nine to thirty pages each. In each case, the first few pages dealt with the purpose, required qualifications of bidders, work requirements, and the bid process. The following three pages described the fund, its powers, confidentiality requirements, and a stipulation that bidders could not alter their proposals during the course of contract negotiations. Thereafter, another ten pages were devoted to the fund's requirements, including certifications by bidding companies and bidders' organization, management, and transaction histories. The last seven pages were devoted to questions on bidders' experience, investment philosophy, and performance in the relevant asset class and related products. The RFP for custodial services had a similar structure but required more information from bidders (spread over nearly eighty pages).

The detail involved in many PERS RFPs is such that the US market for financial services has become Balkanized, or differentiated according to the willingness of industry providers to deliver information on their business models and expertise. Furthermore, the structure and contents of these documents emphasize procurement policies and procedures rather than the realities of investment in global financial markets. It is notable that the Los Angeles PERS RFP for document photocopy services is similarly extensive, running to nearly eighteen pages, with many of the same headings and items as the investment RFPs (excluding the pages devoted to matters such as asset classes). In effect, formalism dominates the RFP process, being insensitive to the substantive nature of the service sought; as the photocopy instance illustrates, bid procedures often lack proportionality, thus treating minor service arrangements as they would service agreements for major items, including investment services.[8]

Templates, Terms, and Conditions

Nonetheless, a number of state and local PERS have formulated their own model contracts or IMAs for investment services. To characterize the contractual templates utilized by US state and local pension funds, an Internet search, and FOI requests for information about IMAs were made to US states and cities with pension and retirement benefit schemes. In the first instance, we identify the PERS that require service providers to respond to model IMAs. In the second instance, we compare model IMAs in terms of their substantive content, referencing categories of terms and conditions as well as the extent to which each fund included or excluded specific items. As to the first issue, in a small number of cases, state and local funds use model IMAs that match standard industry IMAs. In one case, the standard IMA, which ran to twenty-two pages, was accompanied by a fund-specific investment policy document that ran for more than seventy pages. The policy document overwhelmed the IMA, emphasizing the duties of providers relative to the prerogatives of the client.

Some twenty-seven funds were identified that either allow the public to view their model RFPs and/or IMAs or responded to our FOI requests (see Appendix). Six of these came from Illinois. Two—the Illinois Universities Retirement System and the Illinois Municipal Retirement Fund—were statewide funds, while four—the Chicago Park Employees' Fund, the Chicago Transit Authority Trust, the Chicago Teachers' Fund, and the Metropolitan Water Reclamation Fund—were Chicago-based. Included in the twenty-seven were some of the country's largest pension funds, such as Los Angeles City Employees' Retirement System (LACERS) and California Public Employees' Retirement System (CalPERS) from California, the Kansas PERS, the Minnesota Teachers' Fund, the Missouri State Employees' Retirement System (SERS), and the Texas Municipal Fund—as well as smaller funds such as the Ohio Police and Fire Pension Fund. More specifically, these funds control as much as $630 billion in assets, representing the Midwest, the southwest, California, and the Mountain States. Most funds had between $10–50 billion and $50–100 billion in AUM, while CalPERS ranks as one of the world's largest funds.

To summarize the size and scope of the model IMAs obtained from our twenty-seven institutions, we undertook a series of assessments of each

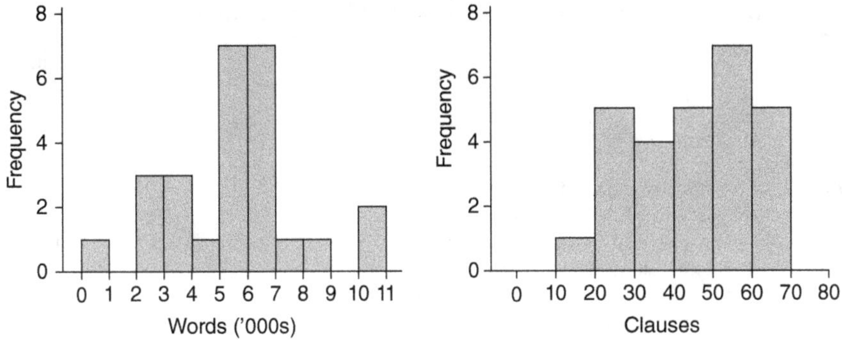

Figure 7.1. Word count and clauses in IMAs

Source: Authors

IMA. In terms of the number of words making up each IMA, Figure 7.1 provides a histogram showing that about 50 per cent of the IMAs were between 5,000 and 7,000 words in length. Less than 20 per cent of IMAs were between 2,000 and 4,000 words while 10 per cent were more than 10,000 words. As for page length (not included in Figure 7.1) 40 per cent were between fifteen and twenty pages, with 20 per cent being either ten to fifteen or twenty to twenty-five pages in length. In what follows, we look in more detail at the categories and items making up the model IMAs. In Figure 7.1, it is shown that IMAs varied widely in terms of their itemized conditions or clauses (within categorical headings). As such, it is possible to conclude that (a) IMA diversity is an important attribute of the sector, and (b) diversity is not only an issue of form (the organizational structure of IMAs), it is also an issue of substance (the content of IMAs).

To illustrate these points, Table 7.1 lists the IMA items or clauses shared by the 27 funds, working from a 100 per cent down to a 60 per cent share of the 110 items or clauses identified across the 27 fund IMAs. The twenty-five shared items are hardly surprising in that they establish the significance of state law, the relevance of fiduciary duty, the start date of contracts, and the means by which an agreement may be terminated. Notably, most of these agreements appear open-ended without an end date (which is normally provided in RFPs). At the other end of the spectrum, Table 7.2 provides a summary of the nine IMA items that do not appear in more than one fund. Model IMAs come with a termination date in only one instance. Many other items appear relevant, though some are more important than others. For example, it is significant that only one fund provided for the resolution of 'problems or disputes'. It is also remarkable that one model IMA would protect the selected investment manager from 'any acts or omissions by . . . a broker dealer'.

Table 7.1. Contractual items shared by state and local pension funds (per cent)

Item	Percentage
Fund name	100
Effective date/contract start date	96
IM name	93
IM subject to fiduciary standards/requirements	93
IMA includes details of how IM is terminated	93
Prior approval required in transferring mandate	89
IM authorized to invest assets under state law	85
IM required to hold errors and omissions insurance	81
IMA covers IM's registration under applicable laws	78
IM shall monitor and report to fund on investments	78
IMA stipulates fund has the right to terminate agreement unilaterally	78
IMA details confidentiality of all fund's documents and proprietary information	78
IMA offers specific details on fee structure	78
The power and authority to enter to the contract	74
IM is authorized to issue 'broker instructions'	74
IM performs duties with care, skill, prudence, and diligence	70
IM shall promptly notify fund of any change in status (i.e. any material change in senior management, etc.)	70
IMA identifies indemnification clauses	70
Governing law (Agreement)	67
IM reports monthly and meets annually with the fund	63
Full authority to purchase/sell/exchange the assets with discretion and subject to the investment strategy	63
IM shall secure and maintain at all times during the term of agreement a bond or bonds protecting the account assets	63
IMA stipulates the entity to register the securities	63
IMA details the process for auditing IM	63

Source: Authors

One way of characterizing commonalities among funds is that those items most often shared are those that refer to the respective powers of the clients (funds) and the investment managers (providers), the obligations imposed on investment managers regarding reporting and transparency, the relevant standards by which investment managers' actions are to be judged, and the rights of funds to terminate agreements (including reference to any notice period). On the other hand, many IMAs include items that refer to specific requirements. For example, some funds require the identification of investment managers' authorized representatives, others require investment managers to ensure the security of deposits, and others still give quite detailed instructions on the nature, scope, and timing of investment manager reporting. Few share requirements regarding conflicts of interest, soft-dollar arrangements, proxy-voting requirements, ethical policies, and the like. It is noteworthy that less than 33 per cent of the funds shared most items.

Table 7.2. Contractual items *not* shared by state and local funds

Expiration date/contract end date
Authorized persons definition
IMA authorizes other services to be performed by IM
IM stipulates that subsidiaries and key officers not in financial distress
IM waives right to assert any claim against fund
IM not responsible for any acts or omissions by broker or dealer
IMA requires gifts and political contributions disclosure
IM to provide list of personnel authorized to act on its behalf
Fund responsible for diversification of investments of the Trust
Fund only incurs liability in co-fiduciary relationships or co-investments
IM to act appropriately to achieve investment objectives
IM shall use a consistent, replicable investment strategy
IM to actively educate fund staff and board
Fund and IM shall meet and negotiate in good faith any disputes
IMA describes how fees and costs litigation are allocated
IM complies with the Americans with Disabilities Act
IM complies with Drug-Free Workplace Act
IM complies with Child Support Compliance Act
IMA proscribes a performance-based fee structure
IM shall manage the assets using a consistent, replicable investment strategy
IMA describes how fees and costs of attorney in terms of litigation are dealt with

Source: Authors

Community Norms

The funds with the most IMA items were the Chicago Teachers' Fund (sixty-eight), the Chicago Park Employees' Fund (sixty-eight), CalPERS (sixty four), and LACERS (sixty-three). Those with the fewest items included the Nevada PERS, the Louisiana State Employees system (twenty-three), the New Mexico Education Board (twenty-four), and the Ohio Police and Fire Fund (twenty-nine). In general, funds with the fewest items tended to have one or two requirements for most categories (such as fiduciary duty), whereas those with many more items tended to have more requirements under each category heading. Funds with the fewest number of items were also those that tended to exclude some categories altogether, such as proxy voting, ethical investment, or provisions against side-payments. The size of fund (AUM) was not associated with the number of categories or items.

We expected to see a close resemblance between local IMAs, reflecting shared learning and experience, and the loose coupling often associated with jurisdiction-specific political coalitions (Grabher 1993; Storper and Venables 2004). When comparing the Illinois state-wide funds, the Universities' fund ($11 billion AUM) and the Illinois Municipal fund ($25 billion AUM), however, we found significant differences both in the numbers of items (fifty-two against twenty-nine) and in the substantive content of each template.

Whereas the Universities' fund required its investment manager to disclose any pending legal proceedings or disciplinary actions against the company or its employees, as well as any subsidiaries and the amounts of monies likely to be transferred through the agreement, the Municipal fund did not. The Universities' fund also required the IMA to specify what entity would have physical control of the assets and cash and how proxy votes were to be handled, while the Municipal fund did not.[9]

As for the Chicago funds, there were obvious similarities (apart from the Transit Authority fund, which had far fewer items than the other three). Where the other funds identified the relevant custodian, the applicability of state law, and the possibility of varying the IMA at the discretion of the fund, these items were not found in the Transit Authority fund. The latter did not include two statements regarding the exclusive interest of the fund relative to the investment manager, which are included in the IMAs of the other three Chicago funds. The Transit Authority fund was also different in that it gave investment managers the discretion to exercise their powers of proxy voting, yet did not require them to keep detailed records of their proxy voting actions. The three funds used categories consistent with the state-wide funds. However, the overlap is not so consistent as to suggest that there was a *common* template shared at the state *and* Chicago metropolitan levels.[10]

There was an intriguing difference between the Illinois Universities' fund and the Municipal one. The Board of Trustees of the former consists of four elected (active) members, two elected (retired) ones, four appointed by the governor, and a chair; the governor appoints the latter who furthermore serves as chairperson of the Illinois State Board of Higher Education. The governor's appointees are, quite obviously, political and, in recent years, they have brought considerable expertise in financial markets to the board. The Municipal fund's Board of Trustees, by contrast, has three elected (active) members, one elected (retired) member, and four who are nominated and appointed via the participating units of the Illinois local government. The Universities' board is less parochial than that of the Municipal fund, for it includes members with knowledge and understanding of financial services.

COMMONALITIES AND DIFFERENCES

Based on our research on state and local PERS procurement procedures, it is apparent that any contract for financial services offered by a US public-sector pension plan is embedded in an ensemble of statutes, policies, and procedures. The substantive content of such contracts are to be found, in the first instance, in requirements that exist prior to the contract for services. In large part, these requirements are *not* subject to negotiation—they are *conditions* by which any service provider must abide when accepting a contract. These requirements reflect the interests of various community groups, as well as a common interest in awarding contracts to those most likely to meet a priori requirements. These types of requirements may or may not be consistent with realizing the financial objectives of public pension funds. Many issues are included in these requirements, reflecting public policies and commitments that often match the character of local jurisdictions. Given the diversity of US states, cities, and communities, it is not surprising that there is considerable variation among jurisdictions in the nature and scope of requirements.

We do not mean to imply that community interest in the investment policies of public pension funds is, in any sense, illegitimate. Rather, the issue is whether local ensembles of statute, policies, and procedures are conducive to the formation and execution of contracts that are consistent with the long-term financial integrity of pension schemes. Also at issue is whether the process of contracting offers enough freedom (discretion and delegation of powers) to use the contract as an effective means of governing ongoing commercial relationships. More often than not, these types of contracts are 'precautionary', in the sense that they are written to forestall any embarrassment that otherwise might be visited on the political sponsors of state and local pension funds. As a consequence, in the US public pension-fund sector it is difficult to use contracts for financial services in flexible and strategic ways within the process by which contracting is framed and executed (as suggested by Weber and Mayer (2011)).

It was also found that a number of large and small public-sector pension funds have adopted an IMA model *not* specific to the jurisdiction. Adoption can be a signal to market providers that, whatever the strictures involved in the procurement process, fund boards and officials expect a level of performance consistent with industry norms. Adoption of an IMA model may also signal a level of expertise and experience relevant to the industry, thereby implicitly discounting the importance of the formal RFP process. This may be especially significant in the larger funds, which have people on their management boards who have experience of and responsibilities in industry. To the extent that boards have the authority and responsibility to select providers from shortlists of qualified contenders, the IMA framework may be used to discriminate between potential providers (in subsequent rounds of review). Nonetheless, it is entirely possible for the overarching procurement process to subsume the substantive significance of IMAs.

It was found that a number of large state-wide public-sector pension plans have adopted model IMAs, suggesting that their size, significance, and ongoing relationships with industry providers have encouraged these institutions to imitate related practices found in the private sector. However, it is not simply an issue of financial size and significance by state of jurisdiction. It was also found that Illinois state-wide and local pension funds have adopted the IMA framework. This is either the result of peer pressure, innovation via a 'follow-the-leader' process of diffusion, or policy initiatives encouraged by the governor, state treasurer, or state legislature. Notice, however, that funds have *not* adopted a standard IMA. Rather, the models vary in terms of their categories and items (substantive content). As such, the commonalities among funds in relation to Illinois RFP procedures are not carried through to the design of a common Illinois IMA. The implication is that fund-specific political considerations drive the IMA design process, even if Illinois RFP procedures encourage formal similarities.

A variety of factors can explain the persistence of state and local PERS. These include the constitutional powers of state governments, the fiscal circumstances of different jurisdictions and their related PERS, and the difficulties associated with coming to an agreement with different groups of public employers, unions, and occupations. It is arguable that the coexistence of state and local PERS in Illinois and elsewhere comes at a cost, although it may be difficult to identify those costs because they are absorbed in the governance and management of specific institutions. Likewise, it is difficult to estimate the costs of RFP procurement policies compared with (possibly) more flexible IMAs. Nonetheless, a number of states have sought to reform the structure and management of their public pension systems, and to impose state-wide investment institutions or platforms shorn of the impediments associated with public procurement policies.

To bypass the possible costs of politicization, the State of Oregon brought to the legislature a proposal to establish the Oregon Investment Council (an advisory body) as the Oregon Investment Corporation (OIC). If Senate Bill 120 had been accepted, the OIC would have been responsible for investing the assets of the Public Employees Retirement Fund (PERF) and a large group of related government funds, including the Oregon University System Fund and the Local Government Employee Benefit Trust Fund. In many respects, the proposed OIC had many of the attributes of institutional best practice, including a relatively small governing body comprised of directors qualified by virtue of their financial experience and skill (see Clark and Urwin (2008a) on best-practice governance). Furthermore, the mandate of the OIC was to be relatively well defined, and the rules governing the behaviour of board members and fund executives were based on prudence and the fiduciary duties of loyalty and impartiality. In this respect, it could have been a model institution, realizing the benefits of scale and with a licence to contract external providers in line with industry norms rather than local standards.

The 2013 legislation required the fund to abide by state regulations regarding its independence from the State of Oregon and the latter's employers, the purpose of the fund, and what would have counted as being a prudent investor. Crucially, the legislation exempted the fund from many existing state regulations, including those relating to personnel relations, public facilities, public contracting and procurement policies, standards of financial administration including budgeting and expenditure, the salaries and expenses of state officers and employees, and the administration of public funds. For example, state policies regarding treatment of specific classes of individuals, categories of service, compensation regimes, and selection processes and procedures would be the responsibility of the OIC. In effect, the OIC would have had the power to establish its own procedures consistent with the tasks and functions attending an investment institution rather than being required to adopt the public procurement policies required of state institutions. The OIC would also have the power to build its own investment capabilities and negotiate contracts for services consistent with industry practice.

However, there was one aspect of the original legislation that would have undercut the best intentions of the sponsors of the legislation. The legislation provided for a governing board consisting of five voting members and one non-voting member. It also gave the state governor the power to appoint four of the voting members, provided they were 'qualified' by virtue of their 'training and experience in the field of investment or finance'. The state treasurer would have been the fifth voting member and the director of the Public Employees Retirement System was identified as the board's sixth (non-voting member). Consistent with past legislation, the terms of the appointed voting members of the board was to be four years (with reappointment for another term possible).[11] However, each member would have 'serve(d) at the pleasure of the governor and may be removed from office with or without cause'. In effect, the governor would have controlled the board, whether directly or through the threat of termination. It is arguable that this is consistent with the precautionary ethos that is evident in the governance practices found in the US state and local pension-fund sector. Nonetheless, it is inconsistent with the principles of best practice evident, for example, in appointment procedures and policies that insulate governing boards from the political cycle and direct political influence (Clark and Monk 2011).

IMPLICATIONS AND CONCLUSIONS

Diversity is a key characteristic of US state and local pension systems (Mitchell and Smith 1994). Many funds utilize rather limited IMAs, and are normally idiosyncratic rather than consistent with sector- or industry-specific norms. In any event, of the 120 larger US public-sector funds that account for the majority of US public employees enrolled in pension saving schemes and the vast majority of AUM, only about 20 per cent of funds have introduced model IMAs. Most funds use the RFP process to set the terms and conditions that govern the provision of investment management services. Our research demonstrates the extent to which the market for financial services in the US public pension-fund sector is Balkanized, implying significant transaction costs for both the buy side and the sell side of the market. While there is evidence of a neighbourhood effect influencing the form and content of public-sector funds' model IMAs, this effect is more often found at the city or metropolitan level than among funds within states or between funds of adjacent states.

In many jurisdictions, state-mandated and local policies dominate the procedures through which public pension funds purchase financial services and products. RFPs and related policy documents set out specific requirements, as well as the rules and regulations that govern bid processes and selection procedures. Contracts written in the shadow of these policies and procedures are shallow documents, more often precautionary in intent and effect than enabling transaction-efficient commercial agreements. Contracts for investment services reflect state and local political interests and commitments, denying the utility of standardized IMAs so as to give effect to the financial interests of communities across the United States. This reinforces the bid *process* rather than the effective execution and realization of value through ongoing contractual relationships. As noted, this also tends to Balkanize the market for investment services across the sector, limiting suppliers to those comfortable with sector and jurisdiction-specific RPF and certification procedures.

In these circumstances, adaptation to changing market conditions has been relatively slow, especially with regard to the mix of asset classes, investment products, and providers. In the open-ended relational contracts typical of the investment management industry, by contrast, adaptation can be quite responsive to market conditions—albeit subject to recurrent rounds of amendment and negotiation. This may account for the fact that state and local pension funds have been slow to revise the expected rates of return downwards, or to change their assumptions about expected discount rates. It is arguable that these assumptions are embedded in inflexible systems of service procurement and sterile contracts for investment services. Many funds would find it difficult to reconcile desired flexibility in investment strategy with a lack of flexibility of asset allocation strategies, the terms and conditions imposed on investment managers, and variation in those arrangements as markets change.

These observations are no doubt familiar to informed commentators on state and local pension funds. However, as Munnell (2012) has observed, differences among funds in terms of their rates of return have proven to be difficult to explain. Econometric models using common independent variables such as board composition have not been particularly successful as predictors of fund-specific rates of return. We have suggested that the differences *between* states in the nature and scope of RFPs, and in the related rules, regulations, policies, and procedures governing the procurement of investment services, are significant. These differences provide insight into how and why some public funds are more adaptive to market conditions than others. If Lo (2012) is correct in arguing that adaptiveness to risk and uncertainty is a prerequisite for superior investment performance, it may also be a prerequisite for the survival of US state and local pension systems.

NOTES

1. Attempts have been made to establish common US standards of public-sector pension-fund management through the National Conference of Commissioners on Uniform State Laws and, specifically, the Uniform Management of Public Employee Retirement Systems Act (1997) (Volume 7A Pt. III). This model code focuses on holding assets in trust, prudent investment rules, and disclosure consistent with ERISA and more recent federal court decisions regarding the nature and scope of fiduciary duty (Willborn 1998). To date, only two states have adopted this regime.
2. FOI conventions rarely apply to state and local PERS. For example, disclosure by the Pennsylvania Public School Employees' Retirement System (PSERS) is governed by the Pennsylvania Right-to-Know (RTK) law (65 P.S. & 67.101 *et seq.*). This means that information requests are 'granted to the extent that the records exist and are public'. Further, according to the RTK legislation, 'agencies are required to provide public records, not answer questions'. See the Response by the Pennsylvania PSERS 29 January 2013 to Public Records Act Request by Stanford University 22 January 2013. In a similar manner, the Missouri Local Government system indicated that they have a model IMA but were unwilling to disclose it to us, indicating 'we believe this document is an attorney–client work paper and therefore falls under the exceptions of public viewing in Missouri's Sunshine Law (Missouri's FOIA law)' (email 23 January 2013).
3. States such as Alaska, Michigan, and Rhode Island have introduced other kinds of pension savings schemes, including 401(k) and hybrid or mixed schemes. Agnew and Hurwitz (2013) provide a comprehensive inventory of state-based pension and retirement saving schemes.
4. It is likely that many older private-sector workers also carry with them DB entitlements from past employers (public and private). Job switching rarely involves consolidating benefit entitlements, unless workers switch between employers in a sector that provides an umbrella pension benefit institution. To the extent that private-sector employees are offered pension benefits, the standard benefit is now DC not DB.
5. Size is not everything. The ratio of retirees to active participants tends to drive the fund risk budgets, asset allocation formula, and equity exposures. Being relatively small can accentuate the opportunity costs of being mature, while being large can provide even mature funds with options not otherwise available to smaller, less mature, and more risk-tolerant institutions (Ambachtsheer 2007).
6. These estimates and the assumptions on which they are based have been widely disputed; see the report of the Government Accountability Office (GAO 2012) and

the commentary published in *Pensions & Investments*, 21 January 2013, p. 10, by Keith Brainard (research director of the National Association of State Retirement Administrators).

7. In some cases, being on the margin of markets has been made into a virtue via the recruitment of skilled employees who are assigned responsibilities in high-value segments of financial markets to which they would not otherwise have access until later in their careers at major investment houses. With continuity of employment, there is an opportunity for skilled staff to invest in their human capital to realize long-term career aspirations. With market turmoil, job security with responsibility is an investment in future career options (Dixon and Monk 2014).
8. Service providers to the sector may prefer highly detailed rather than open-ended terms and conditions. This is because the former provide explicit limits to the nature and standard of services required, while the latter may mean that the service provider becomes hostage to the changing preferences of clients. With political intrusion in matters relating to service provision and providers, precaution may be as important to providers as it is to the sponsors of retirement plans.
9. The Houston Firefighters fund, Maine PERS, North Dakota Investment Office, Kentucky PERS, and San Diego County fund all indicated that they do not use model RFPs or IMAs. The Ohio PERS indicated that it uses a model RFP and the Missouri Local Government fund and Pennsylvania PSERS indicated that they use a model IMA. The Public Safety System of Arizona indicated that while the state has a procurement code, it was exempt from its provisions.
10. This is not surprising given the tensions occasioned by the often different party affiliations of the Illinois governor and Mayor of Chicago, as well as differences in the party-political make-up of the Illinois legislature and City of Chicago assembly. One way of characterizing these differences is to refer to 'downstate' Republicans and big-city Democrats. Similar tensions are found in many US states where rural and ex-urban interests are at odds with those of the major metropolitan centres.
11. See, for instance, Oregon Laws and Resolutions 1967 (Chapter 335, Sec. 2) and Oregon Laws and Resolutions 1987 (Chapter 877, Sec. 1) referring to the constitution of the board of the Oregon Investment Council.

APPENDIX

State and local retirement benefit systems included in the analysis of model IMAs

State and local retirement benefit systems		US dollars in 000s (as at 30 June 2011)			Actuarial funding ratio (%)	Types of plans offered
		Asset market value	Annual contributions	Annual benefit payments		
California	California Public Employees' Retirement System	243,015,119	0	14,670,473	83.40	DB
California	Los Angeles County Employees' Retirement Association	39,452,011	1,407,917	2,269,791	83.30	DB
Colorado	Fire and Police Pension Association of Colorado	3,135,997	133,603	221,314	79.50	DB
Florida	City of Orlando General Employees' Pension Fund	251,429	–	–	82.00	DB
Florida	City of Orlando Other Post-Employment Benefits Trust					
Idaho	Public Employee Retirement System of Idaho	11,673,428	484,651	616,612	89.90	DB
Illinois	Chicago Teachers' Pension Fund	10,312,762	394,473	1,077,980	59.70	DB
Illinois	Chicago Transit Authority Retiree Health Care Trust					
Illinois	Illinois Municipal Retirement Fund	24,837,061	1,657,643	1,317,305	83.00	DB
Illinois	Metropolitan Water Reclamation District Retirement Fund					
Illinois	Park Employees' Annuity and Benefit Fund of Chicago	452,810	20,658	61,191		
Illinois	State Universities' Retirement System of Illinois	10,970,753	1,382,088	1,529,640	35.50	
Illinois	Teachers' Retirement System of the State of Illinois	37,471,267	3,235,606	4,304,870	46.50	DB
Kansas	Kansas Public Employees' Retirement System	13,468,853	868,952	1,213,140	62.20	DB
Kentucky	Kentucky Teachers' Retirement System	15,130,606	1,340,199	1,419,861	57.40	DB
Louisiana	Louisiana State Employees' Retirement System	9,703,497	755,388	957,395	57.60	DB

(continued)

Continued

State and local retirement benefit systems		US dollars in 000s (as at 30 June 2011)			**Actuarial funding ratio (%)**	**Types of plans offered**
		Asset market value	Annual contributions	Annual benefit payments		
Louisiana	Teachers' Retirement System of Louisiana	14,577,211	1,286,003	1,658,783	55.10	DB
Minnesota	Teachers' Retirement Association	17,303,576	463,548	1,484,650	77.30	DB
Missouri	Missouri State Employees' Retirement System	7,866,917	294,738	640,659	79.20	DB
Nevada	Public Employees' Retirement System	25,255,268	1,393,341	1,438,359	70.60	DB
New Mexico	New Mexico Educational Retirement Board	9,588,563	555,776	736,858	63.00	DB
Ohio	Ohio Police and Fire Pension Fund	9,688,358	455,626	1,049,874	69.40	DB
Oklahoma	Teachers' Retirement System of Oklahoma	10,156,357	925,120	1,038,167	56.70	DB
Pennsylvania	Public School Employees' Retirement System	51,199,994	1,701,218	5,298,918	75.10	DB
Pennsylvania	Pennsylvania, State Employees' Retirement System	24,377,179	742,601	2,705,263	65.30	DB
Texas	City of Austin Employees' Retirement System	1,665,789	108,221	129,842	65.80	DB
Texas	Texas Municipal Retirement System	18,599,039	1,029,743	873,609	85.10	Hybrid

Source: Authors

8

Advisers and Consultants

Pension funds depend on a network of intermediaries that are linked in sequence to frame and implement their investment strategy. In many cases, asset owners try to find and make contracts with multifunctional financial service organizations, discounting, where possible, the costs and consequences of going to the market for each separate but related financial service. Even multifunctional financial service companies combine insourcing with outsourcing by subcontracting those activities that they cannot produce internally in an effective manner to specialist service providers (see Chapter 5). In this respect, intermediation has at least three dimensions—between savers and financial institutions like pension funds, between financial institutions and service providers, and between service providers (paraphrasing Diamond 1984).

Planning the production of financial returns typically involves entities that advise pension funds on the selection of organizations that provide investment-related services (Goyal and Wahal 2008). This is another dimension of intermediation, describing how the demand for financial services is intermediated, as is the supply of financial services. It is standard practice for asset owners such as endowments, foundations, pension funds, and sovereign wealth funds to rely on intermediaries, including actuaries and investment consultants, to determine the nature and scope of the financial services needed to realize their investment objectives. It is also standard practice for these types of intermediaries, which we define as 'consultants', to search the marketplace (local and global) for relevant service providers, ranking them in terms of performance and reliability, and conducting 'beauty parades' at which shortlisted providers pitch their virtues to clients (Shleifer 1985).

In this chapter, we focus on the role of the consultants who advise clients on investment strategy and implementation.[1] There is a significant literature on the global consulting industry and management consultants (McKenna 2006). Here, though, there is less research, although there are strong opinions. Some critics view investment consultants as gatekeepers standing between asset owners and the global financial services industry, thereby controlling access to the ultimate decision-making on a preferential basis (Coffee 2006). Going further, Youngdahl (2013) contended that investment consultants have undue influence over clients, often exploiting their privileged position to gain long-term contracts, high fees, and even kickbacks. Knight and Dixon (2011) argued that investment consultants have stifled innovation because they have little incentive to go beyond industry norms and conventions. Doubts have also been raised about the value of investment consultants, and the money management industry in general, as revealed by the performance of investment managers and products (Gennaioli et al. 2015; Jenkinson et al. 2015).

Investment consultants do more than sell 'solutions to problems specified by the client' even if 'consultants are represented as independent, objective advisers with superior know-how' (Glückler and Armbrüster 2003: 277). Investment consultants are essential to the investment performance of small and medium-sized asset owners, and even for some large investment institutions. They tend to have long-term relationships with these organizations and provide crucial services, including skills and expertise either unavailable in these organizations or, if available, insufficient in relation to financial risk and uncertainty. Contract is one of the threads holding these relationships together. Many funds are limited in their power to bargain the terms and conditions of service agreements. Yet, investment consultants often place a higher premium on equitable relationships than on exploiting their market position, so seek to maintain market share via standardized contracts (see Choi and Triantis (2013: 55) on the ways in which market strategy mediates bargaining power in contract negotiation).

In this chapter, we provide an analytical account of the various roles of investment consultants; we examine how and why their roles vary in relation to the size (assets under management (AUM)) of clients and the ways in which they can foster or stand in the way of innovation. The chapter begins with a discussion of the theory of intermediation, based on landmark papers in the field including Allen (1990), Allen and Santamero (1998), and Diamond (1984), as well as Gorton and Winton's (2003) survey of the field as it relates to banking and finance. This is augmented by reference to the management literature on organizational capabilities and resources (Helfat and Peteraf 2009). There are useful synergies between these fields that deepen our understanding of the role of consultants in general and the role and responsibilities of investment consultants in particular. The third section of the chapter focuses on what investment consultants do, which touches on our earlier discussion (see Chapter 5) of what senior managers do in asset owning and asset management companies.

This is followed by a stylized representation of the contractual relationships between asset owners and consultants, distinguishing between small, medium-sized, and large asset owners. We bring to light the subtleties of these relationships given the capabilities and resources of differently sized institutions. Going beyond functionalist conceptions of intermediation, we suggest that ambiguity is characteristic of these relationships. We argue that both parties may desire ambiguity because the production of investment rate of return is subject to market risk and uncertainty. Ambiguity in these relationships provides a space in which to adjust investment strategy and its implementation to unexpected changes in market conditions. This account of the virtues of ambiguity is informed by Hachigian (2015), and recent research on the importance of reflexivity in modern economies (Bathelt and Glückler 2011). In the penultimate section, we observe that the benefits of ambiguity must be judged against its possible costs, particularly where industry norms and conventions entrench advisory relationships to the detriment of innovation.

THEORY OF INTERMEDIATION

For many analysts, the rationale for intermediation is best understood via the theory of transaction costs. In his treatise on the theory of the firm, Spulber (2009) argued that firms exist because consumers cannot get what they want from separate suppliers in a cost-efficient manner. This argument is obviously inspired by Coase (1937), who argued that the size of any firm is a function of what can be done efficiently within its boundaries, as opposed to outsourcing to organizations that provide intermediate goods and services. In this section, we consider two versions of this argument—one found in financial theory and the other in management science. We show that these arguments converge on a number of counts.

Financial Intermediation

In the finance literature, the issue of intermediation is conceptualized in terms of the existence and functions of banks (or bank-like institutions) (Mayer and Vives 1993). Diamond (1984) began by asking why savers do not lend to investors directly: why are banks needed to manage the relationship between savers and investors? Diamond provided a set of interlocking answers. First, given that there are many savers, searching for investors and then overseeing or monitoring their actions can be, in the aggregate, very expensive. Second, there are likely to be free-riders who shirk responsibility for their share of the costs of searching and monitoring. Third, monitoring is an expensive business, with a premium on information—savers may be poorly placed to collect the needed information to make effective decisions.[2] In effect, it is assumed that banks provide two functions. First, utilizing their skills and expertise to realize investment objectives, they bring together and coordinate savers. Second, they expend scarce resources on monitoring the performance of entrepreneurs to the point where further monitoring is not repaid by better performance.

This model has been developed in many ways—see, for example, Gorton and Winton (2003), who looked at the related research on the various functions of banks. Much like banks, institutional investors bring dispersed savers together, coordinate their interests in terms of desired investment returns, and then go about the business of investing the stock of assets in relevant and available opportunities according to target rates of return. Having realized investment gains or losses, these are then returned to savers. As we show in Chapter 5, many theorists believe the make-or-buy choice unproblematic, notwithstanding the very different implications attending the use of employment contracts (for the make option) and service contracts (for the buy option). Whereas Coase (1937) provided a rationale for insourcing versus outsourcing by focusing on the transaction costs of one mode of organization versus another, we have challenged his assumptions and the implications drawn thereof.

Capabilities and Resources

The theory of intermediation presupposes that financial organizations are flexible in that the switching costs between modes of organization are not a constraint on the choice of modes. In management science, transaction costs are also significant—witness the importance attributed to Williamson's (1975) theory of markets and hierarchies. Here, the issue is whether an organization or set of organizations facing a changing environment has the internal capabilities and resources necessary to respond in an effective manner. In our analysis, capabilities include the decision-making protocols by which organizations frame and implement strategies consistent with their goals and objectives. Resources are defined as the tangible and intangible assets of an organization.

There is some debate about the distinction to be drawn between the terms 'capabilities' and 'resources'. Amin and Cohendet (2004) do not use these terms but refer to an organization's competencies—how it processes and distributes information and knowledge given the premium on coordination. We have noted that coordination is a significant issue for many financial organizations, especially where senior managers are reliant on task- and domain-specific expertise. Helfat and Peteraf (2009) would merge the two terms, especially in a changing environment. Even so, we believe there is merit in maintaining the difference even if in certain situations investment consultants can be seen as 'resources' as well as 'capabilities'. As resources, intermediaries like investment consultants add information and knowledge not otherwise available within the sponsoring organization. As capabilities, investment consultants provide skills and expertise to underwrite the investment decision-making process (Clark and Urwin 2008a).

By this logic, intermediation adds to an existing organization's capabilities and resources. This can be important because the latter are either unavailable to the relevant organization by virtue of its size and position in the market, or are so task-specific and expensive that few managers can justify holding them internal to the organization. At the same time, intermediaries can bring information and knowledge of the competitive environment that few financial organizations would be able to gather themselves. As such, the management literature on intermediation ends up in a similar place as the finance literature, for both suggest that search costs provide a rationale for intermediation.

Organizational Form

The theory of intermediation prioritizes functions over organizational form (see Merton and Bodie 2005). As such, we run the risk of functional essentialism in that this logic tends to ignore the histories and geographies of organizations and the ways these shape the conception and delivery of certain functions. This is not just an issue of degree; it is about the extent to which there is a match between an organization's capabilities and resources and its functional performance in realizing its objectives. In some settings and in some types of organizations, capabilities and resources may be so inadequate as to compromise the realization of their missions. Furthermore, a close match between functions and organizational form can be self-defeating. To the extent that the organizational structure lags behind functionalist imperatives, for instance because of management entrenchment and rent-seeking behaviour, organizational form can be a constraint on the nature and pace of innovation.

In any event, functionalism is hardly an adequate representation of the evolution of organizations, financial or otherwise. As Roe (2006) observed, organizations are normally created for a variety of reasons, some of which cohere and some of which conflict with one another. For example, the express purpose of a pension fund is to reap the benefits of scale and scope in the provision of retirement income not available to individuals acting on their own account. However, few pension funds stand alone: their activities and interests are subject to their sponsors' separate and collective interests as well as the balance that must be struck between different generations of workers (savers) who participate in such organizations. Functionalist conceptions of organizations decry the costs associated with embedded claims and counter-claims for priority. Nonetheless, these types of organizations exist because they are coalitions of interests, notwithstanding the ambiguity about their proper purpose and functions.

Vagueness about the purpose of an organization may be the price paid for its existence. Lack of clarity is one meaning of ambiguity (see Heath and Tversky 1991; cf. Ellsberg 1961). Ambiguous goals and objectives can have adverse consequences for decision-makers and their performance in financial markets (Epstein and Schneider 2008). Ambiguity often characterizes an organization's decision space, where issues and possible solutions are left unstructured to facilitate negotiation and agreement. In this chapter, we suggest that ambiguity about consultants' roles and responsibilities vis-à-vis their client organizations can be beneficial to both parties and desired as such (*contra* Fox and Tversky 1995). There need not be one 'right' organizational form if uncertainty is characteristic of the environment (Hachigian 2015).[3]

WHAT DO ADVISERS DO?

In what follows, we provide a schematic framework of what investment consultants do in three different types of pension funds—small, medium, and large. Our framework is also applicable to endowments, foundations, family offices, and sovereign wealth funds, though it is not our intention to demonstrate empirically its relevance to these organizations. Size matters because it is, in part, a proxy for organizational capabilities and resources. Nonetheless, we are mindful that size can be a significant constraint on realizing the value of embedded capabilities and resources. Size begets complexity and complexity can adversely affect coordination, thereby discounting the notional advantages of size—these points were developed in previous chapters, notably Chapters 3, 4, and 5.

Case 1: Small Fund, Representative Board, Wholly Outsourced

We assume that a small fund is an organization that manages less than US$5 billion in assets and liabilities. This assumption is somewhat arbitrary given that being 'small' does vary in relation to the jurisdiction and origin of an organization. We also assume that a board, representing the fund's stakeholders and including its sponsor and beneficiaries, governs the fund. Again, the composition of such boards can vary by jurisdiction and type of sponsor (Tilba and McNulty 2013). Finally, we assume that, to fulfil its mission, this type of organization buys the functions it needs from the market for financial services. While the fund has employees, it is assumed that they help to administer the process of selecting providers, including their oversight.

In this case, our stereotypical fund works through a two-tiered model of governance in which the board delegates the implementation and oversight of investment strategy to an investment subcommittee comprised of a select number of board members. Ultimately, the board receives the subcommittee's recommendations, which it either accepts or rejects. In this case, the investment adviser provides the relevant capabilities and resources appropriate to framing investment strategy and its implementation through the selection of asset managers and related service providers. In other words, the investment adviser *enables* investment decision-making. Indeed, given the composition of the board—and often a lack of relevant capabilities and resources—the investment adviser is the *means* by which investment strategy is conceived and realized.

This arrangement has three dimensions. First, the relationship between the client and consultant is one of mutual dependency. Without the investment adviser, the board would be unable to make effective investment decisions and would lack the means by which to implement its investment strategy. Even so, the nature of the contract binding the parties together is framed in such a way as to provide the client with the right to terminate the relationship 'at will' (for example, subject to a month's notice). It is assumed that the client's threat of termination is what 'controls' the adviser. Second, a conservative culture tends to dominate investment decision-making. Widely accepted concepts and tools, appropriate to the investment subcommittee if not the entire board, are used to frame investment strategy. Third, therefore, the relationship between the client and adviser references industry norms and conventions. Boards and their advisers find comfort in benchmarking investment strategy and fund performance against similar organizations (Shleifer 1985).

Case 2: Medium Fund, Representative Board, Mixed Sourcing Strategy

In this case, we could think of our idealized fund as responsible for assets and liabilities in the region of $10–30 billion. This is, by necessity, a crude approximation. Nonetheless, in relation to Case 1 and Case 3 insights are to be derived from elaborating the relationship between clients and investment consultants in this type of fund. In this case, the fund has a three-tiered model of governance—the board, the investment subcommittee, and an investment management committee. Whereas the board is representative of sponsors and beneficiaries, its members are selected, in part, for their knowledge and understanding of finance in general and, perhaps, investment in particular. Even at the lower end of the size category, the fund may have sufficient assets to manage a portion of its assets in-house, rather than out-of-house. In-house investing tends to be based on public markets and it utilizes the standard toolkit of investment management techniques, including portfolio diversification. Here, investment consultants are less concerned with *enabling* than with *facilitating* investment decision-making. They may also be important in providing information about the *scope* of market opportunities for investment. This can complement the implementation of investment strategy.

Here, the relationship between the fund and the investment consultant is best understood in relational terms, rather than in terms of the asymmetrical logic evident in Case 1. While the fund *relies* on the investment consultant, it does not *depend* on the adviser for investment decision-making. In effect, responsibility for investment decision-making and determining the means by which investment strategy is to be realized is shared. Furthermore, the investment adviser is able to act as a *resource* for the investment committee and, by extension, for the board as well as the management committee. One implication is that this type of fund can develop a process of investment decision-making to ensure that only strategic issues, rather than the day-to-day business of overseeing the performance of providers internal and external to the fund, come to the board. A second implication is that continuity and mutual learning mark the relationship between the client and the adviser.

Case 3: Large Fund, Representative Board, Reliant on Insourcing

In this case, our idealized fund has more than $40 billion in AUM. Because of its size, and its importance to the sponsor or sponsors, the board is likely to be comprised of individuals who have a representative role *and* knowledge of financial issues consistent with the mission of the fund, if not specifically about investment management. These rare individuals often command terms and conditions of appointment consistent with being a board member of a large corporation (Clark and Urwin 2010). This type of fund has a four-tiered governance structure with significant investment capabilities and resources located within the organization. The relationship between the board's investment subcommittee and the management investment committee is an essential element in the framing and realization of investment strategy. While the board is ultimately responsible for investment strategy, the knowledge located in the management committee and the governance of the relationship between the management investment committee and the investment subcommittee are crucial in setting the mandates for the fund's teams of portfolio managers, the fourth tier of the organization.

Here, investment consultants can have two rather different roles. At one level, they can provide members of the investment subcommittee with 'independent' insight and knowledge—a not-entirely welcome reality check on the aspirations of the fund's senior executives. To do so effectively, however, investment advisers must be embedded in the investment process to the extent that they understand both the issues and the logic, or rationale, underpinning the fund's investment strategy and implementation. Otherwise, consultants may start to compete with senior management, especially if they have a willing audience on the board of the fund. By necessity, such investment consultants are highly skilled individuals with a reputation to uphold. At another level, they also provide information and knowledge about the investment strategies of other similarly placed organizations.

Three implications are to be drawn from this particular case. First, the relationship between the client and consultant appears symmetrical in that the investment process honours the skills and expertise of the investment adviser in relation to those of the in-house team. Second, in reality, the relationship may be discrete in that its continuity depends on the consultant demonstrating value to the organization in which they serve. This is not a relationship of dependency or reliance; it is a relationship cast in terms of cost and benefit. Note that the board, through its investment subcommittee, may come to rely on the investment consultant to provide a critical perspective on investment strategy, otherwise absorbed by the institutionalization of the fund's investment decision-making process. Third, there remains a role for investment consultants that can bring to the client insight, information, and opportunities that the latter is unable to produce in the short or medium term. In this respect, the relationship is one of complementarity via substantive knowledge rather than dependence (Case 1) or reliance (Case 2).

CONTRACTS AND SERVICES

In the previous section, 'What Do Advisers Do?' we provided a brief framework for understanding the role of investment consultants in which we emphasized the size of clients and their systems of governance and management. This is one way of conceptualizing what consultants do. It is equally important, however, to acknowledge that investment consultants, like other service providers, do what they do through the medium of contracts for services. In principle, contracts for services provide both parties with legally enforceable agreements through which to pursue their mutually advantageous but separate interests (Bolton and Dewatripont 2005). In practice, however, contracts for services must be flexible enough to accommodate the various ways in which clients and consultants work together, while providing each party with a degree of detachment consistent with evaluating the costs and benefits of such relationships (Kimel 2005).

Framing and implementing investment strategy involves networks of consultants and service providers, each of which has a role in the process. In the United Kingdom, for example, actuaries clarify the goals and objectives of investment strategies with reference to asset plans and liabilities (or obligations). Once they have established the investment goals and objectives of an organization via a strategic asset allocation model, investment consultants provide information on the performance of various asset classes, investment managers, and opportunities. Legal advisers, in conjunction with the representatives of investment managers, formulate contracts for investment management services and, ultimately, the agreement of both parties. In many cases, a custodian holds and switches assets between clients and investment managers, while providing assurance that those organizations holding assets on behalf of clients do so effectively and efficiently. In some cases, a reporting agency collects performance data from the investment managers and reports back to the client. Overseeing this entire process are accountants and internal administrators.

This characterization of the types of organizations that make up the investment management process is, no doubt, simplistic. Nonetheless, it provides a way of situating investment consultants in the financial services ecosystem. Notice that a separate contract governs each link in the chain. In many respects, these contracts are rather similar in form, if not in the function-specific expectations of clients and providers. The global financial services industry relies on the laws of England and Wales to formalize the process of intermediation and govern the flow of capital around the world. This is also apparent in Europe, notwithstanding that the legal systems of some countries do not cohere with the laws of England and Wales (La Porta et al. 1998). The contractual templates for services provided by associations or organizations representing different types of intermediaries are also under this umbrella. In that they favour accepted norms and conventions to counter the high costs of negotiating bespoke contracts, these templates allow parties to economize on transaction costs.[4] To avoid the costs of going to court, private agencies often offer arbitration mechanisms to help clients and providers resolve disputes (McCormick 2010).

Standard contracts covering accountants, actuaries, investment consultants, investment managers, and information providers share three common characteristics. First, they are typically open-ended in terms of duration, but give clients the power to terminate at will. Second, they are typically silent on the precise nature of the services provided and, more often than not, refer to its *type*—for example, 'actuarial services'. Third, they typically provide a statement of fees. In these ways, they are rather shallow documents that rely on industry norms and conventions on matters such as what comes with an agreement between a client and an actuary, or a client and an investment consultant. Industry respondents report that side letters and/or appendices with detailed terms and conditions, covering topics such as the liability of service providers, the protection of intellectual property, non-disclosure to third parties, and much else besides, often accompany standard contracts.[5] In sum, contracts are more than signed agreements: they are sets of documents that map the scope of engagement while providing frameworks for collaboration (Davis 2013).

At one level, it could be argued that clients have a powerful lever over service providers, especially investment consultants and investment managers, when the instrument binding the parties together enables the client to terminate the agreement with minimum notice. It would seem that this type of standard contract is, or should be, in the vernacular of contract theory, a bilateral contract that can be voided and/or renegotiated as the client desires. It might also be argued that the threat of termination is sufficient to ensure that the relationship between the client and its provider is equitable, even if it does not favour the client. However, the termination of such service contracts can come with significant transaction costs, including the winding down of service provision; the search for, and recruitment of, another provider; the transition between providers; and the upfront costs involved in situating the new provider in the chain of intermediaries that together manage the investment management process.[6]

Notice that contracts for services are typically between those nominated to represent the client and those nominated to represent the company that is providing the services. On the client side, assuming that the pension fund is the legal entity, those authorized to sign such agreements are likely to include the chair of the board and a subset of board members. On the service provider side, those authorized to sign such agreements are likely to include the company secretary, or the nominated officers of the company legally entitled to sign such agreements. In substance, the service provider's 'client' is, more often than not, the board of the fund, whereas the 'service provider' is an individual or set of individuals whom the service provider employs. Those involved may change over time as board members leave their positions and new members are appointed, and as employees of the service provider either leave to take on other responsibilities within the company or leave employment with the company. Recognizing that the continuity of advisory relationships in part determines market share, investment-consulting companies are mindful of the value of maintaining these relationships, even if the individuals involved take on other responsibilities.

Given the transaction costs involved in switching providers, as well as possible changes in the membership and composition of boards, what appears to be a bilateral relationship favouring the client can become, by necessity, a contract marked by continuity rather than disjuncture. This is a significant issue for any fund, whatever its size. Nevertheless, consider the case of a small fund governed by a representative board that outsources the production of investment returns. As demonstrated, the fund may have limited skills and expertise on its board and lack experienced staff through which to manage its assets and its relationships with service providers. In such cases, consultants provide clients with the needed capabilities and resources to function as organizations. Not surprisingly, to economize on the costs of providing services to any individual client, the consultants standardize the services they provide. Both sides of the market acknowledge, but rarely explicitly recognize, that customization in accordance with the needs of clients is an expensive proposition; by this logic, industry norms and conventions are, on average, functionally efficacious.

In a medium-sized fund, by contrast, where the client *relies* on the investment consultant to facilitate investment decision-making and its implementation, the relationship between the client and the service provider is more equitable, if not entirely symmetrical. The costs of termination could be high, given the lack of suitable internal capabilities and resources that could compensate for the termination of such a crucial service. Nonetheless, a medium-sized fund may be able to plan for long-term changes in the nature and composition of the intermediaries that make up the investment management process. Furthermore, this type of fund may be able to bring relevant expertise in-house to ensure that reliance is mediated by informed judgement on the board and/or among its senior officers. This may be a win-win proposition in that external advisers are able to develop relationships with knowledgeable officers who favour innovation in the process of investment decision-making and the nature and scope of investment management. Alternatively, both parties may have a common interest in entrenching their positions.

In large funds with developed investment-related capabilities and resources, the relationship between consultants and clients arguably favours clients over consultants. It would be possible to terminate consultants' services with due notice without an immediate or appreciable loss of value to clients. What is valuable about an investment adviser in these circumstances? There are three possibilities. First, consultants and their companies may have specialized skills and expertise unavailable to organizations internally. Second, independent advisers may be a useful medium through which to interrogate the investment strategies of senior managers, testing assumptions and the plausibility of expected outcomes based on alternative sources of information. Third, consultants may be able to bring to investment strategies knowledge and understanding of the strategies of similar organizations otherwise treated as competitors. Continuity in these relationships depends on the value consultants bring to investment performance.

In Figure 8.1 we summarize this discussion by reference to six criteria that describe how fund size affects the relationship between asset owners and investment consultants. Ranging from left to right across the figure, these are status (the nature of the relationship), function (what consultants provide clients in each instance), content (the material basis of the relationship), knowledge (what consultants add to any discussion of the issues), contract (the nature of the formal relationship between the parties), and value (the net contribution of the consultant to the client). Clearly, these criteria are related, overlap, and reinforce one another. For instance, a large fund is likely to value its relationship with an investment consultant to the extent that the latter's

Size of Fund	Criteria					
	Status	Function	Content	Knowledge	Contract	Value
Small	Dependent	Enable	Process	General	Asymmetrical	Unquantified
Medium	Reliant	Facilitate	Expertise	Market	Relational	Beneficial
Large	Contingent	Complement	Substance	Specific	Discrete	Measurable

Figure 8.1. Stylized account of the consultant–client relationship
Source: Authors

knowledge of key issues makes a substantive difference to the fund's investment performance. Having a contingent relationship based on adding value, clients could seek discrete rather than relational contracts.

Notice the differences between small and large funds across the six criteria. To enable investment decision-making, small funds depend on their advisers being focused on managing the process rather than the substantive content of the investment issues the clients face. Because clients have limited capabilities and resources, they expect consultants to have a wide knowledge of the field. At the other end of the spectrum, large clients are not dependent on consultants but treat the relationship as contingent and substantive, demanding specific knowledge in relation to their ongoing investment programmes and projects. That is, the value of the adviser to a large fund is measurable and may be subject to a performance-oriented contract. In between, medium-sized funds tend to treat consultants as resources, relying on their expertise for framing and implementing investment strategy rather than depending on them for the process of decision-making itself. While in some cases the difference between dependence and reliance may be slight, reliance can be managed whereas dependence may imply capture.

AMBIGUITY, CONTRACT, AND FINANCIAL MARKETS

In the section 'Contracts and Services', we argued that the relationships between institutional investors like pension funds and investment consultants are governed by a type of contract that is open or ambiguous about the specific tasks and functions required by the client.[7] Commonplace conceptions of ambiguity associate the term with something lacking coherence, precise definition, or accepted meaning. Presumably, it is something to be avoided or at least something to guard against. If so, it is perhaps surprising that contracts governing clients' relationships with financial intermediaries are ambiguous about the precise tasks and functions an investment consultant must perform to be rewarded by fees and the reimbursement of costs. Here, however, are three objections to the commonplace presumption against ambiguity.

The first objection comes from Merton and Bodie (2005). In their analysis of the institutional structure of modern financial markets, they argue that, notwithstanding the primacy accorded to individual behaviour in neoclassical economic theory, institutions play a key role in mediating and even resolving evident problems of coordination in episodes of market irrationality. By their account, the institutional structure of financial markets is a response to problems of coordination and agent behaviour: institutions provide a decision-making framework within which agents can go about realizing their separate goals and objectives. By necessity, the institutional structure of financial markets must have a degree of continuity or resilience that individual agents are unable to realize on their own account. The implication is plain: the open-textured or ambiguous nature of many service contracts is a desirable attribute rather than something problematic.

The second objection comes from Keynes (1948), Knight (1921), and scholars who believe that financial markets, more than many other types of markets, are subject to risk *and* uncertainty. By this account, the open-textured or ambiguous nature of clients' service contracts with intermediaries is a necessity rather than evidence of poor governance, given that sometime in the future the client and the service provider might need room for manoeuvre to respond adequately to changing circumstances. For financial organizations that either depend or rely on investment consultants for investment decision-making and its implementation, an itemized contract specifying the tasks and functions of the consultant would be both expensive to oversee *and* a constraint on an organization's ability to respond to unanticipated shifts in financial markets. This objection links together the existence of uncertainty with the nature and scope of the transaction costs involved in repeatedly re-contracting.

The third objection is entirely situational. Industry observers note that if contracts for services are ambiguous, they give the client opportunities to gain access to consultants' skills and expertise that go beyond the normal expectations of any such relationship. Here, two elements are in play. At one level, industry norms and conventions typically provide clients with ready-made expectations about the nature and scope of advice available through investment consultants. While it is a reference point, available at low cost to most clients, it need not be determinate. Clients can exploit the interest of investment consultants in the continuity of contract by pushing them beyond industry norms and conventions on a case-by-case basis. Put slightly differently, investment consultants can become the medium through which institutional investors learn about developments in the field. In doing so, investment consultants can empower their clients, so allowing them to change the relationship into one that is more equitable in terms of clients' knowledge and understanding of market performance and investment strategy.

These three objections suggest that there is virtue to be had in open-textured or ambiguous contracts with investment consultants. Returning to Merton and Bodie (2005), it is arguable that this feature is common to the relationships between clients and intermediaries in financial markets and is a vital component of the institutional structure of the global financial services industry. It facilitates coordination over time; it mediates apparent tendencies towards under- and overreaction to financial market volatility; and it sustains flexibility within contractual relationships. A fixed contract with an explicit menu of roles and responsibilities could impose high transaction costs on agents, which may, in periods of significant market turmoil, threaten the stability of the entire financial system.[8]

Even so, ambiguity can bring significant costs. Norms and conventions, by their nature, reflect established practice, providing the yardstick by which to decide what is acceptable, unacceptable, and contested. Norms and conventions, by definition, also lag behind the leading edge of best practice, even if professional bodies and organizations legitimize them by certifying their efficacy. Lacking the skills and expertise to make their own judgements about the utility or otherwise of what are deemed contested modes of investment management practice, small and medium-sized funds cling to past practices until the latter fail in the face of changed circumstances. Clients then seek 'new' ways of doing things from consultants who, buttressed by industry best practice, reinforce their reliance on these organizations. There are three kinds of costs in these arrangements—the costs of convention, opportunity costs (relative to what may have been achieved), and the costs of coming late to the market where premiums have already been realized.

In any event, contracts with consultants are typically silent on the *performance* of investment consultants, but not on issues such as best endeavours, conflicts of interest, and due diligence. Once again, norms and conventions shape client expectations in relation to what counts as a 'good' or 'bad' adviser. Moreover, in terms of investment performance, advisers do not take responsibility for the decisions that boards and committees take on investment strategy and its implementation. Enabling and facilitating decision-making is not the same as setting a short or long-term investment strategy. Investment consultants are deliberate about policing the boundaries of their responsibilities in this regard. Ambiguity on this matter is unacceptable to investment consultants, their companies, and the sector.

Being embedded in epistemic communities of practice and entrenched in long-term advisory relationships protects investment consultants from the vagaries of financial markets and the possible arbitrary decisions of clients. This means that investment consultants are normally neither rewarded nor penalized for investment performance. This is also true of many institutional investors. Pension funds, sovereign wealth funds, endowments, and family offices typically have an exclusive relationship with the ultimate beneficiary—in effect, they have exclusive control over the assets they manage. Merton and Bodie (2005) suggest that the 'permanent' nature of these organizations and their relationships to beneficiaries is a response to the probable costs of overreaction to short-term events.

Neither investment consultants nor the boards of institutional investors directly suffer the effects of poor performance, which insulates the former from accountability in the face of adverse events. It also minimizes any incentives that consultants might have to promote innovation and change in the face of market dislocation.

MODES OF INNOVATION

In theory, changes in the 'environment' in which organizations operate drive innovation (Rosenberg 1995). Most relevant to our interests, however, is the widespread belief that it is market disjuncture or failure that drives it (Scott 2008). By this account, shortfalls in financial performance should prompt clients to demand solutions from their investment consultants that break with the past and offer an alternative path or means for realizing their goals and objectives (Birkinshaw et al. 2008). Innovation can be found in the process of investment decision-making, in the mechanisms linking investment strategy and its implementation (for example, insourcing or outsourcing), and in the choice of service providers and investment products. None of this need be 'new' in the sense of 'invented'. There may be options that have been ignored because their salience was not apparent or proven.

Market Disjuncture

It is arguable that shifts in financial market performance over the past couple of decades have driven innovation in client–consultant relationships. This is not a new story; it has been told and retold over the past couple of decades in the aftermath of various financial crises. Institutional investors and policy-makers alike have responded, in part, by rethinking their modes of practice and behaviour (Akerlof et al. 2014). Here, though, we focus on two aspects of the relationship between clients and consultants—innovation in organizational form and function, and innovation in the norms and conventions underpinning the framing and implementation of investment strategy.

The problem facing investors is that of distinguishing noise from signal—namely differentiating between market information that is simply a jumble of data in need of sorting and sifting for value on the one hand, and market information that is unequivocal about its implications for framing and implementing investment strategy on the other (Clark 2014). Previously, we have drawn attention to the path of the FTSE100 stock market index since 1984. There appear to have been three rather different episodes over the past thirty years. Episode 1, 1984–98, which saw a steady trend in stock market appreciation; episode 2, 1998–2007, characterized by an extended cycle from a peak (bubble) through a trough to another peak (bubble); and episode 3, post-2008, which the Bank of England characterizes as dominated by systemic risk. Left to the reader is the latest, episode 4, the period since markets were stabilized and economic growth returned to the UK and US economies only to be dampened by the euro crisis, Brexit, and the slowdown in the Chinese economy.

In retrospect, one can readily describe each episode, but *during* each episode it was much more difficult to 'call' its characteristics and to frame investment strategy and its implementation. In the course of episode 1, it would have been relatively easy to make money via a passive index tracker. This period was, as intimated, dominated by benchmarking performance and switching between providers within asset classes according to relative performance (Shleifer 1985). As data accumulated on market performance, it became clear to academic researchers and investment consultants alike that switching between providers in a growing market was consuming scarce resources, including the time devoted to managing the switching process (Litterman et al. 2004). It was more effective to concentrate on longer-term asset allocation than on benchmarking performance. As large funds adopted this strategy, the practice became accepted in the industry and the investment consultants of medium-sized and smaller funds started to mimic the early adopters.

The technology, media, telecommunications (TMT) bubble marked the end of an era (Shiller 2005). As global markets lost value, emerging market investment products came into their own. Initially, these products were amorphous in that there was little in the way of shared attributes or ways of summarizing their characteristics. Information about, and knowledge of, their underlying characteristics was at a premium. Investment consultants took the opportunity to compare options and tout winning products. Larger asset owners tended to adopt these types of products, deploying their own capabilities and resources to inform decision-making. This changed when Goldman Sachs coined the acronym 'BRICS' (Brazil, Russia, India, China, and South Africa)—a marketing device that gave emerging markets a recognized meaning and a benchmark from which to evaluate competing products. In effect,

Goldman Sachs sought to make a market for its emerging market product in an attempt to bypass investment consultants. Consequently, it brought many small and medium-sized funds into the market for emerging market products.

Another narrative became important: labelled the great moderation, it foretold a future of economic growth and stability underwritten by low inflation and global integration (Blinder 2015). Asset owners were asked to look forward, rather than backwards, in framing their investment strategies. Lacking data on the performance of related investment products, vendors simulated performance. Seeking investment returns in the face of declining discount rates, asset owners, large and small, were receptive to alternatives. In this environment, investment consultants were often bystanders as the narrative gained credibility, as this story was justified by a theory of stock market capitalism that discounted the likelihood of market instability (Clark 2011). The global financial crisis (GFC) punished those who stayed too long in the bull market. Even so, it is hoped that the market will soon return to 'normal'.

Innovation in Form and Function

Market volatility has taught us three important things about the relationship between asset owners and investment consultants. First, more is expected of investment consultants, especially their ability to assess the likely performance of 'new' asset classes and investment providers. Even the smallest pension funds have re-evaluated their dependence on advisers in the light of low funding levels and the collapse in discount rates. Second, it has become apparent that while their business models depend on maintaining relationships with clients, investment consultants do not share the costs of poor performance, whether caused by market movements or by factors specific to individual funds. Third, there is a premium on innovation. In part, this is about recovering lost ground, but it is also about diversifying risk. Accordingly, the skills and expertise of investment consultants and their companies have become more important.

One response has been to reconsider the 'form' of the relationship between investment advisers and clients. Here, asset owners foreground the contract binding the parties together rather than leaving it in the background as is typical of most contracts (Kimel 2005). By doing so, clients signal that the industry norms and conventions underwriting expectations of consultants' roles and responsibilities are not necessarily consistent with asset owners' particular interests. As well, it suggests that the ambiguity inherent in these relationships is insufficient for clients to remake investment strategies in ways that take into account new market realities. Put slightly differently, where market disjuncture breaks with past industry practices and the available scope for incremental adaptation, asset owners are forced to confront their own inadequacies and the costs and consequences of conventional behaviour.

For small pension funds, whose governing bodies are conscious of their dependence on consultants to frame and implement investment strategy, one response has been to outsource those functions via fiduciary management (FM) agreements. In effect, such outsourcing changes the organizational form of funds, leaving in its stead a new contract for services rather than the functions normally associated with a pension fund. This gives asset consultants an opportunity to frame and implement investment strategy more effectively. In essence, the related contract is for management 'performance' rather than for facilitating the process of fund decision-making *as if* the managers of such funds were able to realize their objective (see Chapter 9).

For medium-sized funds, also aware of their reliance on investment consultants in a changing environment, one response has been to intensify their relationships with service providers. Rather than maintain a relationship that is only periodically evaluated in terms of its efficacy, medium-sized funds have sought closer relationships with their investment consultants. This has had a number of effects. At one level, it has subtly changed the relationship from reliance to mutual engagement. At another, by intensifying the process of investment decision-making and drawing on the expertise of their asset consultants, medium-size funds have sought to understand the substantive issues better. In effect, asset owners have sought to redefine their relationships with consultants and go beyond the acknowledged ambiguity inherent in the scope of these relationships.

For large funds, aware of their internal capabilities, resources, and possible power over investment consultants, their relationships with these service providers have been subject to review. In many cases, insourcing has raised questions about the benefits of asset consultants who have less knowledge and understanding of the issues relevant to such funds than the investment professionals that such funds employ. Equally, the identity of the 'client' is less clear in these cases, especially if management committees have considerable scope in framing and implementing investment strategy. In such cases, contracts for services can be revised to focus on adding value to the knowledge of investment staff rather than facilitating the process of decision-making. As funds develop their own legal services, contracts with asset consultants have become bespoke rather than merely reproducing industry norms and conventions.

Innovation in Products and Services

Over the past twenty years, emerging markets were brought to the global marketplace via products that packaged securities from selected regions of the world. For example, longer-term trends in middle-class consumption were brought to market via value-focused stock selection investment strategies, and hitherto untraded positions via investment partnerships and closed-end funds.

Some product innovations are notorious; witness the misleading risk-rated collateralized debt obligations (CDOs) based on the US housing market packaged and brought to market in the lead-up to the GFC. Nonetheless, product innovation has provided asset owners with valuable opportunities to diversify risk and gain access to certain types of investments that match their long-term objectives.

Even so, investment consultants are often identified as barriers to the diffusion of new products and new investment strategies. In part, this is because they are more often concerned with the process of framing investment strategy and its implementation than with the nature of investment in its own right. Small funds depend on investment consultants for investment decision-making, and industry norms and conventions provide a baseline from which clients evaluate the utility of their options. It would be unusual for an adviser to break with standard practice. Medium-sized funds are more attuned to alternatives in that having a modicum of knowledge and understanding of investment strategy allows asset owners to look beyond the standard formula linking investment strategy with investment products. As such, medium-sized funds have often given investment consultants an audience for innovation. This has been especially effective in circumstances where funds have intensified their relationships with investment consultants.

The ambiguity at the heart of the relationship between asset owners and investment consultants has also come under scrutiny, especially from large asset owners. As such, for large asset owners, the issue of innovation has evolved from one dominated by assessing investment options against investment objectives, to one dominated by taking control of the investment process, improving knowledge of market dynamics, and reaching beyond the norms and conventions of the industry to concepts and tools that promote performance. In these circumstances, investment consultants have been asked to add value by bringing to the table innovative ideas and strategies. In such cases, the value of any contract for consulting services is to be had in the skills and expertise of advisers. Here, then, the onus is on the consultant to demonstrate value.

IMPLICATIONS AND CONCLUSIONS

This chapter began with the observation that intermediation is a key characteristic of the global financial services industry; standing between individual savers and investment returns on those savings are organizations that collect, manage, and assign to investment vehicles the assets of large groups of individuals. These organizations take a variety of legal forms, including pension funds, sovereign wealth funds, insurance companies, endowments, and family offices. It was also observed that these types of organizations typically use intermediaries to frame investment strategy and its implementation. There are, of course, other intermediaries involved, including actuaries, custodians, legal advisers, accountants, and banks. The framework underpinning this chapter can be applied to a wide variety of intermediaries. Nonetheless, given recent criticism of investment consultants, the substantive focus of this chapter has been on delineating their roles and responsibilities.

The nature and scope of financial intermediation in any jurisdiction is determined in part by the legacy of norms and conventions specific to that country or region. Even so, it is entirely plausible to argue that the functional effectiveness of intermediation is the true test of the relevance of history and geography (Merton and Bodie 1995, 2005). To the extent that matching savers with investors is fundamental to modern economic systems, it does not matter how it is done as long as it is done in an effective manner. Likewise, it is arguable that it does not matter whether or not a financial organization depends on related but external service providers, so long as its long-term financial performance meets the requirements of its beneficiaries (Dixon 2012). If so, one might expect to see various models of management in the financial services industry, particularly in the relationships between asset owners and investment consultants. There is some variety in management models. There are also remarkable commonalities in those models across jurisdictions and types of organizations, but variable between financial institutions, depending on size.

At the heart of our analysis is the assumption that the relationship between asset owners and investment consultants is under-determined. We might have expected to see well-defined contracts governing the relationships between clients and consultants, with clear descriptions of their respective roles and responsibilities. We find, in fact, that these types of contracts are open-ended, ambiguous about the nature and scope of services to be provided, and virtually silent on issues such as performance. These contracts masquerade as discrete bilateral agreements where, in fact, both parties use them as relational frameworks that have no effective termination date. Ambiguity often suits both parties. For small and medium-sized financial institutions that rely on investment consultants to frame and implement their investment strategies, ambiguity about their roles and responsibilities provides clients with flexibility in the face of changing market conditions. For investment consultants concerned to maintain market share, ambiguity about what counts as 'performance' enables them to focus on the process of decision-making rather than its substance.

Industry norms and conventions set what investment consultants do. At the same time, contracts for services are normally quite explicit about what they do not do and the potential liabilities they and their companies are unwilling to assume. In many jurisdictions, industry norms and conventions reflect the evolution of the global financial services industry, the nature and scope of services, and the segmentation of the industry by size of client. As is often observed, norms and conventions summarize the state of play at any point in time rather than setting goals for the future. Merton and Bodie (2005) supposed that financial institutions inevitably converge on organizational forms that have the virtue of functional efficacy. Here, we have identified the reasons why relationships between clients and consultants remain locked in the past. Models of best practice seek to shift norms and conventions towards higher standards of functional efficacy than those evident in customary practice (Clark and Urwin 2008a, 2010).

We explained why norms and conventions have become embedded and entrenched in the industry. It is also suggested that medium-sized asset owners have had opportunities to reframe their relationships with consultants, in part by building up their own internal capabilities and resources, and in part by seeking new ways of adapting to market turmoil. It was observed that size allows clients to discount reliance in favour of more equitable relationships that allow investment consultants to provide knowledge and insights that go beyond what is available to these organizations internally. This argument suggests, however, that the implementation of principles of best practice and the search for innovative ways of investing over the long term depend on the client rather than the consultant. As such, we would shift the focus of attention from investment consultants to clients and ask whether, in fact, the segmentation of the industry into small, medium, and large asset owners is consistent with a collective interest in promoting innovation and excellence in long-term investing (as the *Kay Review* (Kay 2012) intimated).

By this account of innovation, many financial organizations respond to rather than anticipate the market. This matches commentary in the academic literature to the effect that 'very few organizations have well-established and specialized expertise in the area of management innovation' (Birkinshaw et al. 2008: 830). However, this fails to capture the momentum among large financial institutions (such as pension and sovereign wealth funds) towards insourcing over outsourcing, towards reintermediation through exerting greater control over external providers, and towards redefining their relationships with advisers and consultants—including insourcing legal services, especially where asset class- and project-specific specialist knowledge is required. Innovation, under these circumstances, can be thought of as endogenous rather than exogenous. It is driven by the capacity to invest in resources as well as the realization that scale brings with it the opportunity to solve conflicts of interest when dealing with consultants who also advise other organizations that could be construed as direct competitors for market opportunities (as in large asset management companies).

It was noted that the ambiguity inherent in the relationships between clients and consultants, which is characteristic of the industry, may be to the advantage of both parties. Just as large financial institutions seek consultants to fulfil specific roles and responsibilities rather than provide the range of services typical of the industry, investment consultants have sought to deepen their skills and expertise in areas that few institutions are able to cover given the current state of play in the market. By this account, investment consultants have also sought to innovate to provide capabilities and resources that complement large clients, rather than pretend that they are a substitute for clients' capabilities and resources. As the processes of disintermediation and reintermediation gather momentum across the industry, we could well see the emergence of more specialized boutique investment consultants, especially at the higher end of the value proposition.

NOTES

1. Investment consultants are people, normally employees of organizations, who sell services. Globally, the firms Mercer and Willis Towers Watson dominate the investment advisory business. Their significance varies, however, by jurisdiction and market segment. For example, Cambridge Associates is important in North America, the United Kingdom, and Europe for charities, foundations, and family offices. In some countries, public-sector pension funds have steered business away from the major investment consultants to smaller companies.
2. Investors need more than a certain quantity of information; to be effective, they also need information distinguished by quality and value. Caplin and Martin (2011: 2899) show that people typically satisfice rather than optimize when searching for information. Consequently, decisions are made without full examination of all the available options, implying that the best available options may be missed. In response, investors may outsource this function to those with the requisite expertise and judgement.
3. Organizational flexibility may be desirable given the nature of financial markets, which are always evolving in ways that are neither entirely predictable nor necessarily consistent with inherited management practices and commitments (Lo 2012). Regime shifts are rarely immediately obvious but demand an adaptive capacity that can bridge short-term responsiveness with long-term adaptation. Few financial organizations, however, are as adaptive as Lo's characterization of them implies.
4. Choi et al. (2013: 1–50) explain the prevalence of standard contracts in commercial relationships, noting that law firms produce and clients consume contracts not so much for their substantive content as for their form. If there are differences between contracts for the same type of service, these differences tend to be marginal, trading on the 'acceptability' of standard contracts. They also observe that, given the risk that the courts might interpret their terms in unpredictable ways, it is difficult for law firms to capture 'returns from contract innovation'.
5. It is standard practice in commercial relationships for contractual provisions to limit or exclude damages for failing to live up to the terms of an agreed contract (Gillette 2013). If commercial relationships are ongoing and involve some measure

of commitment, then these contracts may involve risk sharing and cost sharing—that is, an equitable distribution of the upside and downside of a relationship. This is rare in the global financial services industry.

6. The dependence and/or reliance of funds on investment consultants, combined with the transaction costs associated with the termination of services, are such that small and medium-sized funds are often locked into these relationships. Investment consultants could exploit their clients by virtue of their privileged positions (Kőszegi 2014). Mediating this possibility is the importance attributed by both sides of the market to the reputation of consultants, whether personal or corporate.
7. See also Hart and Moore (1990: 1122), who suggest that where 'it is costly for agents to write detailed long-term contracts that precisely specify current and future actions as a function of every possible eventuality... the contracts written are incomplete and will be subject to renegotiation later on'. The implication here is that since firms are unable to write 'complete' contracts with providers, these activities are held within the firm. By contrast, in the financial services industry, ambiguity is underwritten by norms and conventions.
8. It is also plausible that ambiguity facilitates the development of trust between parties to contracts in that the resolution of ambiguity on an issue-by-issue basis builds confidence in one another's commitment to the overarching project. By this account, trust thrives in these situations because neither party desires the alternative (a complete contract). See Kimel (2005) on the relationship between trust and contract.

9

Outsourcing and the Principal–Agent Problem

As we have seen, there are various ways of managing the investment process, including insourcing the investment of pension-fund assets. Rather than managing providers through service contracts, set in accordance with industry norms and conventions, insourcing utilizes employment contracts with terms and conditions that reflect the goals and objectives of the organization and the market premium available to those who have scarce skills and expertise. There may, in fact, be a discount applied to any premium if pension funds offer employment contracts with terms and conditions that favour collective over individual interests (Chapter 5). Disintermediation and reintermediation are favoured strategies when a fund is of a certain size in assets under management (AUM) with concomitant capabilities and resources (Chapter 6). Size can also give these types of organizations sufficient leverage to rewrite the terms and conditions of service and employment contracts (Chapter 7).

Another model of pension-fund governance and management has recently claimed attention: variously labelled, this model of management involves outsourcing the framing and implementation of investment strategy to another entity. The outsourced chief investment officer (OCIO) model of pension-fund management locates the authority and responsibility for investment strategy, along with the option to insource or outsource its implementation, with an external agent. In this chapter, we explain how and why the OCIO model has emerged in the global institutional investment industry. In doing so, we observe that it is an organizational innovation driven, in part, by factors external to the conventional hub-and-spokes model of pension-fund governance and management. We situate this model in relation to other possible models, suggesting that it has certain advantages for smaller pension funds that do not have the options available to larger funds.

In some jurisdictions, the OCIO model is called the delegated chief information officer (DCIO) model, whereas in other jurisdictions it is identified as fiduciary management (FM). Whatever the label, it is a mode of management defined by its functions (Merton and Bodie 2005). Van Nunen (2008: xii, 1–2) indicated that these types of managers take responsibility for 'comprehensive risk management, strategic decision-making, and effective organizational governance' while 'overseeing a decentralised, outsourced array of investment managers'. His analysis did not distinguish between the type of pension institution, the nature of pension benefits, or its jurisdictional particularities. In some jurisdictions, OCIO management could involve the transfer of legally enforceable obligations like the duty to act solely in the interests of pension-plan participants. This is possible, but it is not the object of this chapter. Rather, whatever the virtues of the OCIO model of management, it is shown that there are important governance issues to be resolved. We show, in fact, that there is an important role for investment consultants and similar types of organization.

We begin this chapter by relating the conventional model of pension-fund governance and management to the theory and practice of investment. Here again we suggest that the search for alternatives is due, in part, to the costs and consequences of the market turmoil leading up to and immediately following the global financial crisis (GFC). We identify the OCIO model as one of a set of related models of management, so explain its significance against the alternatives. This provides a reference point for nine principles of best-practice OCIO management (along the lines suggested by Clark and Urwin (2008a)). One key finding from our research is that, notwithstanding the virtues of OCIO management, it requires governance. Using the principal–agent model, we explore this issue in the penultimate section of the chapter, 'The Principal–Agent Problem'. Here, though, the principal–agent model is reconceived through the interaction between information and skill, as well as expertise demonstrating the crucial role that advisers and consultants can play in realizing the benefits of OCIO management. In conclusion, we draw implications for the nature and scope of pension-fund management.

Following our previous discussion, we utilize an analytical framework embedded in theories of the firm. It brings to light principles and practices by eschewing detailed knowledge of the industry and its organizations in favour of the building blocks needed to understand recent developments in the institutional investment industry. More specifically, the approach taken in the chapter brings together many of the lessons drawn from our collaboration with Roger Urwin on the relationship between governance and the management of investment risk and return, and the ways in which institutional investors have responded to the GFC and its aftermath.

CONVENTION AND FINANCIAL MARKETS

By focusing on the hub-and-spokes model we begin with a recognized organizational type and use it as a benchmark to explain how and why a rather different organizational form has gained traction in the industry. In doing so, it should be acknowledged that, as in any industry, there is considerable organizational diversity, notwithstanding the apparent dominance of one or two organizational types (Hannan and Freeman 1989). Our argument goes further to suggest that the status of one model versus another is owed, in part, to its efficacy in dealing with or adapting to changing circumstances. We follow organizational theorists who argue that any model of management can become so entrenched in convention that it becomes an impediment to change (see Chapter 8 and Gans 2016).

Board Authority and Governance

Pension funds and pension-fund boards are similar to corporations in that they are entitled, at their discretion, to own property and a wide variety of financial instruments. Pension-fund boards use those property rights to frame and implement investment strategy. In many jurisdictions, pension-fund board members are expected to have relevant skills and expertise and are subject to similar legal rules and standards of behaviour applicable to corporate board members.

There are three important differences between corporations and most pension funds. First, in many jurisdictions, pension funds have a well-defined and single purpose—to manage and invest pension contributions on behalf of their members in the interests of their long-term financial well-being. Second, although a pension fund's tasks and functions are less pliable than those of a corporation, in that it has a specific purpose, the organizational shape of a fund can change, for example, from insourcing to outsourcing. Finally, whereas a corporation can switch its assets between chosen activities, pension funds typically do not 'own' members' assets. Rather, pension funds act on behalf of members who either have a legal right to those assets should they wish to switch providers, or have legal rights to retirement benefits or a derived income sometime in the future.

The hub-and-spokes model of investment management and governance is a bridge between the flexibility of a corporation and the fixed purpose of a pension fund.[1] In this model of management, the board and its executive team, as the members' representatives, use their authority to frame and implement investment strategy to ensure that members' interests are protected and commitments honoured. When funds place members' assets with investment providers, they do so to take advantage of the scope of the market for financial services and the flexibility of providers in adapting to changes in financial markets. By holding multiple service contracts according to asset class and investment style, it is presumed that there is a premium to be had in switching assets between providers according to their relative performance.

Investment Models and Expectations

Throughout the 1960s and 1970s, accompanying the growth in pension-fund assets in many Organisation for Economic Co-operation and Development (OECD) countries were a deregulation of financial markets and a liberalization of rules on investment by and across asset classes. Underpinning these developments was the reconceptualization of the theory and practice of investment led by Markowitz (1952a) modern portfolio theory (MPT). In essence, MPT shifts the focus from the risks associated with a specific investment to evaluating investment risk in accordance with asset-specific portfolios. One implication of MPT is that asset classes are more important than individual investments. A second is that, insofar as asset classes vary by risk and return, the framing of a fund's investment strategy depends on its overall risk and return objectives (Campbell and Viceira 2002).

As the theory and practice of investment developed, MPT was joined by a programme of research that assumed that financial markets were *ipso facto* efficient (Fama 1970, 1991). In combination, these developments provided a recipe for investment management (Ho and Lee 2004). Instead of detailed knowledge of specific investments, the touchstone for realizing value was found in the design of optimal portfolios and efficient frontiers (Litterman et al. 2004). Likewise, instead of knowing a market and/or having at hand a list of key informants, investment practice shifted towards identifying product providers who had the insight and information that processing technology needed to outperform their competitors (Shleifer 1985). Since outperformance is unlikely to persist, investment management became preoccupied with the timely switching of mandates between competing providers by asset class. As we have seen indicated in the previous section, 'Board Authority and Governance', with the expertise required to design an investment strategy and to switch between providers, investment consultants became integral to the investment management process.

Market Position and Performance

Pension-fund governance and management came to maturity in a rather benign environment: notwithstanding a handful of noteworthy events, such as the Asian financial crisis of 1997 and the long-term capital management (LTCM) debacle of 1999, year-to-year stock market performance in London and New York was systematically positive over the 1985–2001 period. The conventional model of pension-fund governance and the MPT recipe were handsomely rewarded. Furthermore, investing at home was rewarded, which reinforced investor belief in the virtues of Western financial markets and light-touch government regulation (Barth et al. 2012). Indeed, as the developed financial markets absorbed each event, confidence in the integrity of the received theory and practice of investment management grew (Shiller 2005). A predisposition in favour of the status quo and a widespread belief in the power of mean reversion concealed the long-term costs and consequences of conventional ways of doing business for pension-fund management.

Lost in the obsession of investors and the public alike with the upward trajectory of developed financial markets were the increasing costs associated with the secular decline in discount rates. See Chapter 4 where we illustrate this point in Figure 4.1. As assumptions were slowly revised, renewed pressure was brought to bear on active stock market investment strategies. At the same time, burgeoning growth in the financial markets of developing economies garnered increasing attention led, in part, by asset managers such as Goldman Sachs (Clark 2014). Realizing the potential of these markets prompted greater reliance by the average pension fund on large investment managers with global reach. The search for higher levels of performance in domestic markets also encouraged pension funds to use opportunities that promised higher returns for minimal risk.

The GFC in the core markets of the global economy undercut, first, long-term global economic growth; second, the stability of major currencies including the euro; and, third, the growth prospects of emerging economies. These events prompted policymakers to observe that systemic risk is embedded in the global economy's most developed financial markets (Haldane 2009). The implication drawn is that financial markets are irrational in the sense that agent behaviour is separately and collectively self-correcting absent regulation (Haldane and May 2011). More generally, there has been a shift in conceptualizing investment decision-making from the axioms underpinning rational expectations to the behavioural paradigm championed, among many others, by Shleifer (2000), Kahneman (2011), and Lo (2012).

MODELS OF MANAGEMENT

By convention, pension funds decide whether to hold internally the tasks and functions necessary to realize a target risk-adjusted rate of return (insource) or go to the market for those tasks and functions (outsource). Where there is a high degree of complementarity between tasks and functions, the orchestration of the production process is fundamental to realizing an organization's risk and return objectives. The management issue is whether the costs of segmenting tasks and functions and having external agents provide them outweigh the benefits of managing each element separately. Here, we restate the key assumptions underpinning our analysis, which are important for what follows.

Economies of Scale and Scope

As suggested, the global financial services industry relies upon economies of scale to deliver value for money. Economies of scale have two dimensions. First, there are the upfront costs involved in establishing the management systems and information infrastructure necessary to allocate the inflows and outflows of financial assets. Maintaining the integrity and efficacy of such systems requires continual upgrading and investment. Spreading the costs of these systems is an essential ingredient in minimizing the unit costs of investment management. Second, the asset management process is labour intensive, requiring high levels of domain-specific skills and expertise. Set-up costs are significant and, once established, portfolio teams can absorb large volumes of assets and thereby pay a premium for the most talented professionals (Clark 2015). There are also diseconomies of scale reflected, for example, in the challenges that large asset managers and owners face when seeking to upgrade their information systems.

Economies of scope are also important, but more nuanced in effect. Large asset managers often proclaim the virtue of having available a wide variety of investment services (Clark 2002). However, going to market for each task and function can incur significant transaction costs, including the time taken to search and assess competing service providers (Caplin and Martin 2011). Furthermore, given the importance of orchestrating complementary tasks and functions for the production of risk-adjusted returns, segmentation of the investment process can impose significant costs on an otherwise well-conceived investment strategy. Notwithstanding the supposed virtues of separate contracts for service providers, pension funds can find it difficult to orchestrate in a timely fashion the implementation and management of investment.[2]

Outsourcing Strategy

Whereas theories of the firm focus on sourcing tasks and functions, few studies have considered the issue of insourcing or outsourcing the firm's central decision-making unit. Nonetheless, there are many instances of owner-entrepreneurs relinquishing direct control of their firms and delegating control to a chosen chief executive officer (CEO) and executive team. This is evident, for example, when a firm is passed from one generation to another and/or when its growing size and complexity is such that a small group of executives is unable to give effect to planned goals and objectives. It is problematic to suppose that CEOs and their teams would give up their authority and responsibility to set firm strategy. If they were to do so, this would threaten the *raison d'être* of their existence and salaries. This happens, though, when a company agrees to be acquired by another, resulting either in redundancy or, in the case of the acquiring company not merging the operations of the target company, the maintenance of a shallow administrative staff.

Nonetheless, the outsourcing of corporate competitive strategy is more common than theorists suppose. Consulting companies exist, in part, to provide advice on corporate strategy. These consultants frame the issues and options, while management consultants take the chosen strategy and develop the means by which the client implements it. Strategy consultants have prospered for a variety of reasons (McAfee 2002). Facing external threats, incumbent boards may feel insufficiently informed or unable to rely on their senior staff to frame a strategy that sets aside past commitments in favour of a different future. Facing internal divisions, incumbent boards rely on (trust) strategy consultants to help resolve internal competing interests that would otherwise paralyse decision-making (Glückler and Armbrüster 2003). Outsourcing the framing *and* implementation of strategy is an important way of adapting to a changing world.

Four Ideal Types

In what follows, we assume that the options that the sponsor of a pension fund faces in responding to the apparent shortcomings of the conventional model of pension-fund governance and management have two dimensions. For a larger fund with a volume of financial assets consistent with insourcing the production of investment returns, the implementation of a chosen investment strategy can be via insourcing or outsourcing or a combination of both. Smaller funds might also consider insourcing some tasks and functions, while recognizing that there will be tasks and functions for which the volume of assets is insufficient to provide those activities internally in a cost-efficient manner. Then there are small funds where insourcing is simply not possible.

These cases, and others, are represented in Figure 9.1. Model A is the larger fund referenced in the previous subsection, 'Outsourcing Strategy'. It combines a well-resourced governance function (framing investment strategy) with insourcing the tasks and functions (services) needed to realize that strategy. Model C is the conventional hub-and-spokes model in which the board, its subcommittees, and advisers frame the investment strategy but outsource its implementation. Model B is less common in that the governance function is outsourced but implementation is insourced. This model has been observed in financial service companies and in some global corporations where the governance function is expected to be independent of the sponsor, its board, and senior executives. In effect, this model of management presupposes that there can be significant conflicts of interest when senior executives dominate the governance of its 'captive' pension fund. At the same time, insourcing

		Fund Governance	
		Insource	Outsource
Services	Insource	A	B
	Outsource	C	D

Figure 9.1. Models of governance
Source: Authors

implementation can be cost-efficient, reinforced by an alignment of interests otherwise not possible when service provision is outsourced.

In Model D, the governance function is outsourced along with the implementation of the chosen investment strategy. Depending on the jurisdiction, the entity responsible for framing and implementing investment strategy is, quite literally, the fiduciary being subject to common law and statute-based standards of behaviour that are consistent with fiduciary duty. In some jurisdictions, however, both the client and the OCIO manager are subject to fiduciary duty in that the client is required to oversee the OCIO manager in a manner consistent with trust law. Notice that a space or set of activities may not be entirely consistent with the particularities of each model. That is, there could be an 'in-between' model at the centre of Figure 9.1. For example, a Model A organization could outsource some activities, just as the Model D organization could insource some.[3]

Here, OCIO managers come in various forms. Some stand-alone companies with the skills and expertise needed to frame and implement investment strategy specialize in OCIO management. Some large multifunctional financial service companies provide OCIO management along with a wide range of other banking and investment services. Yet other companies have entered the market for OCIO management from the consulting side of the asset management industry, thereby deploying skills and expertise normally offered to Model A and Model C types of pension funds. In many cases, specialist OCIO management companies and asset consulting companies rely on the market for financial services when implementing investment strategy. By contrast, large financial companies expect to provide needed investment management services, albeit subject to market standards of performance and value for money.

There are advantages and disadvantages to each type of OCIO manager. Specialist OCIO management companies may excel at framing investment strategy, *yet* face significant transaction costs when searching for, evaluating, and managing the service providers needed to implement the strategy. In this respect, they may rely on asset consultants to cut through the maze of market claims and counterclaims. Asset consultants are skilled at framing investment strategy and have at their fingertips extensive knowledge of the market for financial services. Indeed, this may be their comparative advantage. However, when it comes to orchestrating the investment process, the costs of managing external providers can constrain their capacity to do so.

PRINCIPLES AND PRACTICES

The principles and practices for best-practice pension-fund governance are well established (Clark and Urwin 2008a). They are arranged hierarchically so that sponsors and funds can assess their standing, the value to be had from the implementation of each principle, and the standards appropriate to different sizes of pension funds and similar organizations. It was shown in the previous section, 'Models of Management', that governance and risk are intimately connected: the resources devoted to governance provide a reference point from which to judge the degree of risk a pension fund can effectively manage. These principles and practices remain important and, arguably, have gained widespread recognition because of the costs and consequences of market volatility over the past decade or so.

Nine Principles

Here, we summarize and briefly explain the key principles underpinning best-practice OCIO management. As indicated in this chapter, these are abstract, albeit not abstract enough to be irrelevant.[4] They should be understood as necessary conditions for best-practice OCIO management and are rank ordered, moving from fundamental and essential to more complex and sophisticated, even if subject to negotiation over the framing and execution of the contract binding the parties together in the fiduciary relationship.

Principle 1: clarity of mandate. Essential to a well-functioning OCIO management programme is the mandate or goals and objectives of the mandate. Most obviously, this could include investment return, risk, and performance objectives set in relation to the client's broader objectives. For example, the long-term objective of the client could be to ensure solvency of the pension fund in relation to its obligations to participants. A subsidiary goal could be to limit calls for more resources from the client or sponsor over the longer term, thereby facilitating the planning of capital expenditures.

Principle 2: simplicity of performance measures. Translating the mandate into performance measures is an essential ingredient in providing the OCIO manager with an unambiguous focus. It is a truism that organizations manage what is measured (Lowenstein 1996). This is important both for the client and for the OCIO manager. For the client, accepted performance measures provide a means of testing the effectiveness of the provider. For the OCIO manager, such measures can be used to impose discipline on the activities of its own organization.[5] Both elements are fundamental to ensuring a well-functioning relationship.

Principle 3: alignment of interests. OCIO management is notionally a long-term commitment by both the client and the provider. Given objectives and performance measures, the client has an interest in ensuring that the provider shares in both the upside and downside of the investment programme. This is one way of reinforcing the link between framing and implementing the investment strategy, providing the OCIO manager with a strong incentive to integrate the investment process. Integration can, for example, make transparent the link between risk management and long-term investment performance.

Principle 4: enhanced complementarity. One of the costs of the hub-and-spokes model of pension-fund governance is the segmentation of the various tasks and functions that make up the framing and implementation of investment strategy. In principle, one of the most important benefits of OCIO management is the opportunity to reap the benefits of complementarity, having direct control over the investment value chain through the integration of investment strategy and its implementation. This is a key test of the efficacy of any OCIO management relationship.

Principle 5: transparent decision rights. To realize the goals and objectives of a fiduciary mandate, to reap the benefits of greater coordination over complementary activities, and to be able to act within the terms and conditions of the agreement without negotiation are key ingredients of success. Transparency is essential in the decision rights of the OCIO manager in relation to the client, and in the manager over the allocation of responsibilities for the performance of the agreement. Lack of transparency on both counts is likely to discount the benefits of outsourcing the framing and implementation of investment strategy.

Principle 6: delegation with deference. By convention, the investment subcommittee advises the board, which has final authority over investment strategy and its implementation. Investment subcommittees often claim a measure of deference for their recommendations by virtue of their members' skills and expertise (Clark 2007). OCIO management involves formally delegating these matters to an external agent; in these circumstances, delegation *requires* deference to the agent's judgement. To second-guess an agent would be to discount the value of OCIO management and put in play the contract setting out the terms and conditions of the agreement binding the parties together.

Principle 7: integration with checks and balances. Ultimately, the success of OCIO management depends on integrating services otherwise provided separately in the hub-and-spokes model. While it is customary to ensure that service providers come from different companies, the virtue of OCIO management is the effective coordination of these services within an organization so that one service provider does not hold the others hostage to its interests. However, this may require an overarching 'manager' whose incentives are consistent with those of the client or clients. In some large multifunctional service companies, this may be difficult to realize.

Principle 8: adaptive capacity and potential. Another test of the efficacy of any OCIO management relationship is the external agent's capacity to adapt to financial market risk and uncertainty. At one level, adaptive capacity can be measured by the responsiveness of the OCIO manager to shifts in market expectations, being both a strategic issue and an issue of orchestrating the investment process. At another level, it reflects one of the key findings of Clark and Urwin (2008a), namely that managers' risk budgets should be aligned with their governance budgets.

Principle 9: certainty with flexibility. A key driver in the adoption of the OCIO management model of investment management has been financial market instability and the erosion of confidence in MPT (Lo 2012). At the same time, both parties desire certainty when writing contracts for services—that is, certainty about their rights and privileges. Nonetheless, any contract must also be flexible to allow for discretion in responding to unanticipated circumstances. Inevitably, any contract for services must be able to evolve without incurring significant delays and transaction costs. In this sense, a contract for services can be interpreted as a governance framework for shared goals and objectives.

It is apparent that these nine principles are interdependent. For example, the clarity of an OCIO management mandate enables simplicity of performance measurement. Likewise, the alignment of interests depends on principles 1 and 2 (Ambachtsheer 2016). With respect to the second group of principles, delegation with deference allows OCIO managers to enhance the benefits of complementarity. Being able to do so, however, depends on clarity over the decision rights of both parties (Clark 2007). As for the third group of principles, we have emphasized the adaptive capacity of any contract for OCIO management services in relation to market movements. Realizing the benefits of adaptive capacity depends on the nature and flexibility of the contract for services.

Practice as Contract

As noted, the hub-and-spokes model of investment management is a conventional mode of organization, relying as it does on standardized contracts for investment services. In doing so, this model of management is a form of organization that tends to minimize transaction costs—that is, the costs associated with negotiating contracts for services, writing contracts, and overseeing performance against expectations (Schepker et al. 2014). This model of management is used to dampen opportunism on both sides of the market, holding both parties to account by reference to recognized standards of behaviour. It is commonplace for clients to ask whether a choice made or a decision taken with respect to an agreement for services is consistent with industry practice.

While the hub-and-spokes model uses organizational oversight, deliberation, and decision-making to govern the investment process, OCIO management would replace it with a single or small set of contracts for services. With a well-defined set of goals and objectives, agreed measures of performance, and transparent decision rights, delegation with deference is the means by which the parties to the agreement realize their common objectives. In this sense, contract stands in place of active management, being as it is a blueprint or framework for action by the party charged with the responsibility for framing and implementing investment strategy (Davis 2013). Here, however, is a matter that goes to the heart of the contractual agreement binding the parties together. At issue is whether contracts for services are incomplete in terms of being a full specification of the privileges and responsibilities of both parties (Argyres et al. 2007).

If OCIOs manage to claim deference for their decision-making, any contracts for services need to be adaptive and responsive to shifts in market expectations rather than hemmed in by convention; in other words, sufficiently flexible to facilitate the manager's best endeavours. Put slightly differently, insofar as checks and balances exist in the relationship between the parties, to realize the potential inherent in the outsourcing of investment strategy and its implementation, OCIO managers require a degree of certainty about their authority and responsibilities. For some analysts, this is an issue of trust (Connelly et al. 2012). In this context, it refers to the degree to which a client willingly defers to the provider's chosen strategies and actions taken, albeit subject to measures of performance against goals and objectives. Note, however, it would seem that trust is earned rather than assumed from the start of a relationship.

Three implications follow. First, a pension-fund board may find it difficult in the early stages of its relationship with an OCIO manager to have a degree of trust consistent with the flexibility desired by both parties. As such, the initial contract binding the parties together may contain reporting protocols that mimic conventional investment management agreements (IMAs). Second, as the client becomes more comfortable with the manager and the discretion inherent in the relationship, the contract may evolve to be more flexible and open-ended than a standard IMA (Mayer and Argyres 2004). Third, over time, the contract may recede into the background and be replaced by an ongoing relationship between the parties. In this respect, rather than defining the relationship between the parties, the contract would then become a tool of last resort.

These implications presuppose that clients have the capabilities and resources to seek and/or design bespoke agreements with service providers. The logic set out also presupposes that OCIO managers are willing to accept such agreements. In fact, small funds neither have such capabilities and resources, nor are they large enough to justify the investment of managers in such agreements. Under these circumstances, potential clients are most likely to be offered a service contract on a take-it-or-leave-it basis (Deakin and Michie 2000: 1–39). On the other hand, larger funds may well have the requisite capabilities, resources, *and* AUM to make them desirable clients. Here, OCIO managers seeking market share may be willing to adapt standard IMAs to garner a bigger client base.

As contracts for services evolve, new types of agreements consistent with the needs of the parties to OCIO management relationships may then filter down to less well-endowed clients, a process that could accelerate in the face of changing market conditions. In these ways, as Choi et al. (2013) implied, innovation in OCIO management agreements could establish industry-wide protocols that are different from standard IMAs.[6]

THE PRINCIPAL–AGENT PROBLEM

The efficacy of OCIO management depends, as in other economic relationships, on the degree to which the sponsor or pension fund (principal) is an effective client and the OCIO manager (agent) is an efficient provider. In economics, the principal–agent problem obtains in any situation where an entity 'delegates an action to an agent' (Laffont and Martimort 2002: 4). Given the significance of delegation in modern economies, and the importance of this issue for the effectiveness of OCIO management relationships, in this section we discuss three aspects of the problem, as well as the various mechanisms used to manage if not expunge it. Some types of OCIO management relationships are more vulnerable to the principal–agent problem than others.

Identity and Responsibility

The principal–agent problem is deeply embedded in the global financial services industry (Ambachtsheer 2016). Consider, for example, the links in the investment chain connecting the pension-fund participant with, in order of importance, the pension fund, the actuary, the asset consultant, the custodian, the asset manager, and the accountant (Black 1992). Each link in the chain is formally constituted through a contract binding the parties together, in which each party has the rights and privileges of a person but is, normally, an organization and not a person per se. The employee representing an organization directs other employees in the fulfilment of the contract and other contracts with similar organizations. Normally, contracts between organizations are mute on intra-organizational matters.

Pension funds that rely on the hub-and-spokes model of investment management often seek to understand how an asset manager, for example, is organized internally to realize a target risk-adjusted rate of return. This is because such organizations are vulnerable to management failures. OCIO management seeks to clarify the respective roles of the principal and agent, where the former is responsible for selecting the OCIO manager and the latter for all matters pertaining to the framing of investment strategy and its implementation. With a clear mandate, simple performance measures, and aligned interests, the client need not intrude on the investment management process and the performance of each element in the process. OCIO management presupposes that the agent bears the costs and consequences of the investment management process.

Two Institutional Factors

Principals and agents differ markedly in terms of their organizational longevity or persistence. Pension funds are expected to last as long as their obligations and commitments, with a long-term planning horizon consistent with their participants' retirement plans. In many jurisdictions, pension funds have an organizational form that is protected by law and regulation. By contrast, there is an active market for corporate control in the global financial services industry. Any deal struck between a principal and its OCIO manager must be robust enough to outlast those responsible for negotiating the deal. At the same time, recognizing that both the agent and its employees may come and go over the course of an agreement, pension funds may well seek a contract that provides for termination should such changes impose costs on the principal.

Equally, it should be recognized that principals and agents are not the only players in these relationships. The hub-and-spokes model of investment management comes with a string of intermediaries, including expert advisers and consultants. Whereas Judge (2013, 2015) disparages consultants because they impose costs on transactions and bring greater complexity to the production of financial services, it is apparent that these agents are often fundamental to framing and realizing goals and objectives (particularly in smaller pension funds and similar institutions). Furthermore, advisers and consultants can provide some continuity in commercial relationships otherwise subject to the flux and flow of the financial services industry. In what follows, we suggest that advisers and consultants can play a key role in providing the expertise necessary for the effective governance of the principal–agent problem.

Governing OCIO Management

In effect, the relationship between pension funds and their OCIO managers must be governed, even if the relevant issues are different from those of the standard hub-and-spokes model. Economic theorists suppose that the fundamental problem affecting relationships between principals and agents is that information is not evenly distributed between the parties (Meckling and Jensen 1976). Because the agent is responsible for framing and implementing investment strategy, it has access to information that the principal cannot directly observe. As such, it can systematically limit the distribution of relevant information to put the principal at a disadvantage. There are two possible effects of information asymmetry—adverse selection ('hidden knowledge') and moral hazard ('hidden action') (Laffont and Martimort 2002).

The standard principal–agent model assumes that information is scarce and the costs of searching for and selecting it are significant.[7] Assuming all organizations, particularly smaller pension funds, face significant budget constraints, it may be impossible for clients to overcome this disadvantage. However, it is reasonable to suppose that, whatever the premium on information, one of the defining characteristics of the global financial services industry is the volume of information available to third parties, whatever their standing in the investment management process. While we should take care not to confuse quantity with quality, the world envisaged by economic theorists has changed markedly over the past fifty years and will continue to do so with the advent of 'big data'.

Access to information is fundamental to the principal–agent problem (Pratt and Zeckhauser 1985). A second element is the skills and expertise available to the principal in overseeing its relationship with providers.[8] A high level of expertise matching that of the agent may empower the client actively to govern its contractual relationship, thereby dampening the costs and consequences of information asymmetry. Conversely, a low level of expertise relative to the

		Information	
		Rich	Limited
Expertise	High	A	B
	Low	C	D

Figure 9.2. Models of management
Source: Authors

agent may mean that the principal does not have the capacity to assess the agent's investment management process. A lack of, or indeed systematic exclusion from, relevant information is likely to accentuate the problems associated with low levels of expertise. In these circumstances, the contractual relationship between the principal and agent is likely to continue until it fails (in dramatic fashion).

In these ways, the principal–agent problem has two dimensions and a set of possible states. In Figure 9.2, we provide a systematic mapping of the principal–agent problem relevant to governing OCIO management. Going beyond the standard way of representing the principal–agent problem, the issue is framed by reference to information and expertise with four ideal types. Clearly, our map of the principal–agent problem is rather abstract, suggesting the existence of categorically different types where, in fact, there is likely to be a continuum along the two dimensions of the problem. Therefore, for example, where we represent the availability of information as either ubiquitous or scarce, this ignores real-world issues such as the quality of information, including its specificity.

Model A represents the best possible situation for a principal governing an agent. A high level of expertise combined with information is likely to empower a pension-fund client in relation to its OCIO manager. How is this possible? A client could employ a knowledgeable consultant or set of consultants, and could hire key employees who have worked on both sides of the market. The danger in this situation is that the client comes to dominate the OCIO manager to the detriment of both sides of the relationship.

Model D, by contrast, is an instance of the OCIO manager capturing the principal, for there is no basis for systematically overseeing its organizational robustness or its short- and long-term performance. Either expert advice is unavailable at a fee the fund can afford, or the provider systematically denies the consultant information on or insight into its strategy and implementation. Model B is entirely possible in that, despite limited information, a high level of expertise can empower a client to be an effective governing party if done on a strategic basis with selective expenditure on needed information. Here, a consultant with experience in this segment of the market could compensate for limited information by referencing information from other sources.[9] Model C, by contrast, would seem to be a losing proposition in that, despite a rich source of information, the principal simply does not have, or cannot afford, the expertise to take advantage of the available information in governing its relationship with the OCIO manager.

In the world observed, among smaller pension funds there are few Model A cases, many Model Ds, an increasing number of Model Bs, but fewer Model Cs. Pension funds that are conscious of their reliance on their OCIO manager, and sensitive to shifts and changes in the global financial services industry that affect the ownership and organization of service companies, have begun to invest in expertise to discount the risks associated with adverse selection and moral hazard. Note, however, that capture is an ever-present danger. In some cases, appointing an OCIO manager is an opportunity for the plan sponsor or sponsors to discount the costs associated with the governance and administration of their pension funds. This is apparent in circumstances where the corporate or government sponsor requires small pension funds to give up their investment management, governance, and implementation functions to a central agency.

IMPLICATIONS AND CONCLUSIONS

OCIO management is one response to the costs and consequences of the hub-and-spokes model of pension-fund governance. At base, it involves outsourcing both the framing and the implementation of investment strategy. In Figure 9.1, other kinds of responses were identified, including retaining responsibility for framing investment strategy and insourcing its implementation. This type of response involves disintermediation and, in some circumstances, strategic reintermediation. Our framework also includes a less familiar case where large financial institutions and corporations outsource the framing of investment strategy but insource its implementation, thereby taking advantage of existing capabilities and resources, including the capacity to monitor closely and oversee the investment process. Given the economies of size and scope that dominate the financial services industry, many smaller pension funds have identified

OCIO management as a viable alternative to the conventional hub-and-spokes model.

Whereas it is suggested that OCIO management is a new phenomenon, there are examples of it in the global pension-fund industry. For example, the large multi-employer pension plans that provide investment services, including the framing and implementation of investment strategy, can be thought of as a form of OCIO management. While participating sponsors and members are normally represented on boards of management, they tend not to be involved in the investment management process. To participate in the schemes may require participating sponsors to give up their rights to monitor and oversee these organizations, delegating this responsibility to their representatives. In the United States, for example, state governments often require lower units of government to participate in these organizations. Once employers join this type of organization, however, they often find it virtually impossible to leave. Nonetheless, despite having relinquished their fiduciary responsibilities to another entity, participating employers frequently retain responsibility for the payment of pension benefits.

A key finding of our research is that the plan-sponsor–OCIO-manager relationship must be managed. Yet, the nature of this relationship is such that the modes of monitoring and oversight typical of the hub-and-spokes model are not especially relevant. Indeed, close oversight of the OCIO manager could discount the advantages of outsourcing the framing and implementation of investment strategy. We provide a set of nine principles and practices that underpin an effective plan-sponsor–OCIO-manager relationship. These principles and practices were allied with previous research on the principles of best-practice pension-fund governance (Clark and Urwin 2008a). Clarity of mandate and delegation with deference resonate with our template and considerations of how best to manage the insourcing of investment services. It was also suggested that, in governing the plan-sponsor–OCIO-manager relationship, a key measure of success is being able to reap the benefits of complementarity and the adaptive capacity of the manager.

Inevitably, a contract formalizes any such relationship. It was noted, however, that smaller pension funds contemplating a relationship with an OCIO manager face the prospect of being offered a standard contract on a take-it-or-leave-it basis. This is not to say that standard contracts are without virtue: they are widely accepted in the industry because of the high costs of negotiating bespoke agreements (see Chapter 8). In some cases, OCIO managers offer standard contracts modelled on industry-accepted IMAs. Larger clients can, of course, claim special treatment because of their significance to providers. Both sides of the relationship may find virtue in a standard contract, particularly in the early phases of a relationship in which trust is yet to be established. In any event, clients may wish to hold in reserve the powers afforded to them by a standard contract, particularly with regard to termination, given the flux and flow of the global financial services market.

This is the realm of the principal–agent problem. The apparent asymmetries in the relationships between many plan sponsors and their OCIO managers are such that the former may well bear the costs of adverse selection and moral hazard. On this issue, we provide an analytical framework that links together the expertise of the client with its access to information. Analytically, the normal way of representing the principal–agent problem is to assume that the agent holds all relevant information, which it discloses to the principal to advantage its position. Rarely do these models consider the issue of expertise and how that may either amplify or dampen the principal–agent problem. Financial markets are so awash with information that an expert client can reasonably assess an OCIO manager's investment strategy if not the choice of the various options related to its implementation. It is shown that a well-informed expert client can be an effective partner in a plan-sponsor–OCIO-manager relationship. A naïve client with inadequate information could well be held hostage by a service provider.

In any event, concern for these issues may well give rise to further segmentation in the market for financial services. There are three different kinds of OCIO managers. These are (i) single-purpose entities established to provide the service, (ii) asset consultants and similar types of organizations that provide OCIO management to established clients and others, and (iii) large asset management companies that provide the service alongside a broad array of complementary services. Each type of entity could attract its own loyal client base. For example, a plan sponsor and/or pension fund that invests in its own expertise and information to govern its relationship with the OCIO manager could effectively seek out a single purpose entity or an asset consultant willing to cultivate a relationship with such a client. By contrast, if the plan sponsor and/or pension fund simply wants to pass on responsibility for framing and implementing investment strategy, this type of client may well seek out a large asset manager.

NOTES

1. The demand for flexibility in the purchase and provision of financial services within and between relevant tasks and functions is one reason why intermediation is so important in the global financial services industry. Other accounts of intermediation in the industry emphasize the existence of information asymmetries (Allen 1990; Allen and Santamero 1998).
2. In this regard, our argument resonates with Holmström and Milgrom's (1991) observation that many economic activities carry with them multiple tasks, and many tasks carry multiple dimensions. In essence, realizing value in investment

management is to be found in the effective coordination of the various tasks that go into framing and implementing investment strategy being mindful of the complexity of each task.

3. Large, multifunctional organizations can find it difficult to remain at the leading edge of innovation in any sector or industry. As such, outsourcing can provide an action space for the senior executives of large financial institutions (asset owners and asset managers) seeking to adapt to, or keep abreast of, new ideas and tactics in the industry. If successful, outsourcing can become insourcing as new initiatives are integrated into the business of the financial institution (Bachher and Monk 2013).
4. Inevitably, given the heritage of an institution and its ongoing commitments, there are limits to the implementation of best practice (Gertler 2003; Granovetter 1985). In addition, the legal environment in which a financial institution operates can structure contractual arrangements, thereby excluding options otherwise judged desirable (La Porta et al. 1998). The latter issue could affect the relevance of principles 7–9.
5. While specificity is a virtue, clients may also seek performance measures that allow for comparison across providers of OCIO management services. Inevitably, a well-functioning market for financial services thrives when comparability is one element of the process of assessing competing providers. Third-party data providers have transformed the global financial services industry.
6. Implied is a mode of innovation in legal form and function that follows the needs of the market rather than being conceived by forward-looking legislators or the courts. Gilson et al. (2013) argue that early on in the formation of a new mode of contract, courts can impede rather than facilitate progress. This logic is consistent with the role of industry associations in facilitating the development of industry norms and conventions.
7. The costs and social consequences of the asymmetrical distribution of information have a long history in economics and the social sciences. See Akerlof (1970) for his seminal treatment of the issue, using a simple example to illustrate how a buyer can be at a disadvantage relative to a seller when assessing the quality of a product. Spence (1977) took the issue further, providing a systematic way of integrating the distribution of information with market phenomena.
8. For Glode et al. (2012: 1724), expertise is required to process 'information about the values of assets traded'. They go on to suggest that 'financial expertise…is the ability to acquire more accurate information'. Thereafter, they observed that complex financial products require a level of expertise that is not readily available in the market, thereby driving compensation and the like. See Clark (2016) on the nature of the distribution of financial expertise in time and space among different types of investors.
9. Standard treatments of the principal–agent problem make little allowance for the systematic 'leakage' of information from agents to principals through repeated engagement and observation of the behaviour of other similarly placed parties. It is widely observed that information cascades through the financial services industry, reinforced by the actions of agents competing with other providers to garner market share. It has also been shown that the interaction between agents, between agents and principals, and between principals promotes the disclosure of information, which, in a settled market, would otherwise be more 'sticky' than observed. See Caplin and Leahy (1994) on the release of information to the market.

10

Cooperation and Collaboration

Throughout the book, we have focused on institutional form and functions, the ways in which financial institutions organize themselves and their service providers, and how they have sought to take advantage of opportunities in global markets. Motivating our research has been an interest in rewriting theories of the firm that focus on commodity-producing companies, favouring financial institutions that depend on intangible assets to produce returns in global markets that are subject to risk and uncertainty. Responding to financial instability is not simple: it requires organizational flexibility, management authority, and mandates, as well as formal and not-so-formal mechanisms for facilitating innovation. In this chapter, we explain how and why new modes of cooperation and collaboration *between* rather than *within* institutions have become important. These options offer senior managers an intermediate action space between their institutions and financial markets to transcend home bias.

In the next section, 'Returning to Fundamentals', we remind the reader about what is distinctive about the global financial services industry. It is noted that there are significant economies of scale and scope in money management, providing a rationale for the in-house provision of financial services. In benign financial conditions, an institution's strategic asset allocation and investment management decisions tend to frame the issue of make-or-buy (being an issue of cost effectiveness and control). However, as financial markets have become hostile environments, in which even the largest institutions find it a challenge to be effective, there is an increasing premium on organizational capacity, whether internal or external to the institution. Cooperation and collaboration give senior managers opportunities to adapt or extend the capacities of their institutions to respond to a changing environment (Helfat et al. 2007: 1–2). In the penultimate section of this chapter, 'Transforming Home Bias', we apply our characterization of cooperation and collaboration to the design of investment platforms that bring together financial institutions across space and time to invest in opportunities that are beyond inherited capabilities and resources.

This chapter provides findings that are relevant to the literature on organizational change and to concerted efforts to understand better the nature and shape of global financial services. It shows that financial institutions often seek partners for cooperation and collaboration outside their home jurisdiction, but recognize that knowing too much about local institutions that may be competitors for talent and market share can create conflicts of interest. We note that institutions seek partners from jurisdictions that are, within limits, different, which allows them to adopt lessons learned without necessitating radical changes in institutional form. Importantly, we also show that institutions seek partners that are, in a sense, symmetrical. For example, being large in terms of assets under management (AUM) relative to other partners enables an institution to assume a significant share of the costs of cooperation and collaboration. Finally, we identify the likely limits associated with cooperation and collaboration, especially with respect to the capacity of senior managers to make commitments on behalf of their organizations.

RETURNING TO FUNDAMENTALS

We return to earlier chapters of the book to re-emphasize key characteristics of the financial services and institutional investment sectors that are important for understanding the logic of organizational change in institutional investors. In doing so, we seek to marry theory and practice with due regard to the world in which institutions frame strategy and facilitate decision-making. At the same time, we refer to the organizing principles underpinning the production of investment returns, while being sensitive to space and time.

Persistence and Competition

At the heart of recent treatments of organizational behaviour and strategic management is a concern with the goodness of fit between the organization and the market in which it must operate (Barnett 2008). While the competitive circumstances of markets vary over space and time, market competition is believed to be a fundamental mechanism with which to reward and penalize companies for their adaptability to changing circumstances. This logic provides a rationale for predatory behaviour and the elimination of rivals through mergers and acquisitions. While there are other explanations for mergers and acquisitions (see Coffee et al. 1988), it is assumed that competition between firms in relation to market share is a key mechanism by which rent-seeking behaviour is contained and disciplined (Jensen 1993).

By contrast, many asset owners have exclusive control over the accumulation, management, and investment of funds. Because of their relationships with fund sponsors and beneficiaries, pension funds and sovereign funds rarely if ever face rivals for control of the flow of funds. In fact, 'capture' on both sides of the relationship between sponsor and institution is an ever-likely possibility. On the other side of the equation, however, it is apparent that while pension and sovereign funds are not in competition with other similar institutions for their asset base, they do compete with one another for risk-adjusted rates of return on financial assets. If this premium is randomly distributed in time above and below industry benchmarks, customary practice is the ruling ethic of management in the sector. Systematic underperformance can lead to significant shifts in strategy, changes to in-house and external service provision, and investment in institutions' capabilities and resources.

At the limit, where systematic underperformance relative to peers threatens the viability of institutions' sponsors, poor performance can precipitate the dissembling or restructuring of the institutions' inherited form and functions.[1] Given the importance of benchmarks and the imputed career risks, there is a premium on learning from other institutions, especially those better able to produce a return premium on investments located at some distance from their home domain (as suggested in Chapter 3).

Economies of Scale and Scope

Textbook treatments of the competitive strategies of firms often begin with the size of the firm relative to its market, and the advantages that accrue to large firms by virtue of scale. That is, relatively low average per unit costs of production and, on the margin, lower per unit costs of production as the volume of production expands. Theorists recognize that, at some point, the unit costs of production begin to increase in the face of increasing complexity, problems of coordination, and inertia (Coase 1937; Williamson 1975). Economies of scope are also important; size allows firms to produce more specialized tasks and functions, discounting the cost of overheads attributed to the core activities of the firm. This is one reason why firms extend the range of products and services offered as they grow in size (measured in terms of, inter alia, the volume of production). Facilitating complementarities can also reduce the appeal of the market for existing consumers, while attracting new consumers interested in a range of options within one commercial relationship (Clark 2002).

Economies of scale and scope are significant in the investment sector. Funds unwilling or unable to incur the costs of being small in AUM terms, outsource the supply of financial services and products. Because the senior executives of such funds spend most of their time on investment strategy, they recruit the help of investment consultants and actuaries to monitor the performance of external investment managers. As AUM grow in volume, funds tend to provide and oversee the relatively inexpensive tasks and functions in terms of skill and expertise in-house. As suggested in Chapters 4 and 5, this can include, for example, investment in certain asset classes such as bonds and equities, where a high level of skill and expertise is less important than the cost advantages of placing them in generic or easily imitated financial products. Large funds can provide most of the tasks and functions needed to manage assets and liabilities internally. Realizing the advantages of complementarity, however, demands organizational skill and management authority—factors that may be in scarce supply among both large *and* small institutional investors.[2]

Contingency and Response

Standard treatments of commodity production suggest that learning by doing is an important element in promoting labour productivity and, ultimately, firm-specific competitiveness within and among industries. However, financial theorists doubt whether these conditions are obtained in financial markets over the long term (Weitzman 2007). To the extent that market expectations are realized, these are moments of stability disrupted by unexpected events that discount the value of past practices, while raising doubts about their applicability in the future. In Chapter 8, we have drawn the attention of the reader to the path of the Financial Times Stock Exchange (FTSE) 100 index over the period 1984 to 2016. We identified a number of seemingly 'self-contained' market episodes or phases. Over the period 1984 to 1997, the FTSE moved steadily upwards with remarkably low volatility. Thereafter, momentum accelerated, then became subject to booms and busts, and most recently brought the global economy to the brink of collapse. In the first phase, holding equities for the long term was rewarded; in the second phase, long termism was not rewarded. Sophisticated time-variant investment strategies were required simply to hold risk and uncertainty at bay.

There are various ways of coping with these conditions. Rather than produce planned risk-adjusted rates of return within an institution, senior executives may outsource asset-management functions. In doing so, they would hope to contain the possible losses associated with changing market conditions by switching mandates among providers in a timely manner based on market performance. Here, there is a premium on institutional decision-making capacity. Alternatively, senior managers can benchmark internal providers against the leading edge found in the industry, varying the allocation of assets between internal and external providers to maintain options should (when) markets change in unexpected ways. Yet another option is to leave the market altogether and establish internal investment offices that rely less on financial markets and more on private placement of investments in untraded opportunities such as infrastructure and private equity. These options are three among many, all of which depend on the authority of senior managers relative to internal and external portfolio managers (see Chapter 9, for example).

OBJECTIVES, CONTRACT, AND AUTHORITY

Having rehearsed key aspects of the investment sector, the next step is to return to the schematic model of our representative financial institution first introduced in Chapter 4. Our reference point is an asset owner, or asset owner with many of the tasks and functions of an asset manager. Through the elaboration of our model, we have explained the nature and scope of the management 'problem' facing senior managers; in this chapter we use this model to explain why senior managers of financial institutions might search for cooperation and collaboration with other entities. In doing so, a theoretical rationale is provided for observed practice (see Bachher and Monk 2013; Guyatt 2013), distinguishing between large and small institutions, their functional scope, and the authority of senior managers in relation to the opportunities for cooperation and collaboration outside their organizations.

Objectives and Constraints

It was assumed in Chapter 4 that our representative institution will maximize the risk-adjusted rate of return on AUM. It does so while seeking to minimize costs even if it is a weak constraint in that sponsors of the institution and its ultimate beneficiaries may have little effective control over the costs incurred in realizing the rate of return. Electronic infrastructure costs, transaction costs, switching costs, salaries, fees, and charges are the responsibility of the institution's board of trustees. Nonetheless, the institution bases its planned rate of return on forecast liabilities and income objectives. In some cases, the sponsor and/or beneficiaries may ultimately be responsible for forecast liabilities and objectives, although this is of limited significance over the short to medium term.

It is apparent, however, that the institution's liabilities and objectives are priced in local currencies. Furthermore, its home jurisdiction normally imposes regulations on the organization to ensure that its effective operating space–time horizon combines local circumstances with global financial markets. To the extent that customary practice is rewarded by a better than average performance over time, local opportunities may claim the centre of our representative institution's investment strategy—even if the original conditions producing those returns no longer prevail. Not surprisingly, the institution's strategic asset allocation exhibits home bias relative to the global map of market capitalization and performance (as with other similarly placed institutions). This tends to reinforce the isolation of local financial institutions and their senior managers—in effect, they are competitors for the premium on local risk-adjusted rates of return. If alliances are sought with other institutions, they tend to come from other jurisdictions.

The Employment Relation

As explained in Chapter 5, the option to make or buy is a choice between insourcing and outsourcing the production of the institution's target risk-adjusted rate of return. For financial institutions, this translates into a choice between directly employing the requisite portfolio managers and entering into service contracts with third-party providers on a fee-for-service basis. In effect, outsourcing bundles together desired resources and capabilities into a service contract that sets the target rate of return, the related costs, and the mechanism for renewing or terminating the contract in the future. Insourcing the production of the target rate of return requires the institution to write a set of employment contracts; these need to distinguish between different classes of employees, their significance to the institution, and the market premium that certain types of employees may command because of their skills and expertise. Being close to or distant from the market for talent may also affect the choice between insourcing and outsourcing (Dixon and Monk 2014).

In financial institutions, it has proven difficult to maintain standardized contracts applicable to the various investment and non-investment employees who are essential to producing the target rate of return. In part, this is because certain types of services, such as the accounting, actuarial, and custodial ones, must be executed whatever the market conditions. By contrast, portfolio managers are literally 'in the market' in the sense that their performance depends on their skill and expertise in making bets for and against the other market participants in their asset class or segment of the financial market. The more transparent a market segment or asset class, the more likely senior managers will be able to rely on chance as opposed to skill and expertise: the more opaque a market segment or asset class, however, the higher the reward that successful portfolio managers can extract from the host institution. At the limit, successful portfolio managers on the margin of markets can trump the authority of senior managers and enterprise-wide employment norms and conventions.

Service Contracts

Smaller financial institutions are unlikely to insource the various tasks and functions that make up their investment strategies and target rates of return.

In Chapter 4, this argument was developed by reference to the principles and practices underpinning the production of investment returns. These types of institutions have neither the economies of scale nor the scope to deliver cost-effective investment strategies; neither do they have the managerial resources and capabilities required to function effectively in the context of market risk and uncertainty. The solution for such organizations is to hire knowledgeable and experienced managers who can hire and fire external portfolio managers in accordance with the institution's investment strategy and asset-specific goals and objectives. Even larger institutions may use external portfolio managers on service contracts. These types of agreements can augment existing asset-specific investment strategies, access financial products not covered by the institution, and impose discipline on internal portfolio managers who (otherwise) may engage in rent-seeking behaviour.[3]

These types of service contracts may be bilateral in the sense that they can be terminated at will. As we explained with reference to Bolton and Dewatripont (2005), bilateral contracts are assumed complete, Pareto optimal, and contestable in that non-performance can bring forth claims for redress that, if necessary, can be realized in court. However, these types of contracts are hardly ever exclusive because the tasks and functions that the external portfolio manager provides are in the sole interest of the institution. The large investment management companies offer pooled investment vehicles by asset class, style of investment, sector, and geographical focus; however, they are available to such a wide variety of clients that they tend to manage the product rather than long-term relationships with clients. Notice that external portfolio managers offer clients a range of services with and without preferential pricing and conditions, depending on the volume of assets placed with the provider. For example, a relatively large placement of assets is likely to attract a discount on costs, private briefings, and direct engagement on issues of relevance.

In effect, smaller clients face significant costs—including the possible ones associated with knowing little about the organization and the real-time performance of external portfolio managers. Predictably, smaller institutions are likely to come late to successful portfolio managers and are prone to stay longer with one whose luck has run out. In any event, large and small clients face significant search costs in discovering appropriate external portfolio managers, estimating their performance in the short and long term, and measuring it against that of their competitors (including internal managers) in circumstances where market conditions are rarely repeated. It is hardly surprisingly, therefore, that smaller institutions tend to favour local opportunities and to want to maintain the status quo.

Mediating the status quo bias are investment consultants employed to widen the geographical and functional scope of any search for internal and external managers. Here, as explained in Chapter 9, the effectiveness of consultants depends on (1) the specification of their mandates, (2) their skills and expertise (in specific domains), (3) their networks, especially beyond the local situation, and (4) the authority of senior managers in relation to the choice of options the consultants present. Staying with a relatively poor-performing provider (whether internal or external to the institution) can be taken as representative of shortcomings at each stage of the search process.

Authority and Convention

Senior managers face a problem in trying to promote innovation among existing in-house portfolio managers in that any radical attempt to alter the process of investment management and/or the nature of investment products is likely to run up against the industry norms and conventions that exist within and between financial institutions, whether these are asset-specific or otherwise. The market for talent offers attractive opportunities to the best performing portfolio managers who are unwilling to put an institution's interests before their own. Then again, external portfolio managers resist at every turn asset owners' attempts to rewrite the terms of engagement. As noted in Chapter 6, in recognition of the transaction costs involved in agreeing to a new kind of contract that concedes significant authority to the client, the vast majority of institutional clients are offered terms and conditions on a take-it-or-leave-it basis.

By our account, senior managers of financial institutions are predisposed to consider joining initiatives that break with local convention; the options of make or buy do not necessarily add to managers' authority or flexibility in terms of promoting organizational innovation in either the process or the nature of investment management. In the aftermath of the global financial crisis (GFC), the ongoing euro crisis, and now a global downturn, senior managers of many large and small financial institutions have actively sought alternatives to the make-or-buy logic that hitherto has dominated the investment management industry. Quantitative easing, stock market appreciation, the rush to and from emerging markets, and sudden shifts to risk-on/risk-off have separately and together raised concerns about the sustainability of past ways of doing business. Senior managers have looked to cooperation and collaboration with other asset owners as a means of breaking with convention.

MODES OF INNOVATION

Cooperation and collaboration offer participants a level of informality missing from conventional modes of contracting, whether with in-house employees or external service providers. Being on the outside of commercial contracts and relationships makes it possible, through cooperation and collaboration, to explore the costs and benefits of organizational innovation, given the fixed form of the participating institutions. The parties to cooperation and collaboration either do not need, or do not require, contracts to participate. It is deemed sufficient to operate in the shadow of mutual obligation, relying on social norms and conventions to govern participation. In this section, we explain what we mean by collaboration and cooperation, and suggest that these strategies are related but different in important ways.

Cooperation

Perhaps the simplest way for senior managers of financial institutions to extend their understanding of innovation is to cooperate with other institutions. As we understand it, cooperation involves shared projects, agreed expected outcomes, and well-defined mechanisms governing entry to and exit from such arrangements. More often than not, senior managers have overlapping interests, so by cooperating on a project they immediately gain knowledge and understanding, even if not in terms of their institution's capacity to realize target risk-adjusted rates of return. In this respect, cooperation is often driven by a specific issue that senior managers who see other financial institutions as peers rather than rivals recognize as important. If cooperation is to be effective, there must be symmetry to ensure that one party does not expropriate the benefits of cooperation that the parties to an agreement share equitably, if not equally (Olson and Zeckhauser 1966).[4]

The mechanism governing cooperation is important. Formalism is a virtue because it forces explicit consideration of the costs and benefits of joining others outside the institution. On the other hand, participants may be more willing to sign a memorandum of understanding (MoU) than a legal contract in that the former tends to be permissive, whereas the latter tends to carry enforceable commitments. For example, the MoU may begin by acknowledging the limits of the agreement, its intended use as a means of encouraging cooperation, the sharing of responsibilities between partners, and the need for timely decision-making in relation to the opportunities for cooperation. To forestall argument after the fact, the MoU may also establish rules about the distribution of the costs and benefits of cooperation (for example, in proportion to commitment). The MoU could also acknowledge the right of any participating institution to exit at will, just as it may provide for the exclusion of any institution that fails to take part in the consortium's activities.

Given the contingent nature and governance of cooperation, as well as the exploratory character of shared projects relative to financial institutions' ongoing operations, it can be difficult for senior managers to devote new resources to cooperative arrangements, especially if they seek to circumvent standard ways of contracting internal and/or external portfolio managers. It is apparent that cooperation is most effective when the parties to such agreements bring something different to the project. Learning is enhanced by difference and distance from related financial institutions, for these might otherwise be regarded as competitors for investment returns (Grabher and Ibert 2013). At the same time, institutions' resources and capabilities must, in some sense, be complementary to ensure that the lessons the participants learn through shared projects are useful to them (Cohen and Levinthal 1990). Complementarity also enables institutions to bring together resources and capabilities that, when combined, provide options and insight for innovation not otherwise available to the participating institutions in whole or in part.

More formally, cooperation provides senior managers with a variety of related benefits. First, it is a means of mobilizing and sharing knowledge of innovation relevant to the formation of strategic planning. Second, it enhances the senior managers' power over their own employees, thus avoiding the compromises involved in relying on existing in-house providers to deliver services *and* information on alternatives. Third, it reduces the power of consultants by providing a check on their value for money (as suggested in Chapter 9). Fourth, it helps to identify and evaluate the 'fit' of a party or parties to a cooperative venture in relation to other possible ventures that require much deeper commitment given market risk and uncertainty. In these ways, cooperation can discount institutional myopia while providing senior managers with options to drive innovation in their own institution (cf. Barnett 2008).

Collaboration

Collaboration involves commitment to a project or projects in terms of both the specification of shared objectives and the means of realizing them. Commitment involves allocating institutional resources and capabilities, monitoring and overseeing the project with respect to its objectives, and supporting the senior managers who sponsor such commitments. Collaboration is likely to require a stronger framework of governance than cooperation, for it is necessary to specify the respective shares of the benefits of collaboration, limits on actual and potential liabilities, and the boundaries of the collaborative agreement with respect to the ongoing operations of project partners. Furthermore, collaboration is also likely to require specification of the mechanisms of objective setting, decision-making, and conflict resolution. Where it involves setting up a separate entity, the powers of that entity and its officers with respect to the collaborating institutions are inevitably well defined (as in a contract).

As in cooperation, the parties to a collaborative agreement are likely to pool their existing resources and capabilities. However, this may involve more than a marginal call on their existing ones; they may even need to invest in new ones consistent with the needs of the shared project. As with cooperation, complementarity between the committed resources and capabilities of the participating institutions may be required to facilitate effective collaboration. However, as collaboration evolves in relation to the shared objectives of the parties, the fit between institutions' resources and capabilities *and* the needs of the project may become a source of tension between (and within) parties. For example, where additional resources are needed to achieve the objectives of a collaborative project, the character and scope of those resources may be such that should the project be wound up, those resources may not be useful if returned to the participating institutions (see Williamson (1975) on the costs of asset specificity). Senior managers have a stake in the success of collaboration. As such, they face the prospect of escalating commitment: realizing the planned outcomes of collaboration may require repeated calls on the resources of participating institutions, perhaps leading to questions about senior managers' authority within their own institutions.

Most importantly, the success of collaboration depends on the choice of partner or partners. Not surprisingly, screening and evaluating potential partners is a vital ingredient in ensuring success. As noted, this can be achieved in a variety of ways, including trial runs through cooperative ventures and purchasing independent advice on the virtue or otherwise of potential partners. However, given the constraints on innovation associated with existing in-house and outsourcing arrangements, there are obvious incentives to take calculated risks on joining partnerships with other, less familiar institutions that may not be subject to the same constraints that bind senior managers in their own institutions. Not surprisingly, given the risks associated with departing from convention, collaborative deals are likely to start with modest commitments, goals, and objectives. In stages, commitment may increase as milestones are realized. Senior managers have an interest in maintaining their authority so that exit remains a viable option.

There are a variety of risks associated with collaboration (Archetti et al. 2011). Where knowledge and understanding of the motives of other institutions' managers are imperfect, collaboration can give some institutions and their senior managers a setting in which to exploit the resources and capabilities of willing partners. Collaboration can prompt shifting alliances and dependencies among partners, especially when the latter cannot (or will not) honour the initial commitments of their own resources and capabilities to shared projects. Just as importantly, some parties to a collaborative agreement may misrepresent the significance of the project to their own constituents and to the parties to the agreement. This can lead to free riding if the establishment of a collaborative partnership is based on trust. Given these possibilities, senior managers may well consider whether, in establishing collaborative agreements, they might begin as one of the dominant partners and thereby hold other parties to account in terms of meeting their commitments and obligations. Just as importantly, collaborative agreements may evolve from statements of shared commitment to mimic the terms of reference and conditions associated with legally enforceable contracts.

Agency and Governance

Considering cooperation and collaboration, it is assumed that senior managers have sufficient authority to initiate and oversee projects in these domains. The scope of authority of senior managers is an issue of considerable importance, especially in the light of recurrent and competing claims for special treatment by talented portfolio managers. As markets move, and as investors become more or less sensitive to market volatility, realizing an institution's target rate of return may become increasingly difficult. Senior managers may persist with existing in-house and out-of-house providers, change the mix, even fire out-of-house providers and bring in-house those activities (see Chapter 5). In these situations, senior managers may have strong incentives to initiate cooperative and collaborative projects. There are significant transaction costs in exercising in-house and out-of-house options; cooperation and collaboration can be seen to sustain discretion in situations where it may be difficult to assess the advantages and disadvantages of other options.

Cooperation and collaboration can flourish in an action space that is less formal and certainly less bound by in-house employment relationships and the legal apparatus that regulates outsourcing agreements. This arena for innovation is both figurative and literal in that it is a space for common action outside the immediate institutional environment of senior managers and, in many cases, is conceived of by partners to bring together institutions from other jurisdictions—thereby avoiding the reputational damage that could come from direct comparison. This action space is only possible, however, if participating institutions allow their senior managers to carry through on these ventures in ways that facilitate experimentation, learning by doing, and alliance formation and deformation.

Over the longer term, it is likely that successful cooperative and collaborative ventures will be absorbed into the institution, whether on an in-house or outsourced basis. This applies especially if these types of ventures claim a significant share of an institution's assets and liabilities, and their risk exposures begin to affect those of the entire institution. Nevertheless, there is a price to be paid for incorporating these ventures into an institution: the favoured status of such ventures may challenge the privileges of incumbent portfolio managers and add a high enough level of complexity to the institution to discount its benefits.

In any event, institutions may prefer to spin off these ventures, given that, because markets move and market agents adapt to changing circumstances, success during one phase of the market is no guarantee of future success (Lo 2012). Indeed, senior managers may wish to initiate new kinds of cooperation and collaboration in response to changing market conditions, thus jettisoning previous ventures that proved to be less resilient than expected in the face of unanticipated circumstances. Larger institutions may contemplate implementing a sourcing strategy that combines insourcing and outsourcing with a series of innovative ventures that seek to solve apparent problems found in the existing arrangement of the investment programme, without committing to those ventures over the long term (either internal to the organization or as privileged external suppliers). This type of innovation strategy presupposes a robust governance framework that simultaneously empowers senior managers and protects against unjustified escalation in commitment and costs that come with functional complexity.

TRANSFORMING HOME BIAS

Here, we move from the logic of cooperation and collaboration to the various ways in which these strategies are realized in practice. We begin with the simplest ways of facilitating senior managers' knowledge and understanding of the options available and move on to more complex modes of cooperation and collaboration that require the mobilization and application of scarce institutional resources and capabilities. These instances are meant to represent the various possibilities on offer rather than being an exhaustive list of what is currently available to the industry.

Conferences and Research Clubs

One of the simplest ways of scoping the available options is to attend international conferences and invited briefings. If commonplace, and an industry in its own right, it is apparent that conferences with specific agendas—tailored to the needs and interests of senior managers in different types of financial institutions—can make a difference to the decisions made about how to proceed. Who is and who is not on the agenda, the topics presented, what can be gleaned from side conversations, and who has something fresh to say are grist for the mill.[5] This type of event gives senior managers information with which to challenge their internal and external advisers, placing proffered advice in the context of the home market for innovation. Importantly, these types of events also allow senior managers to discriminate between what is widely accepted and conventional and what is unconventional and subject to dispute.

Recognizing the costs and benefits of attending such events, research clubs were formed to explore together the interests of related institutions at a price that does not automatically engage the procurement procedures of participating institutions. These clubs tend to be relatively small, with no more than a dozen members, thereby allowing for the realization of benefits otherwise lost when clubs become too large (Buchanan 1965: 8). Crucially, they are comprised of members who can learn from one another; in fact, they often offer the first ones to join an opportunity to invite other institutions with resources and capabilities that are consistent with, but different from, those of the initial participants. As Grabher et al. (2008: 262) observed when discussing communities of learning, these types of organizations include those that are 'deeply involved and widely focused at the same time', switching the focus from the relationship between senior managers and internal and external suppliers to what senior managers can learn about innovation in different jurisdictions. These organizations tend to have a limited life and often depend on the flow of fresh ideas offered to participants that are consistent with their interests.

Seeding-related Ventures

Having identified the issues to be resolved, one way forward for senior managers is to provide the start-up capital needed to carry forward investment programmes. Seeding start-up ventures are investments in the skills and expertise of those who claim a different perspective on problems that affect much larger investment institutions (*contra* Barnett's 2008 discounting of the benefits of alliances). Typically, these ventures begin within an established institution, whether an asset owner or asset manager, and then seek independence from the host institution and its priorities and decision-making mechanisms. Seeding gives the new entity assets to manage, services, and sponsorship, which, in the longer term, can attract other institutions. For the sponsoring institution, the new entity can be a site for testing out ideas and solutions without disturbing the existing arrangement of roles and responsibilities. In some instances, geography is the key to success—for example, seeding a new hedge fund in London, a database designer in Silicon Valley, or an emerging market manager in Hong Kong.

This mode of innovation supposes that the needs of the sponsor, as well as the skills and expertise embedded in the new entity, mediate the apparent imbalance of power between the sponsor and the new entity. Nonetheless, there are obvious dangers in such relationships: the sponsor could simply walk away with the ideas that the new entity has generated, or its principals could exploit the senior managers' commitment. If successful, these new entities are likely to cast aside the shackles of the sponsor sooner rather than later. Another possible approach is to set up a jointly owned entity for which the investment responsibilities fall outside the scope of existing in-house and out-of-house portfolio managers. This type of entity could be domiciled in another jurisdiction and could be the site for experimenting with new forms of compensation, a style of investing that runs counter to portfolio managers in the sponsor's home jurisdiction, or a system of decision-making that is less hierarchical and reliant on a de-centred team-based approach. Inevitably, these types of ventures run the risks (or costs) of being out of sight and out of mind.

Partnerships, Informal and Formal

In many jurisdictions, financial institutions coexist with one another with many of the same functions, even if in the final instance they compete over realizing target rates of return. As noted, larger institutions can be more cost-efficient than smaller ones in providing the services associated with investment management. Equally, the larger ones can claim significant discounts from external service providers. In these circumstances, senior managers of small institutions may seek cost-sharing and service-sharing agreements with larger ones, piggybacking on the functional scope of the latter to maintain their cost effectiveness. These types of agreements are informal in the sense that the larger institution is willing to enter into them because sharing services does not conflict with their existing priorities or operational performance.

These types of arrangements can form a basis for establishing formal partnerships between local institutions with an interest in compensating for their peripheral location relative to the global market for financial services (Dixon and Monk 2014). In these circumstances, large and small institutions often face the prospect of making deals with external providers, which, because of the size of the local market, effectively control the terms and conditions for financial services. In addition, the nature and scope of proffered services may be rather limited compared with those of the financial centres at the core of the global financial industry. Enhancing the size and scope of the client side of the local market may be necessary if beneficial institutions are to bypass local providers in favour of the bulge-bracket global providers and the myriad of smaller institutions that offer boutique services from, for example, London or New York. Whether these types of partnerships are possible depends, in part, on the home jurisdiction's competition policies and practices, the balance of power between the buy side and the sell side of the market, and the rivalries among senior managers representing local institutions.

For larger institutions, concerned about the organizational complexity that comes with providing the full range of services needed for effective investment management, being a partner in a captive supplier can be a way of externalizing the supply of services, while remaining in control of the costs and quality of those services. For smaller institutions unable to produce their own services, so subject to the market for them, these partnerships provide an equitable relationship with other institutions, which is often missing in fee-for-service agreements. Notice, however, the inherent tensions between large and small partners; the former are always likely to consider the opportunity costs of remaining in such partnerships whereas the latter may have no real alternative. How these entities are governed, the allocation of voting rights, and the degree to which proffered services are innovative are key elements in any long-term partnership.[6]

Investment Clubs and Shared Equity

Going beyond partnerships, asset owners have formed investment clubs to accomplish three separate but related objectives. In the first instance, these clubs have sought to join members whose interests are aligned, and whose goals and objectives are consistent over a sequence of deals extending into the future. In the second instance, these types of clubs often depend on relationships with investment managers whose own incentives are demonstrably consistent with those of members of investment clubs. In the third instance, the size and scope of the deals involved are such that they can justify the commitment of time and effort of senior managers of investment institutions in realizing shared goals. Here, the make-or-buy option is subsumed by a third option, which is a form of collaboration underwritten by transparency and accountability within institutions, among institutions, and between an institution and its partners. These types of entities can be found, for example, in the private provision of urban infrastructure.[7]

This mode of promoting innovation in the investment process is closely related to the private equity industry where general partners (GPs) organize a stream of investment opportunities orchestrated through the fund or funds they control, and in which asset owners or limited partners (LPs) invest. In some cases, these types of funds bring LPs with previous knowledge and experience together with each other and with the sponsoring GP. Even so, the relationship between the GP sponsor and the participating LPs can be variable—depending on the volume of assets committed, shared expertise and knowledge, and past relationships with one another. Indeed, notwithstanding common contracts and letters of commitment, side deals are often struck between the sponsoring GP and privileged LPs, thus excluding the less privileged LPs. It is arguable that these types of deals are less about cooperation and collaboration than about fees and the disbursement of benefits. Nonetheless, to the extent that senior managers control entry and exit from these deals, these arrangements can provide opportunities to remake or realign the make-or-buy option spread.

IMPLICATIONS AND CONCLUSIONS

The premise underpinning this chapter is that asset owners have shown a surprising lack of institutional innovation. The current organization and management of these institutions typically reflects their establishment, in many cases looking back over fifty to seventy years. This is remarkable given the transformation of the investment management industry over the past twenty-five years, and the rate of product innovation found in global financial markets. The stasis of the sector has been such that these types of financial institutions have, on the margin, taken higher levels of risk in the hope of realizing returns that could compensate for low rates of institutional adaptation and development. At the limit, the crisis facing the US state and local public pension-fund sector is illustrative of the costs and consequences of institutional stasis (see Chapter 7).

In this chapter, we focused on the senior managers of a representative financial institution. These agents have been identified as key to realizing investment goals and objectives; we suggest that the option to make or buy (namely in-house management versus outsourcing) has not always provided an adequate action space for innovation. Reliance on employment contracts has sometimes resulted in manager entrenchment, while reliance on external providers is often accompanied by difficulties in systematically discriminating between luck and skill (given informal alliances between asset managers, consultants, and advisers). In any event, industry-wide norms and conventions that favour continuity over innovation can compromise the senior managers' authority and control over portfolio managers. We have emphasized the benefits for senior managers of cooperation and collaboration, which in effect bypass the make-or-buy option and provide an action space for experimentation and learning that can then be applied to their own operations or to their relationships with external providers.

We noted that cooperation facilitates learning and innovation, even if inherent limits on longer-term commitment can discount the implementation internally and externally to the institution. We also noted that collaboration requires commitment, as well as the application of scarce institutional resources and capabilities. As has been widely observed, it is commonplace for institutions in the sector to economize on governance and management, assuming that professional standards are sufficient to carry decision-making in a rather benign financial environment (Clark and Urwin 2010). Recurrent crises in the core markets of the global financial system have challenged this assumption; indeed, recent research suggests that crises are endemic to developed economies' financial markets (Haldane and May 2011). Ultimately, the value of collaboration is found in the enhancement of institutions' investment-related capabilities (Helfat et al. 2007).

Much of the research on innovation in the social sciences is on product innovation. Here, we are less concerned with what prompts the transformation of products, with how the flow of product innovation is channelled and communicated, or with the status of communities or networks of innovation (Von Hippel 2005). Rather, we are concerned with the emergence of new modes of organization, given continuity in institutional form and functions (Padgett and Powell 2012: 1–2). Perhaps surprisingly, in this chapter we suggested that current practices (make or buy) are a constraint on the nature and scope of innovation. Whether reliant on employment contracts (insourcing) or service contracts (outsourcing), senior managers face significant constraints on institutional innovation associated with the entrenchment of past practices. On the other hand, we also showed that senior managers can create for themselves and for their institution action spaces that facilitate innovation, which, if not particularly revolutionary, may well be transformative over the longer term.

In any event, financial institutions are, more often than not, reactive to events. Even if senior managers are able to anticipate changing market conditions and the realignment of internal and external relationships, there is sufficient noise in financial markets to ensure that doubts can always be raised about the urgency of 'agendas for change'. On the other hand, big events such as the GFC, the ongoing euro crisis, and the slowing global economy can fundamentally alter perceptions about the desirability of the status quo. In these circumstances, senior managers may be empowered to rewrite the terms of employment contracts and service agreements with external providers. Indeed, entirely new initiatives may claim centre stage. Here, innovation in institutional form and functions is perceived to be the solution to the apparent disconnection between what is inherited and the new realities of global markets.

NOTES

1. Gennaioli et al. (2013: 1331) suggest that shadow banks 'originate or acquire both safe and risky loans, and can finance these loans from [their] own resources as well as by issuing debt'. By contrast, the legal form and responsibilities of pension funds and the like are quite different from shadow banks, which operate quite literally in the shadow of their corporate sponsors in either offshore or onshore jurisdictions.

2. Whether beneficial financial institutions face competition for the flow of funds varies by jurisdiction. Even in countries like Australia, where pension-plan participants have the right to switch between 'competing' funds, the rate of switching is low, concentrated among a few participants, and mixed in terms of the benefit that comes with it. As Samuelson and Zeckhauser (1988) note, inertia is characteristic of pension-plan participants.
3. See recent moves in the United Kingdom not only to outsource the management of pension funds, but also to shift fiduciary responsibilities to commercial entities. In a similar manner, there have been moves to sell both the management of assets and the obligation to pay future benefits off to insurance companies and special purpose vehicles. These developments are explained in Clark and Urwin (2010).
4. With its focus on the costs of inertia for organizational innovation in the absence of a market for institutional control, this chapter can be read as an analysis of the consequences of size in the financial industry. As such, it resonates with related treatments of large organizations, including Jensen (2000), even if our representative institution is fundamentally different from commodity-producing firms.
5. Institutions enter into cooperative agreements to realize some benefit, even if marginal, to the status quo; such agreements are assumed Pareto optimal (Olson 1965). However, any cost–benefit analysis of cooperation needs to be mindful of the differing time horizons of participating parties and the variable nature of expected benefits. It also needs to be mindful of the trade in costs and benefits within and among cooperative arrangements by parties that may seek longer-term relationships that promote common benefits rather than the immediate payoffs that each party claims (Fehr and Schmidt 1999).
6. Some events mix together asset owners and managers, whereas others discriminate against asset managers in the hope of building coalitions or alliances among clients. See Bathelt and Glückler (2011: chapter 9) for an extensive treatment of the benefits and orchestration of what they term 'temporary clusters'. At the limit, these are networks rather than places in the manner suggested by Benkler (2006).
7. In a related vein, Hachigian (2013) argues that public–private partnerships (PPPs) joining together financial institutions, governments, and construction companies in the provision of urban infrastructure and other similar large-scale projects have often failed to realize the promised benefits for all parties because of misalignments of interest and poor governance procedures and processes. Whether to join a partnership can be seen as a different problem from that of realizing the benefits of a partnership over time.

11

Reframing Finance

With the relative slowdown of the Chinese economy and the concomitant slowdown in economic integration and trade, institutional investors are unlikely to reap a rate of return anything like that of the past twenty-five years. At the same time, the global financial crisis (GFC) and its aftermath has disrupted confidence in existing models of institutional investment, leaving many institutional investors questioning their core assumptions and beliefs, many of which have persisted for half a century. Accordingly, a lot of investors are re-evaluating the manner in which they will attempt to hit their (high) expected return targets. As such, we are now seeing, for the first time in decades, a sincere interest among institutional investors, such as pension funds, sovereign funds, and endowments, in new and innovative models of investing. As such, the asset-owner industry, which has been focused on efficiency for the better part of a century, is now faced with the challenge of figuring out how to be innovative, which seemingly goes against the DNA of many of these organizations.

This is largely because there are fewer pressures on institutional investors to change and innovate than there are on their private, commercial counterparts. Most asset owners have a legal right to represent the interests of 'captive' beneficiaries. To be fair, some funds have sought to disintermediate, or simply to reintermediate, asset managers in the pursuit of more aligned, long-term models of investment (Clark and Monk 2011; Monk et al. 2017). However, this type of behaviour has been rare (Ambachtsheer 2014). The large majority of pension funds have made no meaningful changes to the way they do business in decades, for they are often embedded in particular economic and political environments that seem to constrain rather than encourage evolution. Even sophisticated institutional investors, like certain endowments, have been slow to change, for they tend to focus their innovative endeavours on the kinds of investments they pursue rather than on questioning the ways in which they themselves invest capital.

In sum, the world of institutional investment is changing too slowly to keep up with either the dynamic underlying economy or the increasingly complex and challenging financial ecosystem. In addition, since the investment world is likely to continue to change at a rapid pace, this stagnation will become progressively more problematic. The rise in artificial intelligence, big data, and social networking are but three technological innovations that could threaten core financial service industries. The business of investing will almost certainly not revert to anything approaching that of the 1980s, or even 1990s, which is when most of the models of institutional investment were founded. Going forward, institutional investors that can be innovative will prosper and succeed (Clark and Urwin 2007, 2008b, 2008c). Those that allow inherited organizational and operational characteristics to dictate their plans may find themselves in trouble.

In this concluding chapter, we thus discuss the ways in which asset-owner investors can catalyse change and innovate prudently. While many articles have been written about the asset management industry and how it is changing in the face of new technological threats, we purposefully view the world through the lens of those institutional investors searching for organizational innovation and reconfiguration to meet their long-term objectives in a challenging world. We examine the forces underpinning change among pension funds and sovereign funds (among others) and consider the imperatives driving these investors towards different forms of management and governance. Moreover, we consider why innovation is necessary and, in turn, focus explicitly on how these funds can, and even should, innovate. In particular, drawing on Teece et al. (1997), we look at the mechanisms that permit dynamic capabilities within an institutional investor and focus on how they can exploit assets today while exploring new assets for the future.

Because the pace of economic and technological change is unlikely to slow down, it will take us even further from the foundations of our current finance and investment ecosystem. As such, we conclude that innovation—and the capacity to innovate prudently—will provide an important competitive advantage to institutional investors in the decades to come. We seek to give asset owners the tools they need to innovate from within (Battilana et al. 2009).

A REASON FOR BEING

Institutional investors, like pension funds, endowments, and sovereign funds, exist because their sponsors decide to manage a set of future liabilities and/or uncertainties by setting aside financial assets for investment in financial markets (see Chapter 2). One can simplify the rationale for doing this by reducing it to two key drivers. First, prefunding provided an assurance that sponsors made credible and legitimate promises, that is, they could actually meet their future obligations. Second, the prefunded financial assets would also, it was hoped, grow faster than either the sponsor or the overall economy, which meant that future liabilities could be met at a relative discount today. Embedded in both these factors was the assumption that financial markets offered a reliable mechanism for managing long-term objectives, thus allowing institutional investors to achieve their corporate and financial goals in the long run. These assumptions are currently being tested.

Despite a clear reliance on financial markets to achieve objectives, the sponsors of the plans we study rarely allow their funds to build up sufficient capabilities to invest assets directly in financial markets. Rather, they believe that they would be better served by seeing their investment organizations as simple conduits into financial markets; in other words, they prefer to buy the talent of the professional financial services industry rather than create it themselves (see Chapter 5). In this respect, the institutional investors' job was (and more often than not still is) to contract investment management services from external asset managers (see Chapters 6 and 7 for a detailed discussion). It was the private asset managers (and not the institutional investors) that made the actual investments in stocks, bonds, or other financial securities. In addition, institutional investors had an array of consultants, accountants, auditors, actuaries, and custodians to help share the oversight and burden of managing these assets (see Chapter 8).

As this suggests, the traditional institutional investor was almost entirely outsourced, so rarely possessed the internal expertise or competence needed to execute even the most basic financial transactions without the help of some external adviser. Put differently, the sponsors of institutional investment organizations were seemingly comfortable with the idea that the success of their funds was a function of the effective oversight and management of a long chain of principal–agent relationships. For example, such relationships might bring together owners (elderly), sponsors (governments), institutional investors (pension funds), asset managers (Wall Street), and advisers (consultants). To orchestrate this complex symphony of risks, products, service providers, and obligations, pension funds were utterly dependent on intermediaries. They used external managers to deploy capital. The boards and senior managers also often relied on consultants to set strategy and asset allocation.

To be fair, this model of institutional investing seemed to work for a while, thanks in large part to a series of bull markets, which seemed to paper over the misalignment of interests growing between asset owners and managers. Over time, however, the extended chain of principal–agent relationships became problematic. In particular, the injection of new incentives and motivations at each link of the chain served to distort the original motives of the asset owners into a signal that maximized value for the managers. In short, the disjointed process of asset allocation and investing often led to suboptimal choices, and the ultimate investment decisions that the asset managers made maximized their own utility rather than that of the asset owners; this phenomenon is referred to as a 'broken agency' problem (Sheffer and Levitt 2010).

Broken agency stems from a misalignment of interests due to an inappropriate distribution of risks and expected returns among the principals and agents. It is most obvious in large-scale construction and infrastructural projects where the agents that bear the short-term risk and receive the short-term rewards are different from those that bear the long-term risks and rewards. In finance, broken agency distorts portfolio construction: the portfolios that long-term investors would like to hold and those that they actually hold are quite different due to an over-reliance on short-term-oriented asset managers. This is the broken agency of institutional investing, and the source of this agency conflict ultimately stems from the silent nature of the ultimate owner of the assets. Some participants or beneficiaries own the actual assets within an institutional investor (Morrison and Wilhelm 2008), but these true principals rarely, if ever, are seen or heard from (Black 1992).

What can be done? The only way to ensure an alignment of interests among all these parties would be to identify intermediaries and service providers that can truly take a long-term view. This is sound in theory, but, in practice, it is difficult to achieve. It is rare to find private-sector asset managers willing to make decisions that will benefit a portfolio twenty or even ten years in the future. In addition, it is rare to see asset owners capable of managing the end-to-end investment process required to take a life-cycle perspective.

THE CASE FOR INNOVATION

Institutional investors organize their production to realize a given objective, typically communicated to management in the form of a return target (see Chapter 2). To achieve this, investors are obliged to make a series of strategic decisions on asset mix, market access points, and the execution of investment strategies (Campbell and Viceira 2002). In making these decisions, institutional investors will tend to have three key resources within the organization—human capital, systems, and processes. It is important to note that the fund's level of sophistication in these three areas will tend to drive the organization's decisions about assets, access, and execution. It is also important that investors balance their ambitions in terms of returns with the organization's resources in these three critical domains.

The problem we find with many of our case studies is that the ambitions of sponsors are often out of line with the investment organization's resources; for example, pension or sovereign funds may be expected to generate a return that is incompatible with the realities of either the market or the fund. In other words, the organizations lack the systems, personnel, or information needed to generate the requested returns. This is manifest, for example, in the case of a government putting undue pressure on a board to maintain a high discount rate, with a view to keeping the reported liability small and freeing space in the government's budget for other spending (or simply maintaining a credit rating). The expected discount rate is a fiction drawn from a goal-seeking exercise, but the rate protects politicians' short-term spending.

To make this fiction plausible, the board has to 'work' with actuaries and consultants to set an asset allocation policy that can actually justify the high discount rate. This means asking the plan to take on high risk, which is the only way to increase the expected return calculation provided by the actuaries as the discount rate. The board may or may not realize that its fund is not equipped to handle this risk, but it is willing to push forward in the hopes of maintaining its funding level. This set of demands from the sponsors (though not the owners) leaves the organization in a very precarious position. Not only are the funds often under-resourced but they are also pushed towards challenging investment environments that can support a high discount rate. Not surprisingly, research shows that these sorts of situations lead to investment underperformance (Andonov et al. 2016).

Given that most institutional investors lack human resources, systems, and processes, it is hardly surprising that many are seduced by complex financial products offered by third-party managers. Financial intermediaries are very adept at packaging the risk and return characteristics of underlying assets into a product that institutional investors can easily digest. These products come with a specific risk-return profile that can be combined with other products to construct a credible portfolio to meet the investors' required rate of return. All this intermediation is deemed necessary to manage the growing complexity of the products that intermediaries offer. The result is a world in which the tables are tilted too far in favour of third-party asset managers.

As evidence of this, research has started to quantify and define the areas of misalignment between the owners and managers of assets. For example, if an asset owner has difficulty getting transparency into a manager relationship, the former is often 'gamed' on fees by the latter (Foster and Young 2010). In addition, the confusing nature of management contracts too often allows managers to overcharge for low or average performance (Phalippou 2009). Robinson and Sensoy (2013) show that managers with higher fees in fact generate higher returns, but do not share the additional returns with limited partners (LPs). Numerous papers show that the incentives that standard compensation contracts give to managers allow them to manipulate returns (see Bebchuk and Fried 2004; Carpenter 2000; Starks 1987). Worse still, most institutional investors are not even aware that they are getting a bad deal (MacIntosh and Scheibelhut 2012; Sharpe 2013); this is because information is distorted along the long chain of intermediaries, which makes oversight all the more difficult (Leiblein et al. 2002).

In sum, plan sponsors often prevented twentieth-century institutional investors from developing the internal capabilities needed to manage these increasingly complex relationships, which has greatly handicapped them vis-à-vis twenty-first-century investing realities. In the wake of the financial crisis, however, the community of institutional investors is increasingly pondering novel business models. To be clear, they are not just considering new and exciting investment products coming from third-party managers; they are considering new ways of investing. In a slowing global economy with diminished confidence in the long-term prospects of public financial markets, many institutional investors are looking to innovation to meet expected return targets. At issue, then, is the degree to which the broader community of long-term, institutional investors will be able to change their organizations enough to be successful in the decades to come.

PRUDENT INNOVATION

In our research, we have found that when people see institutional investment organizations' large pools of assets under management (AUM), they assume that they can be tapped for internal resources in the three key domains underpinning the production of returns—process, people, and information. However, that is an incorrect assumption because there are often strict firewalls between the investment capital of these funds and their operating budgets, which means that the latter are usually inadequate for managing the former. There is also often little short-term pressure to develop competitive capabilities within these funds, for there are no competitive threats. In general, institutional investors enjoy a monopoly in that they have a legal right to represent the interests of a 'captive' beneficiary, which further erodes the impulse to professionalize and equip the organization properly.

In our view, governance will be crucial in overcoming the deficiencies of investor innovation. The independence of the organization, its resources and systems, and an ability to identify areas of opportunity and challenges are all crucial elements of governance that can have a dramatic impact on the success of any innovation policy. Therefore, before investors can take on innovative challenges and make operational changes, the organization should first assess its governance capabilities to determine whether a given investment strategy is commensurate with its organizational skills. The idea is to root the fund's investment style and strategy in a clear assessment of the organization's capabilities and the resources at the disposal of its staff. Much like using a 'risk budget' to guide portfolio construction and investment decision-making, institutional investors should use a 'governance budget' to guide the process of investing, the development of the organization, and the guidance of management (Clark and Urwin 2008a, 2010).[1]

Governance budgets are comprised of three ingredients. These are (1) the amount of time that a fund's board can apply to a given investment problem, (2) the level of expertise that can be called upon at the level of the board, and (3) the commitment of the board, which refers to its effectiveness at getting things done. This refers to the dynamic capabilities of the board (for example, real time versus calendar time meetings). We can look at each of these as being scarce resources that can be drawn down as a fund engages in more innovative or risky behaviour. Thinking about governance budgets, then, should become just as important as thinking about asset allocation or manager selection, especially for funds interested in bringing assets in-house.

Developing a governance budget first requires cataloguing the resources and assets that can drive sustainable returns. In general, these include the talent and skills of portfolio managers; the processes and protocols of decision-making; and the information-processing tools that support judgements. In other words, the people, processes, and protocols are what seem to matter most in this business (Clark and Monk 2014), but from where do these people, processes, protocols, and systems ultimately come? The board makes these resourcing decisions and controls the strategic levers of success. A fund's governance budget, which ultimately refers to the resources available to it to build investment operations, is thus a crucial determinant of an investor's capacity to innovate and has clear relevance to insourcing. In sum, any fund considering an innovation policy should first check to ensure that its governance budget aligns with its new risk budget. If the required levels of governance exist, then the fund can begin to develop the organization in accordance with the strategy.

Unfortunately, most of the investors reading this will recognize that their governance is often underprepared for innovation. As Clark (2015) notes, instead of looking forward and being part of a process whereby community norms and conventions adapt to a changing environment, trustees may seek refuge in the past where certainty prevails, albeit at the cost of reinforcing convention. To execute an innovative investment strategy successfully, many funds will have to restructure their own internal governance. Changing a fund's governance, however, is not easy, which is why it helps to assess what strategies are possible in the context of an existing governance budget (Clark and Urwin 2010).

CATALYSTS FOR INNOVATION

The key ingredient driving the long-term success of an institutional investor is its governance. As noted, governance is the mechanism that can mobilize an institution's resources to realize its objectives. It can also create new resources (or further develop existing ones). Whether the fund is considering creative products or developing certain products of its own, new resources will be required. The real question, then, is how a management team can actually get its board to mobilize the resources needed to be creative and innovative. In our research, we uncovered four ways in which an organization can secure the resources it requires to be innovative. These are (i) extra-financial objectives, (ii) fees and cost transparency, (iii) collaboration and cooperation, and (iv) competitive advantages.

Extra-financial Objectives

Many long-term investors have stakeholders that want them to consider extra-financial criteria in their investment process. While this is generally viewed in the pension community as a distraction and potential drag on returns, it is also an opportunity to innovative. Take the world of sovereign development funds (SDFs) as an example. SDFs are strategic, government-sponsored investment organizations with dual objective functions—to deliver high financial performance while fostering development. Our research has found that some SDFs have used this dual objective to develop innovative investment approaches that have, in turn, driven attractive investment returns (Clark and Monk 2016). An SDF requires innovation because there are no off-the-shelf products that these funds can buy that will deliver on the investment and development objectives simultaneously, which means that they are obligated to develop novel skills and expertise. In short, the extra-financial mandate helps a management team justify the development of internal expertise, which, in turn, helps it realize investment returns from a proprietary knowledge of local opportunities, privileged access to those opportunities, and trusted relationships with other investors. Moreover, SDFs are not the only ones to take advantage of this; other investors can use similar extra-financial constraints, be they environmental or governance, to develop unique and commercially valuable competencies.

Fees and Cost Transparency

Helping institutional investors get fees, and cost transparency is, in our view, a very effective way of unlocking additional resources for internal innovation and change. This is because most asset-owning boards have no real understanding of the scale of the fees and costs they are paying to external service providers. Accordingly, neither the boards nor the sponsors of these organizations have invested in the professionalization and innovation of their investment teams, for they have not yet seen the true cost of the outsourced investment model. The present value of the average fees that asset owners paid to asset managers over a thirty-year period amounts to approximately one-third of the assets invested, which is a lot to pay a manager who is not, on average, going to beat passive benchmarks (Greenwood and Scharfstein 2013). Paying an internal investment team $20 million dollars may seem costly on its own, but it is cheap if you consider that the same service and performance costs $200 million a year when paid to a team outside a pension fund (CEM Insights 2010). Our logic here is simple: if a pension fund or endowment board—let alone its sponsor or the general public—saw how much its plans were paying Wall Street for its products, asset owners would be forced to change the way they operate (Ellis 2012). Importantly, our research has found many pension funds that have used fee and cost transparency to secure greater internal resources for innovative projects.

Collaboration and Cooperation

We have found that cooperation and collaboration among investment organizations facilitate innovation because they offer participants an 'action space' in which to be informal and yet in some way committed to a project (see Chapter 9). As it turns out, resources cobbled together on the margin from a handful of organizations can end up being sufficient to take on a new project of some importance. This type of informal interaction is unavailable in conventional contracting with either internal employees or external service providers, for it generally allows participants to wind down and reduce commitments quickly if the innovation proves unsuccessful (Williamson 1975). In sum, cooperation and collaboration facilitate the pooling of numerous small resource commitments to achieve a large objective. This is done by bringing like-minded organizations and managers together around mutual problems with a view to developing common solutions. This lowers the barrier to commencing a project, for the expenses and resources are shared among parties. It is also worth noting that if a pension can convince its peers, which are also fiduciaries, to work with it on something innovative, it has, almost by definition, fulfilled its obligations under the prudent person rule. It can also smooth the process of doing something innovative.

Competitive Advantages

Institutional investors face a challenging market in which their expected return targets are high, but future market returns are projected to be low. This means that investors will have to do something different from what they did to achieve their objectives. One mechanism that we have seen investors focus on is their own competitive advantage and the ways they use this to drive higher returns. Some investors catalogue their competitive advantages to build a case for innovation in certain privileged domains in which they alone can invest with less competition. To do this, investment organizations must understand and know how to promote their unique characteristics and acquire the resources needed to develop novel access points. Generally, the advantages that these investors enjoy come from scale, time, liquidity, social acceptance, and even privileged access to deals within the sponsor's area of oversight. Without a detailed list of these advantages, it can be very challenging for investors to secure the resources they require.

We have found asset owners using all four of these catalysts to drive their innovative strategies or policies. In all cases, management teams used each of these to secure needed resources—and to expand the governance budget—with a view to pursuing innovation.

INNOVATION IMPLEMENTED

Financial markets are akin to 'innovation machines' that test investors' fitness to succeed; investors who can move quickly to identify and exploit opportunities can reap large rewards. Having reviewed in this chapter the importance of good governance and how to mobilize the needed resources via catalysts, we now reflect on the actual implantation of innovation. Numerous constraints prevent these organizations from actually being innovative.

It is very difficult to study how innovation policies might be implemented among asset owners, as there are almost no case studies from which to draw inspiration. Indeed, few investment organizations 'have well-established and specialized expertise in the area of management innovation' (Birkinshaw et al. 2008: 830). In fact, in our fieldwork over the past ten years, we have only come across one institutional investor with a dedicated group focused exclusively on the research and development (R&D) of innovative investment approaches, tools, methodologies, or even technologies. There are, to be sure, 'special opportunity' groups and 'special situation' teams; in fact, most investment organizations will have a strategy team that can do some applied R&D work. However, none of these groups can be accurately characterized as delivering innovation to the overall investment organization. How, then, should institutional investors implement innovation? In this case, we are forced to draw inspiration and insights from other industries.

As the literature points out, organizations that are skilled at exploiting value are often ill equipped to explore new value (Lubatkin et al. 2006; O'Reilly and Tushman 2004; Rivkin and Siggelkow 2003). You can think of an organization that is adept at exploitation as highly efficient, while one that is successful at exploration is good at searching for and understanding variations that can affect performance. The latter would be seen as innovation. As March (1991) noted, most organizations are poor at combining efficiency and innovation. Yet, both factors are required for survival among firms. 'The basic problem confronting an organization is to engage in sufficient exploitation to ensure its current viability and, at the same time, devote enough energy to exploration to ensure its future viability' (March 1991: 105). While this may be a pervasive problem for all industries, it affects institutional investors especially strongly because of their focus on being extremely efficient with internal resources. Put another way, a key challenge facing institutional investors is to bring innovation into a world dominated by efficiency. Moreover, as markets have moved towards shorter and shorter time horizons, investors have been pushed more towards exploitation than exploration (March 2003).

Research shows that, over time, the source of a firm's competitive advantage may be the very thing that drives its demise. Tushman and O'Reilly (1996) called this the 'success syndrome'. Yet, some particularly innovative companies in the private sector have managed to evolve and compete for more than two hundred years. Moreover, in explaining the survival of these companies, we see some useful points of departure for investors, namely the importance of dynamic capabilities and the role that leaders play in adapting, integrating, and reconfiguring the assets and resources within an organization (Eisenhardt and Martin 2000; Lavie and Rosenkopf 2006; Teece 2006; Teece et al. 1997). Indeed, there has been a great deal of research on how mature organizations can change to meet new demands (O'Reilly and Tushman 2008) and sustain competitive advantages as environments change around them.

The core idea emerging in the literature is that success demands finding ways to combine innovation and efficiency—exploration and exploitation—in the context of a single firm. Bringing these two contradictory dynamics together is referred to in the literature as 'organizational ambidexterity', and it is very difficult. Organizational ambidexterity calls for managers to experiment proactively in schemes with long-horizon payoffs (if they ever pay off). This is a challenging thing to do if the resources used could be used to achieve additional short-term profits through exploiting an existing asset base. Because of the unique nature of each organization, reflecting the set of historical decisions that has put it on its unique path, developing dynamic capabilities is itself a dynamic and challenging process. In fact, in his seminal book, Christensen (1997) suggested that exploration and exploitation were so difficult to combine that they required spinning out a subunit.

Notwithstanding, we use Teece's (2006, 2011) work on dynamic capabilities to highlight the areas in which an investment organization could work to improve its chances of being ambidextrous. These are termed sensing, seizing, and transforming.

Sensing

An organization has to be able to sense threats and opportunities if it wants to be able to respond to them. This requires intelligence gathering, with a focus on peers, technologies, and changing market factors. This implies that an organization has a plan for where this intelligence needs to be collected, which means having a vision of the future. Investors will want to get as close as possible to a market's edge to be able to appreciate the nuanced or low-volume signals. Management teams will need to cultivate an interest in long-term challenges and opportunities, for those focused on short-horizon exploitation have found it difficult to 'sense' threats and opportunities emerging over time (Jackson and Dutton 1988; Tripsas and Gavetti 2000). As Teece (2009: 208) rightly noted, 'the skills that result in the identification and/or development of an opportunity are not the same as those required to profit from or exploit the opportunity'. In short, without a powerful sensing mechanism, investors will struggle to combine efficiency with innovation (Chapter 3).

Seizing

Having sensed threats or opportunities, ambidextrous organizations must be able to make smart decisions about which choices to pursue and then to execute them fully (Harreld et al. 2007). For an investor, this generally means having organizational buy-in for a given strategy, which allows resources to be mobilized quickly in the pursuit of opportunities or in defence against threats. This may require investors to develop an explicit capability around learning and even to relearn how to learn. Seizing implies developing a sophisticated set of internal incentives to prioritize long-termism and innovation, which means leadership is a critical component of organizational ambidexterity among investors (Chapter 4). In this context we believe that investors could benefit from a formal R&D team that has a mandate to seize opportunities and move them towards execution and implementation.

Transforming

Even with sensing (adept intelligence, knowledge) and seizing (honed leadership, R&D) capabilities, organizations that want to be ambidextrous always have to be renewing themselves in the face of an environment that is, itself, constantly evolving. This is particularly challenging for institutional investors, for most of them have no existential threats that could jeopardize their survival. They have monopolies over their asset base, which limit the need for permanent renewal and change altogether. Moving assets from mature businesses and refocusing them on emerging opportunities goes against the grain. Again, this is about committing resources to long-term projects that are not necessarily going to produce returns in the short or medium term (Danneels 2002). According to the research, this may require meta-routines in which an organization develops routines that can be used to change other routines (Adler et al. 1999). An example of a meta-routine may be asking people to change jobs on a rotation. In any case, the objective is to institutionalize the allocation of resources to long-horizon projects and opportunities.

When these three components are combined within an investment organization, we expect to see dynamic capabilities emerge. Sadly, we cannot think of a single investment organization that has yet fully applied all three components of organizational ambidexterity. Some are close on these counts, but none has institutionalized policies around sensing, seizing, and transforming. To be fair, there are plenty of innovative investors in the world today, but we should not confuse launching an innovative product or strategy with having dynamic capabilities (Dew et al. 2006; Ebben and Johnson 2005); they are not the same.

This is the paradox of long-term investing; these organizations have to be good at two things that seem in direct contradiction with one another (Lewis and Andriopoulos 2009; Slaatte 1968). We hope, however, to find ways of making innovation and efficiency more in tune with each another. Indeed, when done very well, exploration and exploitation cease to be competing activities and can come to complement one another (Chen and Katila 2008).

A REAL-WORLD EXAMPLE

Over the past five years, we, the authors, have worked closely with a variety of endowments, pension funds, and sovereign funds around the world. In all cases, the organizations with which we worked were seeking to improve their governance and management and to launch innovative modes of operation. One fund in particular stands out to us as having displayed many of the concepts and ideas that underpin this book—developing a governance budget, using the catalysts, and beginning the process of institutionalizing dynamic capabilities and organizational ambidexterity. This organization, which due to confidentiality requirements will remain anonymous, has a long history and has been managing money for decades.

With a new leader on board, fresh eyes saw the challenges facing this fund. This person sensed that the fund was underperforming because of a lack of alignment with managers and its blind pursuit of an investment model that had worked well in the past but would unlikely do so in the decades to come. After taking stock of the organization, it was determined that innovative projects could deliver value on a number of different levels. After reviewing the capabilities of the organization and its governance, the team agreed that new resources would be required to change the fund. This raised the question of how the management team would secure the resources from the board with which to effect the change.

In making the case, the team reminded the board of the challenging return environment ahead and the need to leverage the fund's unique competitive advantages. The chief information officer (CIO) also engaged a fee and cost consultant, which allowed the management team to demonstrate to the board the high cost of the external service providers and remind his staff and sponsor that alternative methods were actually not only desirable but also a requirement. At the same time, all its stakeholders were pushing the investment organization to take on some non-financial projects, specifically on the environment. The team used these requests to build a more robust investment decisions framework rooted in long-horizon risk management. While this ticked the boxes for environment, it also helped the fund in core commercial areas. Finally, the organization sought to work closely with peers to develop novel investment strategies, so sharing the costs of some of the most audacious innovations. Using these four factors, the CIO secured the crucial resources and buy-in from all stakeholders to be able to pursue the innovation that was necessary for the organization to thrive in the twenty-first century.

Significantly, peer collaboration was also the first step towards institutionalizing organizational ambidexterity to implement the innovation. Indeed, the fund saw its peer relationships as useful in 'sensing' opportunities and threats. The team then began trying to seize certain opportunities, using consultants and advisers to scale up and down where needed. In addition, the CIO was willing to take a personal career risk to seize these new opportunities; and so began the implementation of this fund's desired changes. To date, the fund has received many accolades for this innovation and is on track to implement a highly professional and flexible operating model. Our last piece of advice to this fund would be to remember that there is no finish line for innovation; it has to remain on this course of transformation.

SOME FINAL THOUGHTS

In the wake of the financial crisis, a growing number of plan sponsors have begun to wake up to the misalignment of interests embedded in their principal–agent-based investment model. In fact, the onslaught of recurring financial crises over the past few years has jolted some sponsors to push their own organizations to seek out more aligned models of institutional investment, as many funds now recognize that the long chain of principal–agent relationships has allowed for a distortion of their overarching objectives (Ambachtsheer et al. 2013). In this concluding chapter—and indeed in this book—we have sought to situate asset-owner investors in the increasingly complex and challenging capitalist system and indeed financial markets.

Very few academic studies have focused like this on asset owners, even though they arguably constitute the foundation of our capitalist system. In Chapter 2, we therefore reminded our readers of the key role of asset managers and of their unique and idiosyncratic nature. In Chapter 3, we set out the rather simple production function of investing by showing that, with the right people, information, and process, all investors generate the same thing—returns. In Chapter 4, we show that the application of these three inputs through leadership, and the decision to make or buy them (Chapter 5), is what truly differentiates investment organizations. However, as we see in Chapters 6 and 7, the process of governing and managing these inputs—whether it be internal or external—is woefully inadequate. Worse yet, we show in Chapter 8 that the traditional sources of advice and counsel, the consultants, have lost touch with the fundamentals of institutional investing. This, in turn, as we show in Chapter 9, has driven many investment organizations to gather intelligence and counsel from peers and other like-minded organizations. All this brings us to this chapter on reframing finance through innovation.

The objective of this chapter—and indeed of the book—has been to remind investors of their core function and show them how they can take charge of their futures. This chapter lays plans for how asset owners can mobilize their innovative ideas and, indeed, catalyse their boards to resource them appropriately. We do not mean to suggest here that investors should innovate for the sake of being new and different. Our objective is simply to remind everybody about the basics and push all investors to think about how best to take money, add people, information, and policies, and then make more money. At issue, then, is the degree to which the broader community of long-term institutional investors will be able to change their organizations and the production of investment returns. The twentieth-century production function is unlikely to work in the twenty-first century. This means that innovation is coming to pension funds, sovereign funds, university endowments, charitable foundations, family offices, and other asset-owner investors. We hope that this book helps them to prepare for the changes to come.

NOTE

1. Here it is important to recognize that governance is a finite and measurable resource, and that the investment style and strategy of the organization should match its available levels. Put slightly differently, a fund's governance budget should be reflected implicitly in its planned and expected performance and, explicitly, in its risk budget.

Bibliography

Abolafia, M. Y. (1996), *Making Markets: Opportunism and Restraint on Wall Street*, Cambridge, MA: Harvard University Press.

Adler, P. S., Goldoftas, B., and Levine, D. I. (1999), 'Flexibility versus efficiency? A case study of model changeovers in the Toyota production system', *Organization Science* 10(1): 43–68.

Aghion, P. and Tirole, J. (1997), 'Formal and real authority in organisations', *Journal of Political Economy* 105(1): 1–29.

Agnew, J. and Hurwitz, J. (2013), 'Financial education and choice in state public pension systems' [mimeo], Williamsburg VA: College of William and Mary.

Aikman, D., Galesic, M., Gigerenzer, G., Kapadia, S., Katsikopoulos, K. V., Kothiyal, A., Murphy, E., and Neumann, T. (2014), 'Taking uncertainty seriously: Simplicity versus complexity in financial regulation', *Bank of England Financial Stability Paper* No. 28.

Akerlof, G. (1970), 'The market for "lemons": Quality uncertainty and the market mechanism', *Quarterly Journal of Economics* 84(3): 88–500.

Akerlof, G. and Shiller, R. J. (2009), *Animal Spirits: How Human Psychology Drives the Economy, and Why It Matters for Global Capitalism*, Princeton, NY: Princeton University Press.

Akerlof, G., Blanchard, O., Romer, D., and Stiglitz, J. (2014), *What Have We Learned? Macroeconomic Policy after the Crisis*, Cambridge, MA: MIT Press.

Alevy, J., Haigh, M. S., and List, J. A. (2007), 'Information cascades: Evidence from a field experiment with financial market professionals', *Journal of Finance* 62(1): 151–80.

Allen, F. (1990), 'The market for information and the origin of financial intermediation', *Journal of Financial Intermediation* 1(1): 3–30.

Allen, F. and Gale, D. M. (1994), *Financial Innovation and Risk Sharing*, Cambridge, MA: MIT Press.

Allen, F. and Santamero, A. (1998), 'The theory of financial intermediation', *Journal of Banking and Finance* 21(11–12): 1461–85.

Ambachtsheer, K. P. (2007), *Pension Revolution: A Solution to the Pensions Crisis*, Hoboken NJ: Wiley.

Ambachtsheer, K. P. (2014), 'The case for long-termism', *Rotman International Journal of Pension Management* 7(2): 6–15.

Ambachtsheer, K. P. (2016), *The Future of Pension Management: Integration Design, Governance, and Investing*, Hoboken NJ: John Wiley & Sons.

Ambachtsheer, K. P., Fuller, R., and Hindocha, D. (2013), 'Behaving like an owner: Plugging investment chain leakages', *Rotman International Journal of Pension Management* 6(2): 18–27.

Ambrosini, V. and Bowman, C. (2001), 'Tacit knowledge: Some suggestions for operationalization', *Journal of Management Studies* 38(6): 811–29.

Amin, A. and Cohendet, P. (2004), *Architectures of Knowledge: Firms, Capabilities, and Communities*, Oxford: Oxford University Press.

Amin, A. and Thrift, N. J. (1992), 'Neo-marshallian nodes in global networks', *International Review of Urban and Regional Research* 16(4): 571–87.

Andonov, A., Bauer, R., and Cremers, M. (2012), 'Pension fund asset allocation and liability discount rates: Camouflage and reckless risk-taking by US public plans?' Netspar Discussion Paper No. 05/2012-061 (3 March), DOI: 10.2139/ssrn.2070054.

Andonov, A., Hochberg, Y. V., and Rauh, J. D. (2016), 'Political representation and governance: Evidence from the investment decisions of public pension funds'. Available at SSRN: https://ssrn.com/abstract=2754820.

Aoyama, Y. and Ratick, S. J. (2007), 'Trust, transactions, and information technologies in the U.S. logistics industry', *Economic Geography* 83(2): 159–80.

Aragones, E., Gilboa, I., Postlewaite, A., and Schmeidler, D. (2005), 'Fact-free learning', *American Economic Review* 95(5): 1355–68.

Archetti, M., Úbeda, F., Fudenberg, D., Green, J., Pierce, N. E., and Yu, D. W. (2011), 'Let the right one in: A microeconomic approach to partner choice in mutualisms', *The American Naturalist* 177(1): 75–85.

Argyres, N. S., Bercovitz, J., and Mayer, K. J. (2007), 'Complementarity and evolution of contractual provisions: An empirical study of IT services contracts', *Organization Science* 18(1): 3–19.

Bachher, J. S. and Monk, A. H. B. (2013), 'Platforms and vehicles for institutional co-investing', *Rotman International Journal of Pension Management* 6(1): 64–71.

Baker, G., Gibbons, R., and Murphy, K. J. (2001), 'Bringing the market inside the firm', *American Economic Review* 91(2): 212–18.

Baker, G., Gibbons, R., and Murphy, K. J. (2002), 'Relational contracts and the theory of the firm', *Quarterly Journal of Economics* 117(1): 39–84.

Barber, B. M. and Odean, T. (2001), 'Boys will be boys: Gender, overconfidence, and common stock investment', *Quarterly Journal of Economics* 116(1): 261–92.

Barnett, W. P. (2008), *The Red Queen among Organizations*, Princeton, NJ: Princeton University Press.

Barro, R. J. (2006), 'Rare disasters and asset markets in the twentieth century', *Quarterly Journal of Economics* 121(3): 823–66.

Barth, J. R., Caprio, G., and Levine, R. (2012), *Guardians of Finance: Making Regulators Work for Us*, Cambridge, MA: MIT Press.

Bathelt, H. and Glückler, J. (2011), *The Relational Economy: Geographies of Knowing and Learning*, Oxford: Oxford University Press.

Battilana, J., Leca, B., and Boxenbaum, E. (2009), 'How actors change institutions: Towards a theory of institutional entrepreneurship', *The Academy of Management Annals* 3(1): 65–107.

Beaverstock, J. (2004), '"Managing across borders": Knowledge management and expatriation in professional service legal firms', *Journal of Economic Geography* 4(2): 157–79.

Beaverstock, J., Smith, R. G., and Taylor, P. J. (1999), 'A roster of world cities', *Cities* 16(6): 445–58.

Bebchuk, L. A. and Fried, J. M. (2004), 'Stealth compensation via retirement benefits', National Bureau of Economic Research Working Paper 10742, DOI: 10.3386/w10742.

Benkler, Y. (2002), 'Some economics of wireless communications', *Harvard Journal of Law and Technology* 16(1): 1–59.
Benkler, Y. (2006), *The Wealth of Networks: How Social Production Transforms Markets and Freedom*, New Haven, CT: Yale University Press.
Bernstein, P. L. (1996), *Against the Gods: The Remarkable Story of Risk*, New York, NY: John Wiley & Sons.
Beshears, J., Choi, J. J., Laibson, D., and Madrian, B. C. (2011), 'Behavioral economics perspectives on public sector pension plans', Working Paper 16728, Cambridge, MA: National Bureau of Economic Research.
Beugelsdijk, S., McCann, P., and Mudambi, R. (2010), 'Introduction: Place, space and organisation—economic geography and the multinational enterprise', *Journal of Economic Geography* 10(4): 485–93.
Birkinshaw, J., Hamel, G., and Mol, M. J. (2008), 'Management innovation', *Academy of Management Review* 33(4): 825–45.
Black, B. (1992), 'Agents watching agents: The promise of institutional investor voice', *UCLA Law Review* 39(4): 811–93.
Blinder, A. S. (2015), 'Can economists learn? The right lesson from the financial crisis', *Foreign Affairs* 94(2): 154–9.
Bolton, P. and Dewatripont, M. (2005), *Contract Theory*, Cambridge, MA: MIT Press.
Bor, D. (2012), *The Ravenous Brain*, New York, NY: Basic Books.
Bowles, S. (2004), 'Microeconomics: Behavior, institutions, and evolution', *Quarterly Journal of Economics* 101: 229–64.
Brennan, G., Eriksson, L., Goodin, R. E., and Southwood, N. (2014), *Explaining Norms*, Cambridge: Cambridge University Press.
Brown, J. R. and Wilcox, D. W. (2009), 'Discounting state and local pension liabilities', *American Economic Review* 99(2): 538–42.
Buchanan, J. M. (1965), 'An economic theory of clubs', *Economica* 32(125): 1–14.
Bunderson, J. S. and Reagans, R. E. (2011), 'Power, status, and learning in organizations', *Organization Science* 22(5): 1182–94.
Calabresi, G. (1982), *A Common Law for the Age of Statutes*, Cambridge, MA: Harvard University Press.
Campbell, J. C., Jackson, H., Madrian, B., and Tufano, P. (2011), 'Consumer financial protection', *Journal of Economic Perspectives* 25(1): 91–114.
Campbell, J. Y. and Viceira, L. M. (2002), *Strategic Asset Allocation: Portfolio Choice for Long-Term Investors*, Oxford: Oxford University Press.
Caplin, A. and Leahy, J. (1994), 'Business as usual, market crashed, and wisdom after the fact', *American Economic Review* 84(3): 548–65.
Caplin, A. and Martin, D. (2011), 'Search and satisficing', *American Economic Review* 101(7): 2899–922.
Carpenter, J. N. (2000), 'Does option compensation increase managerial risk appetite?' *Journal of Finance* 55(5): 2311–31.
Casson, M. (1997), *Information and Organization: A New Perspective on the Theory of the Firm*, Oxford: Oxford University Press.
CEM Insights (2010), 'Internal management does better after costs', CEM Benchmarking Inc. Available at: http://www.cembenchmarking.com/Files/Documents/October_2010_CEM_Insights.pdf.

Centina, K. and Preda, A. (eds) (2006), *The Sociology of Financial Markets*, Oxford: Oxford University Press.

Che, Y.-K. and Yoo, S.-W. (2001), 'Optimal incentives for teams', *American Economic Review* 91(3): 525–41.

Chen, E. L. and Katila, R. (2008), 'Rival interpretations of balancing exploration and exploitation: Simultaneous or sequential'. In Shane, S. (ed.), *Handbook of Technology and Innovation Management* (pp. 197–214), Chichester: John Wiley & Sons.

Chen, J., Hong, H., Huang, M., and Kubik, J. D. (2004), 'Does fund size erode mutual fund performance? The role of liquidity and organization', *American Economic Review* 94(5): 1276–302.

Choi, S. J. and Triantis, G. (2013), 'Market conditions and contract design: Variations in debt contracting', *New York University Law Review* 88(1): 51–82.

Choi, S. J., Gulati, M., and Posner, E. A. (2013), 'The dynamics of contract evolution', *New York University Law Review* 88(1): 1–50.

Christensen, C. M. (1997), 'Making strategy: Learning by doing', *Harvard Business Review* 75(6): 141–56.

Čihák, M. and Nier, E. (2012), 'Need for special resolution regimes for financial institutions: The case of the European Union', *Harvard Business Law Review* 2(2): 396–433.

Clark, G. L. (1998), 'Stylized facts and close dialogue: Methodology in economic geography', *Annals of the Association of American Geographers*, 88(1): 73–87.

Clark, G. L. (2000), *Pension Fund Capitalism*, Oxford: Oxford University Press.

Clark, G. L. (2002), 'London in the European financial services industry: Locational advantage and product complementarities', *Journal of Economic Geography* 2(4): 433–53.

Clark, G. L. (2007), 'Expertise and representation in financial institutions: UK legislation on pension fund governance and US regulation of the mutual fund industry', *21st Century Society: Journal of the Academy of Social Sciences* 2(1): 1–23.

Clark, G. L. (2008), 'Governing finance: Global imperatives and the challenge of reconciling community representation with expertise', *Economic Geography* 84(3): 281–302.

Clark, G. L. (2011), 'Myopia and the global financial crisis: Context-specific reasoning, market structure, and institutional governance', *Dialogues in Human Geography* 1(1): 4–25.

Clark, G. L. (2013), 'Mapping financial literacy: Cognition and the environment', *Geografiska Annaler B* 95(2): 131–45.

Clark, G. L. (2014), 'Information, knowledge, and investing in offshore financial markets', *Journal of Sustainable Finance and Investment* 4(4): 299–320.

Clark, G. L. (2015), 'The components of talent: Company size and financial centres in the European investment management industry', *Regional Studies* 50(1): 168–81.

Clark, G. L. and Monk, A. H. B. (2008), 'Conceptualizing the defined benefit pension promise', *Benefits Quarterly* 25(1): 7–18.

Clark, G. L. and Monk, A. H. B. (2011), 'Pension reserve funds: Aligning form and function', *Rotman International Journal of Pension Management* 4(2): 18–25.

Clark, G. L. and Monk, A. H. B. (2013), 'The scope of financial institutions: In-sourcing, outsourcing and off-shoring', *Journal of Economic Geography* 13(2): 279–98.

Clark, G. L. and Monk, A. H. B. (2014), 'Principles and policies for in-house asset management', *Journal of Financial Perspectives* 1(3): 39–47.

Clark, G. L. and O'Connor, K. (1997), 'The informational content of financial products and the spatial structure of the global finance industry'. In Cox, K. (ed.), *Spaces of Globalisation* (pp. 89–114), New York, NY: Guilford.

Clark, G. L. and Thrift, N. (2005), 'The return of bureaucracy: Managing dispersed knowledge in global finance'. In Knorr-Cetina, K., and Preda, A. (eds), *The Sociology of Financial Markets* (pp. 229–49), Oxford: Oxford University Press.

Clark, G. L. and Urwin, R. (2007), 'Best-practice investment management: Lessons for asset owners from the Oxford-Watson Wyatt Project on governance', SSRN paper, October, DOI: 10.2139/ssrn.1019212.

Clark, G. L. and Urwin, R. (2008a), 'Best-practice pension fund governance', *Journal of Asset Management* 9(1): 2–21.

Clark, G. L. and Urwin, R. (2008b), 'Leadership, collective decision-making, and pension fund governance', SSRN paper, 14 May, DOI: 10.2139/ssrn.1133015.

Clark, G. L. and Urwin, R. (2008c), 'Making pension boards work: The critical role of leadership', *Rotman International Journal of Pension Management* 1(1). Available at SSRN: http://ssrn.com/abstract=1290633.

Clark, G. L. and Urwin, R. (2010), 'Innovative models of pension fund governance in the context of the global financial crisis', *Pensions: An International Journal* 15(1): 62–77.

Clark, G. L. and Wójcik, D. (2007), *The Geography of Finance: Corporate Governance in the Global Marketplace*, Oxford: Oxford University Press.

Clark, G. L. and Wrigley, N. (1997), 'Exit, the firm and sunk costs: Re-conceptualising the corporate geography of disinvestment and plant closure', *Progress in Human Geography* 21(3): 338–58.

Clark, P. B. and Monk, A. H. B. (2016), 'Sovereign development funds: Designing high-performance, strategic investment institutions', SSRN paper, 30 September, DOI: 10.2139/ssrn.2667974.

Coase, R. H. (1937), 'The nature of the firm', *Economica* 4(16): 386–405.

Coase, R. H. (1992), 'The institutional structure of production', Occasional Paper 28, Chicago: University of Chicago Law School.

Coe, N. M. (2014), 'Missing links: Logistics, governance and upgrading in a shifting global economy', *Review of International Political Economy* 21(1): 224–56.

Coe, N. M. and Yeung, H. W. (2015), *Global Production Networks: Theorizing Economic Development in an Interconnected World*, Oxford: Oxford University Press.

Coe, N. M., Dicken, P., and Hess, M. (2008), 'Global production networks: Realizing the potential', *Journal of Economic Geography* 8(3): 271–95.

Coffee, J. (2006), *Gatekeepers*, Oxford: Oxford University Press.

Coffee, J. C., Lowenstein, L., and Rose-Ackerman, S. (1988), *Knights, Raiders, and Targets*, Oxford: Oxford University Press.

Cohen, W. and Levinthal, D. (1990), 'Absorptive capacity: A new perspective on learning and innovation', *Administrative Science Quarterly* 35(1): 128–52.

Cole, C. (2012), 'Volatility of an impossible object: Risk, fear and safety in games of perception', Artemis Capital management letter to investors.

Connelly, B. L., Miller, T., and Devers, C. E. (2012), 'Under a cloud of suspicion: Trust, distrust, and their interactive effects in inter-organisational contracting', *Strategic Management Journal* 33(7): 820–33.

Cyert, R. and March, J. G. (1963), *A Behavioral Theory of the Firm*, Upper Saddle River, NJ: Prentice Hall.

D'Agostino, L. M., Laursen, K., and Santangelo, G. D. (2013), 'The impact of R&D offshoring on the home knowledge production of OECD investing regions', *Journal of Economic Geography* 13(1): 145–75.

D'Arcy, S. P., Dulebohn, J. H., and Oh, P. (1999), 'Optimal funding of state employee pension systems', *Journal of Risk and Insurance* 66(3): 345–80.

Dale, R. (2004), *The First Crash: Lessons from the South Sea Bubble*, Princeton, NJ: Princeton University Press.

Danneels, E. (2002), 'The dynamics of product innovation and firm competences', *Strategic Management Journal* 23(12): 1095–121.

Davis, E. P. and Steil, B. (2001), *Institutional Investors*, Cambridge, MA: MIT Press.

Davis, G. F. (2015), 'Editorial essay: What is organizational research for?' *Administrative Science Quarterly* 60(2): 179–88.

Davis, K. E. (2013), 'Contracts as technology', *New York University Law Review* 88(1): 83–127.

Deakin, S. and Michie, J. (2000), 'The theory and practice of contracting'. In Deakin, S. and Michie, J. (eds), *Contracts, Cooperation, and Competition: Studies in Economics, Management, and Law* (pp. 1–39), Oxford: Oxford University Press.

Demsetz, H. (1968), 'The cost of transacting', *Quarterly Journal of Economics* 82(1): 33–53.

Dew, N., Goldfarb, B., and Sarasvathy, S. (2006), 'Optimal inertia: When organizations *should* fail'. In Baum, J. A. C., Dobrev, S. D., and van Witteloostuijn, A. (eds), *Ecology and Strategy: Advances in Strategic Management Volume 23* (pp. 73–99), Bingley: Emerald.

Diamond, D. (1984), 'Financial intermediation and delegated monitoring', *Review of Economic Studies* 51(3): 393–414.

Dicken, P. (1997), 'Places and flows: Situating international investment'. In Clark, G. L., Feldman, M. P., and Gertler, M. S. (eds), *The Oxford Handbook of Economic Geography* (pp. 275–91), Oxford: Oxford University Press.

Dicken, P. (2011), *Global Shift: Mapping the Changing Contours of the World Economy* (6th edn), London: Sage.

Dicken, P. and Malmberg, A. (2001), 'Firms in territories: A relational perspective', *Economic Geography* 77(4): 345–63.

Diebold, F. X., Doherty, N. A., and Herring, R. J. (2010), *The Known, the Unknown, and the Unknowable in Financial Risk Management: Measurement and Theory, Advancing Practice*, Princeton, NJ: Princeton University Press.

Dimson, E., Marsh, P., and Staunton, M. (2002), *Triumph of the Optimists: 101 Years of Global Investment Returns*, Princeton, NJ: Princeton University Press.

Dixon, A. D. (2012), 'Function before form: Macro-institutional comparison and the geography of finance', *Journal of Economic Geography* 12(3): 579–600.

Dixon, A. D. and Monk, A. H. B. (2014), 'Frontier finance', *Annals of the Association of American Geographers* 104(4): 852–68.

Dore, R. (2000), *Stock Market Capitalism: Welfare Capitalism. Japan and Germany versus the Anglo-Saxons*, Oxford: Oxford University Press.

Durand, C. and Wrigley, N. (2009), 'Institutional and economic determinants of transnational retailer expansion and performance: A comparative analysis of Wal-Mart and Carrefour', *Environment and Planning A* 41(7): 1534–55.

Dworkin, R. (1986), *Law's Empire*, Cambridge, MA: Harvard University Press.

Easterbrook, F. H. and Fischel, D. R. (1991), *Economic Structure of Corporate Law*, Cambridge, MA: Harvard University Press.

Ebben, J. J. and Johnson, A. C. (2005), 'Efficiency, flexibility, or both? Evidence linking strategy to performance in small firms', *Strategic Management Journal* 26(13): 1249–59.

Eisenberg, M. A. (1998), *The Nature of the Common Law*, Cambridge, MA: Harvard University Press.

Eisenhardt, K. M. and Martin, J. A. (2000), 'Dynamic capabilities: What are they?' *Strategic Management Journal* 21(10–11): 1105–21.

El-Erian, M. (2008), *When Markets Collide: Investment Strategies for the Age of Global Economic Change*, London: McGraw-Hill.

Ellis, C. D. (2012), 'Murder on the Orient Express: The mystery of underperformance', *Financial Analysts Journal* 68(4): 13–19.

Ellsberg, D. (1961), 'Risk, ambiguity, and the Savage axioms', *Quarterly Journal of Economics* 75(4): 643–69.

Engelen, E. and Glasmacher, A. (2013), 'Multiple financial modernities: International financial centres, urban boosters and the Internet as the site of negotiations', *Regional Studies* 47(6): 850–67.

Epstein, G. and Schneider, M. (2008), 'Ambiguity, information quality, and asset pricing', *Journal of Finance* 63(1): 197–226.

Fama, E. F. (1970), 'Efficient capital markets: A review of theory and empirical work', *Journal of Finance* 25(2): 383–417.

Fama, E. F. (1991), 'Efficient capital markets: II', *Journal of Finance* 46(5): 1575–618.

Faulconbridge, J. R. (2006), 'Stretching tacit knowledge beyond a local fix? Global spaces of learning in advanced professional service firms', *Journal of Economic Geography* 6(4): 517–40.

Faulconbridge, J. R. (2008), 'Negotiating cultures of work in transnational law firms', *Journal of Economic Geography* 8(4): 497–517.

Faulconbridge, J. R. and Muzio, D. (2009), 'The financialization of large law firms: Situated discourses and practices of reorganization', *Journal of Economic Geography* 9(5): 641–61.

Faulconbridge, J. R., Engelen, E., Hoyer, M., and Beaverstock, J. V. (2007), 'Analysing the changing landscape of European financial centres: The role of financial products and the case of Amsterdam', *Growth and Change* 38(2): 279–303.

Fehr, E. and Schmidt, K. M. (1999), 'A theory of fairness, competition, and cooperation', *Quarterly Journal of Economics* 114(3): 817–68.

Florida, R. (2002a), 'The economic geography of talent', *Annals of the Association of American Geographers* 92(4): 743–55.

Florida, R. (2002b), *The Rise of the Creative Class: And How It's Transforming Work, Leisure, Community and Everyday Life*, New York, NY: Basic Books.

Florida, R. and Mellander, C. (2014), 'The geography of inequality: Difference and determinants of wage and income inequality across US metros', *Regional Studies* 50(1): 79–92.

Foster, D. P. and Young, H. P. (2010), 'Gaming performance fees by portfolio managers', *Quarterly Journal of Economics* 125(4): 1435–58.

Fox, C. and Tversky, A. (1995), 'Ambiguity, aversion, and comparative ignorance', *Quarterly Journal of Economics* 110(3): 585–603.

French, S., Leyshon, A., and Wainwright, T. (2011), 'Financializing space, spacing financialization', *Progress in Human Geography* 35(6): 798–819.

Fried, C. (1981), *Contract as Promise: A Theory of Contractual Obligation*, Cambridge, MA: Harvard University Press.

Friedman, J. and Kraus, W. (2011), *Engineering the Financial Crisis: Systemic Risk and the Failure of Regulation*, Philadelphia, PA: University of Pennsylvania Press.

Gabaix, X. and Laibson, D. (2006), 'Shrouded attributes, consumer myopia, and information suppression in competitive markets', *Quarterly Journal of Economics* 121(2): 505–40.

Galbraith, J. K. (1967), *The New Industrial State*, Princeton, NJ: Princeton University Press.

Gans, J. (2016), *The Disruption Dilemma*, Cambridge MA: MIT Press.

GAO (Government Accountability Office) (2012), 'State and local government pension plans: Economic downturn spurs efforts to address costs and sustainability', GAO-12-322, Washington, DC.

Geithner, T. (2014), *Stress Test: Reflections on Financial Crisis*, New York, NY: Random House Business.

Gennaioli, N., Shleifer, A., and Vishny, R. W. (2013), 'A model of shadow banking', *Journal of Finance* 68(4): 1331–63.

Gennaioli, N., Shleifer, A., and Vishny, R. W. (2015), 'Money doctors', *Journal of Finance* 70(1): 91–125.

Gertler, M. S. (2001), 'Best practice? Geography, learning and the institutional limits to strong convergence', *Journal of Economic Geography* 1(1): 5–36.

Gertler, M. S. (2003), 'Tacit knowledge and the economic geography of context, or the undefinable tacitness of being (there)', *Journal of Economic Geography* 3(1): 75–99.

Gertler, M. S. (2017), 'Institution, geography and economic life'. In Clark, G. L., Feldman, M. A., Gertler, M. S., and Wójcik, D. (eds), *New Oxford Handbook of Economic Geography*, Oxford: Oxford University Press (forthcoming).

Giertz, J. F. and Papke, L. E. (2007), 'Public pension plans: Myths and realities for state budgets', *National Tax Journal* 60(2): 305–23.

Gilboa, I., Postlewaite, A., Samuelson, L., and Schmeidler, D. (2014), 'Economic models as analogies', *The Economic Journal* 124(578): F513–F533.

Gillette, C. P. (2013), 'Tacit agreement and relationship-specific investment', *New York University Law Review* 88(1): 128–69.

Gilson, R., Sabel, C., and Scott, R. E. (2013), 'Contract and innovation: The limited role of generalist courts in the evolution of novel contractual forms', *New York University Law Review* 88(1): 170–215.

Glaeser, E. L. and Ponzetto, G. A. M. (2013), 'Shrouded costs of government: The political economy of state and local public pensions', No. w18976, National Bureau of Economic Research.

Glaeser, E., Resseger, M., and Tobio, K. (2009), 'Inequality in cities', *Journal of Regional Science* 49(4): 617–46.

Glasmeier, A. (2000), *Manufacturing Time: Global Competition in the Watch Industry, 1795–2000*, New York, NY: The Guilford Press.

Glode, V., Green, R. C., and Lowery, R. (2012), 'Financial expertise as an arms race', *Journal of Finance* 67(5): 1723–59.

Glückler, J. and Armbrüster, T. (2003), 'Bridging uncertainty in management consulting: The mechanisms of trust and networked reputation', *Organization Studies* 24(2): 269–97.

Gorton, G. and Winton, A. (2003), 'Financial intermediation'. In Constantinides, G. M., Harris, M., and Stultz, R. (eds), *Handbook of the Economics of Finance* (pp. 431–552), Amsterdam: Elsevier.

Goyal, A. and Wahal, S. (2008), 'The selection and termination of investment management firms by plan sponsors', *Journal of Finance* 63(4): 1805–47.

Grabher, G. (ed.) (1993), *The Embedded Firm: On the Socioeconomics of Industrial Networks*, London: Routledge.

Grabher, G. and Ibert, O. (2013), 'Distance as asset? Knowledge collaboration in hybrid virtual communities', *Journal of Economic Geography* 14(1): 97–123.

Grabher, G., Ibert, O., and Flohr, S. (2008), 'The neglected king: The customer in the new knowledge ecology of innovation', *Economic Geography* 84(3): 253–80.

Granovetter, M. (1985), 'Economic action and social structure: The problem of embeddedness', *American Journal of Sociology* 91(3): 481–510.

Greenwood, R. and Scharfstein, D. (2013), 'The growth of finance', *Journal of Economic Perspectives* 27(2): 3–28.

Greif, A. (2006), *Institutions and the Path to the Modern Economy*, Cambridge: Cambridge University Press.

Grossman, G. M. and Helpman, E. (2004), 'Managerial incentives and the international organization of production', *Journal of International Economics* 63(2): 237–62.

Grossman, G. M. and Helpman, E. (2005), 'Outsourcing in a global economy', *Review of Economic Studies* 72(1): 135–59.

Grossman, G. M. and Rossi-Hansberg, E. (2008), 'Trading tasks: A simple theory of offshoring', *American Economic Review* 98(5): 1978–97.

Grossman, S. J. and Stiglitz, J. (1980), 'On the impossibility of informationally efficient markets', *American Economic Review* 70(3): 393–408.

Grossman, S. J., Kihlstrom, R. E., and Mirman, L. J. (1977), 'A Bayesian approach to the production of information and learning by doing', *Review of Economic Studies* 44(3): 533–47.

Guyatt, D. (2013), 'Effective investor collaboration: Enlarging the shadow of the future', *Rotman International Journal of Pension Management* 6(2): 56–64.

Hachigian, H. (2013), 'Markets hierarchies and exchange platforms: The geography of impact investing' [mimeo], University of Oxford.

Hachigian, H. (2015), 'The consequences and management of ambiguity for long-term investors'. Doctoral dissertation. Oxford: University of Oxford.

Hagerman, L., Clark, G. L., and Hebb, T. (2006), *Massachusetts Pension Reserves Investment Management Board: Urban Investing through a Transparent Selection Process*, Cambridge MA: Labor & Worklife Program, Harvard Law School.

Haldane, A. (2009), 'Rethinking the financial network', Bank of England Speech delivered at the Financial Student Association, Amsterdam.

Haldane, A. and May, R. (2011), 'Systemic risk in banking ecosystems', *Nature* 469 (7330): 351–5.

Hall, P. A. and Soskice, D. W. (2001), *Varieties of Capitalism: The Institutional Foundations of Comparative Advantage*, Oxford: Oxford University Press.

Hannan, M. T. and Freeman, J. (1989), *Organizational Ecology*, Cambridge, MA: Harvard University Press.

Harreld, J. B., O'Reilly, C. A., and Tushman, M. L. (2007), 'Dynamic capabilities at IBM: Driving strategy into action', *California Management Review* 49(4): 21–43.

Hart, H. L. A. (1961), *The Concept of Law*, Oxford: Oxford Clarendon Press.

Hart, O. (1995), *Firms, Contracts, and Financial Structure*, Oxford: Oxford University Press.

Hart, O. and Holmström, B. (2010), 'A theory firm scope', *Quarterly Journal of Economics* 125(2): 483–513.

Hart, O. and Moore, J. (1990), 'Property rights and the nature of the firm', *Journal of Political Economy* 98(6): 1119–58.

Hart, O. and Moore, J. (1999), 'Foundations of incomplete contracts', *Review of Economic Studies* 66(1): 115–38.

Hart, O. and Moore, J. (2008), 'Contracts as reference points', *Quarterly Journal of Economics* 123(1): 1–48.

Harvey, D. (1989), *The Condition of Postmodernity*, Oxford: Blackwell.

Harvey, N. (2012), 'Learning, judgement and decision making from feedback'. In Dhami, M., Schloffmann, A., and Waldmann, M. R. (eds), *Judgment and Decision Making as Skill: Learning, Development and Evolution* (pp. 119–226), Cambridge: Cambridge University Press.

Hawley, J. P. and Williams, A. T. (2007), 'Universal owners: Challenges and opportunities', *Corporate Governance: An International Review* 15(3): 415–20.

Heath, C. and Tversky, A. (1991), 'Preference and belief: Ambiguity and competence in choice under uncertainty', *Journal of Risk and Uncertainty* 4(1): 5–28.

Hebb, T. and Wójcik, D. (2005), 'Global standards and emerging markets: The institutional-investment value chain and the CalPERS investment strategy', *Environment and Planning A* 37(11): 1955–74.

Helfat, C. E. and Peteraf, M. A. (2009), 'Understanding dynamic capabilities: Progress along a development path', *Strategic Organization* 7(1): 91–102.

Helfat, C. E., Finkelstein, S., Mitchell, W., Peteraf, M. A., Singh, H., Teece, D. J., and Winter, S. (2007), *Dynamic Capabilities: Understanding Strategic Change in Organizations*, Oxford: Blackwell.

Helper, S. (2000), 'Economists and field research: You can observe a lot just by watching', *American Economic Review* 90(2): 228–32.

Helpman, E., Marin, D., and Verdier, T. (2008), *The Organization of Firms in a Global Economy*, Cambridge, MA: Harvard University Press.

Hilton, D. (2003), 'Psychology and the financial markets: Applications to understanding and remedying irrational decision-making'. In Brocas, I. and Cartillo, J. D. (eds), *The Psychology of Economic Decisions. Volume 1: Rationality and Well-Being* (pp. 273–97), Cambridge: Cambridge University Press.

Hirschman, A. (1971), *Exit, Voice and Loyalty: Responses to Decline in Firms, Organizations, and States*, Cambridge, MA: Harvard University Press.

Ho, T. S. Y. and Lee, S. B. (2004), *The Oxford Guide to Financial Modelling: Applications for Capital Markets, Corporate Finance, Risk Management, and Financial Institutions*, Oxford: Oxford University Press.

Holmström, B. and Milgrom, P. (1991), 'Multitask principal–agent analyses: Incentive contracts, asset ownership, and job design', *Journal of Law, Economics, & Organization* 7(1): 24–52.

Hong, H., Kubik, J., and Stein, J. (2005), 'Thy neighbour's portfolio: Word-of-mouth effects in the holdings and trades of money managers', *Journal of Finance* 60(6): 2801–24.

Huberman, G. (2001), 'Familiarity breeds investment', *Review of Financial Studies* 14(3): 659–80.

Jackson, S. E. and Dutton, J. E. (1988), 'Discerning threats and opportunities', *Administrative Science Quarterly* 33(3): 370–87.

Jenkinson, T., Jones, H., and Martinez, J. V. (2015), 'Picking winners? Investment consultants' recommendations of fund managers', *Journal of Finance* 71(5): 2333–70.

Jensen, M. C. (1993), 'The modern industrial revolution, exit, and the failure of internal control systems', *Journal of Finance* 48(3): 831–80.

Jensen, M. C. (2000), *A Theory of the Firm: Governance, Residual Claims, and Organizational Forms*, Cambridge, MA: Harvard University Press.

Jones, B. (2012), *Navigating the 'Long Run': A Strategic Asset Allocation Framework for Pensions, Insurers, Endowments, and Sovereign Wealth Funds*, Hong Kong: Deutsche Bank.

Judge, K. (2013), 'Fee effects', *Iowa Law Review* 98(4): 1517–74.

Judge, K. (2015), 'Intermediary influence', *University of Chicago Law Review* 82(2): 573–642.

Kahneman, D. (2011), *Thinking, Fast and Slow*, London: Allen Lane.

Kahneman, D. and Tversky, A. (1979), 'Prospect theory: An analysis of decision under risk', *Econometrica* 47(2): 263–91.

Kay, J. (2012), *The Kay Review of UK Equity Markets and Long-term Decision Making: Final Review*, London: HM Government, Department for Business, Innovation and Skills.

Kennedy, D. (1976), 'Form and substance in private law adjudication', *Harvard Law Review* 89(8): 1685–778.

Keynes, J. M. (1948), *Treatise on Probability*, New York, NY: Macmillan & Co., originally published 1921.

Kimel, D. (2005), *From Promise to Contract: Towards a Liberal Theory of Contract*, Oxford: Hart Publishing.

King, R. G. and Levine, R. (1995), 'Financial intermediation and economic development'. In Mayer, C. P. and Vives, X. (eds), *Capital Markets and Financial Intermediation* (pp. 156–89), Cambridge: Cambridge University Press.

Knight, E. R. W. and Dixon, A. D. (2011), 'The role of investment consultants in transforming pension fund decision-making: The integration of environmental, social, and governance consideration into corporate valuation'. In Hawley, J. P., Shyam, J. K., and Williams, A. T. (eds), *Corporate Governance Failures: Role of Institutional Investors in the Global Financial Crisis* (pp. 217–41), Philadelphia, PA: University of Pennsylvania Press.

Knight, F. (1921), *Risk, Uncertainty, and Profit*, Boston, MA: Houghton Mifflin Company.

Kőszegi, B. (2014), 'Behavioural contract theory', *Journal of Economic Literature* 52(4): 1075–2118.

Krugman, P. R. (1991), *Geography and Trade*, Cambridge, MA: MIT Press.

Kurz, M. (1994), 'On rational belief equilibria', *Economic Theory* 4: 859–76.

La Porta, R., Lopez-de-Silanes, F., Shleifer, A., and Vishny, R. W. (1998), 'Law and finance', *Journal of Political Economy* 106(6): 1113–55.

Laffont, J. J. and Martimort, D. (2002), *The Theory of Incentives*, Princeton, NJ: Princeton University Press.

Lamont, M. (1992), *Money, Morals and Manners: The Culture of the French and the American Upper-Middle Classes*, Chicago, IL: University of Chicago Press.

Lancaster, K. (1975), 'The theory of household behaviour', *Annals of the American Academy of Political and Social Science* 422: 77–86.

Lavie, D. and Rosenkopf, L. (2006), 'Balancing exploration and exploitation in alliance formation', *Academy of Management Journal* 49(4): 797–818.

Leiblein, M. J., Reuer, J. J., and Dalsace, F. (2002), 'Do make or buy decisions matter? The influence of organizational governance on technological performance', *Strategic Management Journal* 23(9): 817–33.

Levin, J. (2002), 'Multilateral contracting and the employment relationship', *Quarterly Journal of Economics* 117(3): 1075–103.

Levitt, S. D., List, J. A., and Syverson, C. (2012), 'Toward an understanding of learning by doing: Evidence from an automobile assembly plant', *Journal of Political Economy* 121(4): 643–81.

Lewis, W. M. and Andriopoulos, C. (2009), 'Exploitation-exploration tensions and organizational ambidexterity: Managing paradoxes of innovation', *Organizational Science* 20(4): 696–717.

Litterman, B. and the Quantitive Resources Group Goldman Sachs Asset Management. (2004), *Modern Investment Management: An Equilibrium Approach*, New York, NY: John Wiley.

Lo, A. (2012), 'Adaptive markets and the new world order', *Financial Analysts Journal* 68(2): 18–29.

Lowe, M. and Wrigley, N. (2010), 'The "continuously morphing" retail TNC during market entry: Interpreting Tesco's expansion into the United States', *Economic Geography* 86(4): 381–408.

Lowenstein, L. (1996), 'Financial transparency and corporate governance: You manage what you measure', *Columbia Law Review* 96(5): 1335–62.

Lowenstein, R. (2008), *While America Aged*, New York, NY: Penguin.

Lubatkin, M. H., Simsek, Z., Ling, Y., and Veiga, J. F. (2006), 'Ambidexterity and performance in small- to medium-sized firms: The pivotal role of top management team behavioral integration', *Journal of Management* 32(5): 646–72.

Lucas, R. E. (2009), 'Ideas and growth', *Economica* 76(301): 1–19.

McAfee, R. P. (2002), *Competitive Solutions: The Strategist's Toolkit*, Princeton, NJ: Princeton University Press.

Macauley, S. (1963), 'Non-contractual relations in business: A preliminary study', *American Sociological Review* 28(1): 55–67.

Macauley, S. (1985), 'An empirical view of contract', *Wisconsin Law Review* 1985(3): 465–82.

MacIntosh, J. and Scheibelhut, T. W. (2012), 'How large pension funds organize themselves: Findings from a unique 19-fund survey', *Rotman International Journal of Pension Management* 5(1): 34–42.

MacKenzie, D. (2006), *An Engine, Not a Camera: How Financial Models Shape Markets*, Cambridge, MA: MIT Press.

Macneil, I. R. (1980), *The New Social Contract: An Enquiry into Modern Contractual Relations*, New Haven, CT: Yale University Press.

Macneil, I. R. (1981), 'Economic analysis of contractual relations: Its shortfalls and the need for a rich "classificatory apparatus"', *Northwestern University Law Review* 75(6): 1018–63.

Macneil, I. R. (1985), 'Relational contract: What we do and do not know', *Wisconsin Law Review* 1985(3): 483–525.

Manski, C. F. (2004), 'Measuring expectations', *Econometrica* 72(5): 1329–76.

March, J. G. (1991), 'Exploration and exploitation in organizational learning', *Organization Science* 2(1): 71–87.

March, J. G. (2003), 'Understanding organisational adaptation', *Society and Economy* 25(1): 1–10.

March, J. G. and Simon, H. A. (1958), *Organizations*, New York, NY: John Wiley & Sons.

Marglin, S. (1974), 'What do bosses do', *Review of Radical Political Economics* 6(2): 60–112.

Markowitz, H. (1952a), 'Portfolio selection', *Journal of Finance* 7(1): 77–91.

Markowitz, H. (1952b), 'The utility of wealth', *Journal of Political Economy*, 60: 151–8.

Martin, R. L. (1999), 'The new economic geography of money'. In Martin, R. L. (ed.), *Money and the Space Economy* (pp. 3–27), Chichester: John Wiley.

Maskell, P. (2001), 'The firm in economic geography', *Economic Geography* 77(4): 329–44.

Maskell, P. (2014), 'Assessing remote knowledge: The roles of trade fairs, pipelines, crowdsourcing and listening posts', *Journal of Economic Geography* 14(5): 883–902.

Maurer, B. (2008), 'Re-regulating offshore finance?' *Geography Compass* 2(1): 155–75.

Mayer, C. P. and Vives, X. (1993), *Capital Markets and Financial Intermediation*, Cambridge: Cambridge University Press.

Mayer, K. J. and Argyres, N. S. (2004), 'Learning to contract: Evidence from the personal computer industry', *Organization Science* 15(4): 394–410.

Meckling, W. H. and Jensen, M. J. (1976), 'Theory of the firm: Managerial behavior, agency costs and ownership structure', *Journal of Financial Economics* 3(4): 305–60.

Merton, R. C. and Bodie, C. (1995), 'A conceptual framework for analysing the financial environment'. In Crane, D. B., Froot, K. A., Mason, S. P., Perold, A. A., Merton, R. C., Bodie, Z., Sirri, E. R., and Tufano, P. (eds), *The Global Financial System: A Functional Perspective* (pp. 3–31), Boston, MA: Harvard Business School.

Merton, R. C. and Bodie, Z. (2005), 'The design of financial systems: Towards a synthesis of function and structure', *Journal of Investment Management* 3(1): 1–23.

Milhaupt, C. J. and Pistor, K. (2008), *Law and Capitalism: What Corporate Crises Reveal about Legal Systems and Economic Development around the World*, Chicago, IL: University of Chicago Press.

Mitchell, O. S. and Smith, R. S. (1994), 'Pension funding in the public sector', *Review of Economics and Statistics* 76(5): 278–90.

Mitchell, O. S., McCarthy, D., Wisniewski, S. C., and Zorn, P. (2000), 'Developments in state and local pension plans'. In Mitchell, O. S. and Hustead, E. (eds), *Pensions in the Public Sector* (pp. 11–40), Philadelphia, PA: University of Pennsylvania Press.

Monk, A. H. B. (2008), 'The knot of contracts: The corporate geography of legacy costs', *Economic Geography* 84(2): 211–35.

Monk, A. H. B. (2009), 'The geography of pension liabilities and fund governance in the United States', *Environment and Planning A* 41(4): 859–78.

Monk, A. H. B., Sharma, R., and Sinclair, D. (2017), *The Re-Intermediation of Finance*, Palo Alto, CA: Stanford University Press.

Morrison, A. D. and Wilhelm, W. J. (2007), *Investment Banking: Institutions, Politics, and Law*, Oxford: Oxford University Press.

Morrison, A. D. and Wilhelm, W. J., Jr. (2008), 'The demise of investment banking partnerships: Theory and evidence', *Journal of Finance* 63: 311–50.

Munnell, A. (2012), *State and Local Pensions. What Now*? Washington, DC: Brookings Institution.

Munnell, A., Aubry, J.-P., and Hurwitz, J. (2013), *Locally Administered Pension Plans: 2007–2011*, Boston, MA: Boston College Center for Retirement Research.

Munnell, A., Aubry, J.-P., and Quinby, L. (2011), 'Public pension funding in practice', *Journal of Pension Economics and Finance* 10(2): 247–68.

Murdoch, J., Martel, T., and Banks, J. (2000), 'Quality, nature and embeddedness: Some theoretical considerations in the context of the food sector', *Economic Geography* 76(2): 107–25.

North, D. C. (1990), *Institutions, Institutional Change and Economic Performance*, Cambridge: Cambridge University Press.

Novy-Marx, R. and Rauh, J. D. (2009), 'The liabilities and risks of state-sponsored pension plans', *Journal of Economic Perspectives* 23(3): 191–210.

O'Barr, W. M. and Conley, J. M. (1992), 'Managing relationships: The culture of institutional investing', *Financial Analysts Journal* 48(5): 21–7.

O'Brien, R. (1992), *Global Financial Integration: The End of Geography*, London: Chatham House.

O'Hara, M. (1995), *Market Microstructure Theory*, Oxford: Blackwell.

O'Reilly, C. A. and Tushman, M. L. (2004), 'The ambidextrous organization', *Harvard Business Review* 82(4): 74–83.

O'Reilly, C. A. and Tushman, M. L. (2008), 'Ambidexterity as a dynamic capability: Resolving the innovator's dilemma', *Research in Organizational Behavior* 28: 185–206.

Olson, M. (1965), *The Logic of Collective Action: Public Goods and the Theory of Groups*, Cambridge, MA: Harvard University Press.

Olson, M. and Zeckhauser, R. (1966), 'An economic theory of alliances', *Review of Economics and Statistics* 48(3): 266–79.

Padgett, J. F. and Powell, W. W. (2012), 'The problem of emergence'. In Padgett, J. F. and Powell, W. W. (eds), *The Emergence of Organizations and Markets* (pp. 1–29), Princeton, NJ: Princeton University Press.

Phalippou, L. (2009), 'Beware of venturing into private equity', *Journal of Economic Perspectives* 23(1): 147–66.

Pitelis, C. and Teece, D. J. (2009), 'The (new) nature and essence of the firm', *European Management Review* 6(1): 5–15.

Porteous, D. (1999), 'The development of financial centers: Location, information externalities and path dependence'. In Martin R. L. (ed.), *Money and the Space Economy* (pp. 96–114), Chichester: John Wiley.

Posner, R. A. (1986), *Economic Analysis of Law* (3rd edn), Boston, MA: Little, Brown.

Posner, R. A. (2003), *Economic Analysis of Law* (6th edn), New York, NY: Aspen Publishers.

Pratt, J. and Zeckhauser, R. (1985), *Principals and Agents: The Structure of Business*, Boston, MA: Harvard Business School Press.

Rajan, R. and Zingales, L. (2001), 'The firm as a dedicated hierarchy: A theory of the origins and growth of firms', *Quarterly Journal of Economics* 116(3): 805–51.

Rapin, C. and Pétermann, C. (2015), 'Banking Switzerland—Financial Services Act and Financial Institutions Act: Results of consultation procedure'. Available at International Law Office: http://www.internationallawoffice.com/newsletters/detail.aspx?g=ff52ee09-3c5a-40f3-afac-09142f63014d.

Rawls, J. (1971), *A Theory of Justice*, Cambridge, MA: Harvard University Press.

Riles, A. (2011), *Collateral Knowledge: Legal Reasoning in the Global Financial Markets*, Chicago, IL: University of Chicago Press.

Rivkin, J. W. and Siggelkow, N. (2003), 'Balancing search and stability: Interdependencies among elements of organizational design', *Management Science* 49(3): 290–311.

Robinson, D. T. and Sensoy, B. A. (2013), 'Do private equity fund managers earn their fees? Compensation, ownership, and cash flow performance', *Review of Financial Studies* 26(11): 2760–97.

Roe, M. J. (2006), 'Legal origins and modern stock markets', *Harvard Law Review* 120(2): 462–4.

Rook, D. P. (2014), 'Aligning representation by negotiating doxastic distances: Relational spaces of financial delegation'. Available at SSRN: http://ssrn.com/abstract=249311.

Rosen, S. (1981), 'The economics of superstars', *American Economic Review* 71(5): 845–58.

Rosen, S. (1986), 'Prizes and incentives in elimination tournaments', *American Economic Review* 76: 701–15.

Rosenberg, N. (1995), 'Innovation's uncertain terrain', *McKinsey Quarterly* (3): 170–85.

Samuelson, W. and Zeckhauser, T. (1988), 'Status quo bias in decision making', *Journal of Risk and Uncertainty* 1(1): 7–59.

Schapiro, R. A. (2005), 'Towards a theory of interactive federalism', *Iowa Law Review* 243: 285–8.

Schepker, D. J., Oh, W. Y., Martynov, A., and Poppo, L. (2014), 'The many futures of contracts: Moving beyond structure and safeguarding to coordination and adaptation', *Journal of Management* 40(1): 193–225.

Schoenberger, E. (1997), *The Cultural Crisis of the Firm*, Oxford: Blackwell.

Scott, A. J. (1986), 'Industrial organization and location: Division of labor, the firm, and spatial process', *Economic Geography* 62(3): 215–31.

Scott, W. R. (2008), *Institutions and Organizations: Ideas and Interests*, Los Angeles, CA: Sage Publications.

Sharpe, W. F. (2013), 'The arithmetic of investment expenses', *Financial Analysts Journal* 69(2), DOI: 10.2469/faj.v69.n2.2.

Sheffer, D. A. and Levitt, R. E. (2010), 'The diffusion of energy saving technologies in the building industry: Structural barriers and possible solutions', Collaboratory for Research on Global Projects, Working Paper 57. Available at: https://gpc.stanford.edu/sites/default/files/wp057_0.pdf.

Shiffrin, S. V. (2007), 'The divergence of contract and promise', *Harvard Law Review* 120(3): 708–53.

Shiller, R. J. (2005), *Irrational Exuberance* (2nd edn), Princeton, NJ: Princeton University Press.

Shleifer, A. (1985), 'A theory of yardstick competition', *RAND Journal of Economics* 16(3): 319–27.

Shleifer, A. (1986), 'Do demand curves for stocks slope down?' *Journal of Finance* 41(3): 579–90.

Shleifer, A. (2000), *Inefficient Markets: An Introduction to Behavioral Finance*, Oxford: Oxford University Press.

Shonfield, A. (1965), *Modern Capitalism*, Oxford: Oxford University Press.

Simon, H. A. (1956), 'Rational choice and the structure of the environment', *Psychological Review* 63(2): 129–38.

Sinn, W. (2010), *Casino Capitalism: How the Financial Crisis Came about and What Needs to Be Done Now*, Oxford: Oxford University Press.

Slaatte, H. A. (1968), *The Pertinence of Paradox*, New York: Humanities Press.

Spence, A. M. (1977), 'Consumer misperceptions, product failure and producer liability', *Review of Economic Studies* 44(3): 561–72.

Spulber, D. (2009), *The Theory of the Firm: Microeconomics with Endogenous Entrepreneurs, Firms, Markets, and Organisations*, Cambridge: Cambridge University Press.

Starks, L. T. (1987), 'Performance incentive fees: An agency theoretic approach', *Journal of Financial and Quantitative Analysis* 22(1): 17–32.

Steger, D. P. (2002), 'Afterword: The "trade and . . . " conundrum—a commentary', *American Journal of International Law* 96: 135–45.

Stewart, F. (2011), The primacy of Delaware and the embeddedness of the firm'. In Willaims, C. A. and Zumbansen, P. (eds), *The Embedded Firm: Corporate Governance, Labor, and Finance Capitalism* (pp. 104–17), Cambridge: Cambridge University Press.

Stiglitz, J. (2014), 'The lessons of the North Atlantic crisis for economic theory and policy'. In Akerlof, G., Blanchard, O., Romer, D., and Stiglitz, J. (eds), *What Have*

We Learned? Macroeconomic Policy after the Crisis (pp. 335–47), Cambridge, MA: MIT Press.

Storper, M. and Salais, R. (1997), *Worlds of Production: The Action Frameworks of the Economy*, Cambridge, MA: Harvard University Press.

Storper, M. J. and Venables, A. J. (2004), 'Buzz: Face-to-face contact and the urban economy', *Journal of Economic Geography* 4(4): 351–70.

Stout, L. A. (2012), *The Shareholder Value Myth: How Putting Shareholders First Harms Investors, Corporations, and the Public*, Oakland, CA: Berrett-Koehler Publishers.

Summers, R. S. (2005), *Form and Function in a Legal System: A General Study*, Cambridge: Cambridge University Press.

Taylor, M. J. and Asheim, B. (2001), 'The concept of the firm in economic geography', *Economic Geography* 77(4): 315–28.

Teece, D. J. (2000), *Managing Intellectual Capital*, Oxford: Oxford University Press.

Teece, D. J. (2006), 'Reflections on "profiting from innovation"', *Research Policy* 35(8): 1131–46.

Teece, D. J. (2007), 'The role of managers, entrepreneurs and the literati in enterprise performance and economic growth', *International Journal of Technological Learning, Innovation and Development* 1(1): 43–64.

Teece, D. J. (2011), 'Dynamic capabilities: A guide for managers', *Ivey Business Journal* 75(2): 29–32.

Teece, D. J., Pisano, G., and Shuen, A. (1997), 'Dynamic capabilities and strategic management', *Strategic Management Journal* 18(7): 509–33.

Thakor, A. V. (1996), 'The design of financial systems: An overview', *Journal of Banking and Finance* 20(5): 917–48.

Thompson, W. (1965), 'Urban economic growth and development in a national system of cities'. In Hauser, P. H. and Schnore, L. F. (eds), *The Study of Urbanization* (pp. 431–90), New York: Wiley.

Tilba, A. and McNulty, T. (2013), 'Engaged versus disengaged ownership: The case of pension funds in the UK', *Corporate Governance: An International Review* 21(2): 165–82.

Torrance, M. (2009), 'The rise of a global infrastructure market through relational investing', *Economic Geography* 85(1): 75–97.

Tripsas, M. and Gavetti, G. (2000), 'Capabilities, cognition, and inertia: Evidence from digital imaging', *Strategic Management Journal* 21(10–11): 1147–61.

Tushman, M. L. and O'Reilly, C. A. (1996), 'The ambidextrous organizations: Managing evolutionary and revolutionary change', *California Management Review* 38(4): 8–30.

Van Nunen, A. (2008), *Fiduciary Management: Blueprint for Pension Fund Excellence*, New York, NY: John Wiley.

Vayanos, D. and Woolley, P. (2013), 'An institutional theory of momentum and reversal', *Review of Financial Studies* 26(5): 1087–145.

Von Hippel, E. (2005), *Democratizing Innovation*, Cambridge, MA: MIT Press.

Wagner, R. K. (2002), 'Smart people doing dumb things: The case of managerial incompetence'. In Sternberg, R. J. (ed.), *Why Smart People Can Be so Stupid* (pp. 42–63), New Haven, CT: Yale University Press.

Wainwright, T. (2011), 'Tax doesn't have to be taxing: London's "onshore" finance industry and the fiscal spaces of a global crisis', *Environment and Planning A* 43(6): 1287–304.

Warf, B. (2006), 'International competition between satellite and fibre-optic carriers: A geographical perspective', *Professional Geographer* 58(1): 1–11.

Warf, B. (2011), 'Evacuating the prehistory of time-space compression', *Geographical Review* 101(3): 435–46.

Weber, L. and Mayer, K. J. (2011), 'Designing effective contracts: Exploring the influence of framing and expectations', *Academy of Management Review* 36(1): 53–75.

Weitzman, M. (2007), 'Subjective expectations and asset-return puzzles', *American Economic Review* 97(4): 1102–30.

Willborn, S. (1998), 'The problem with pension portability', *Nebraska Law Review* 77(1): 352.

Williamson, O. E. (1975), *Markets and Hierarchies: Antitrust Analysis and Implications*, New York, NY: Free Press.

Williamson, O. E. (1999), 'Strategy research: Governance and competence perspectives', *Strategic Management Journal* 20: 1087–108.

Wilson, J. Q. (1989), *What Government Agencies Do and Why They Do It*, New York, NY: Basic Books.

Wilson Report (1980), *The Functioning of Financial Institutions, Cmnd. 7937*, London: HM Stationery Office.

Wójcik, D. (2009), 'The role of proximity in secondary equity markets'. In Clark, G. L., Dixon, A., and Monk, A. H. B. (eds), *Financial Risk Management: From the Local to the Global* (pp. 140–63), Oxford: Oxford University Press.

Wójcik, D. (2011), *The Global Stock Market: Issuers, Investors, and Intermediaries in an Uneven World*, Oxford: Oxford University Press.

Wójcik, D. (2013), 'Where governance fails: Advanced business services and the offshore world', *Progress in Human Geography* 37(3): 330–47.

Wójcik, D., Kreston, N., and McGill, S. (2013), 'Freshwater, saltwater and deepwater: Efficient market hypothesis versus behavioural finance', *Journal of Economic Geography* 13(2): 257–77.

Woods, C. (2011), 'The environment, intergenerational equity and long-term investment', DPhil thesis, University of Oxford.

Yang, T. and Mitchell, O. S. (2007), 'Public pension governance, funding, and performance: A longitudinal appraisal'. In Evans, J., Orszag, M., and Piggott, J. (eds), *Pension Fund Governance: A Global Perspective* (pp. 157–78), Cheltenham: Edward Elgar.

Yates, J. F. and Angott, A. M. (2012), 'Aiding judgement and decision making'. In Dhami M. K., Schlottmann, A., and Waldmann, M. R. (eds), *Judgement and Decision Making as a Skill: Learning Development and Evolution* (pp. 259–88), Cambridge: Cambridge University Press.

Youngdahl, J. (2013), 'Investment consultants and institutional corruption', Working Paper 7, Cambridge, MA: Edmond J. Safra Centre for Ethics, Harvard University.

Index of Names

Abolafia, M. Y. 112
Adler, P. S. 220
Agnew, J. 141n3
Aikman, D. 69
Akerlof, G. 6, 160, 188n7
Alevy, J. 10
Allen, F. 146, 187n1
Ambachtsheer, K. P. 141n5, 179, 182, 208, 222
Amin, A. 11, 59, 125, 148
Andonov, A. 122, 127, 212
Andriopoulos, C. 220
Angott, A. M. 101n5
Aoyama, Y. 100n1
Aragones, E. 18n3
Archetti, M. 199
Argyres, N. S. 14, 120n1, 180–1
Armbrüster, T. 146, 175
Asheim, B. 38, 59, 85

Bachher, J. S. 188n3, 193
Baker, G. 11, 29, 40, 56n2, 86
Barber, B. M. 7, 8
Barnett, W. P. 190, 198, 202
Barro, R. J. 18n1
Barth, J. R. 172
Bathelt, H. 13, 34, 38, 47, 56n2, 60, 73, 82, 86, 105, 147, 207n6
Battilana, J. 209
Beaverstock, J. 56n3, 78, 113
Bebchuck, L. A. 212
Benkler, Y. 30, 41, 207n6
Bernstein, P. L. 3
Beshears, J. 122
Beugelsdijk, S. 62
Birkinshaw, J. 160, 166, 217
Black, B. 182, 211
Blinder, A. S. 162
Bodie, C. 127, 149, 158–60, 165–6, 169
Bolton, P. 13, 34, 61, 103–4, 113, 119, 153, 195
Bor, D. 18n3
Bowles, S. 26, 56n3
Brainard, Keith 142n6
Brennan, G. 24
Brown, J. R. 122, 127
Buchanan, J. M. 202
Bunderson, J. S. 127

Calabresi, G. 110
Campbell, J. C. 10
Campbell, J. Y. 43, 172, 211
Caplin, A. 167n2, 174, 188n9
Carpenter, J. N. 212
Casson, M. 47
Che, Y.-K. 43
Chen, E. L. 220
Chen, J. 68, 81n5
Choi, S. J. 146, 167n4, 181
Christensen, C. M. 218
Čihák, M. 21
Clark, G. L. 4, 7, 12, 14, 18n2, 22, 32, 36n5, 38, 40–1, 45, 57n8, 58, 90, 95, 99–100, 105–6, 108–9, 114, 120n2, 123, 125, 138, 148, 152, 161–2, 166, 170, 173–4, 177–9, 186, 188n8, 191, 206, 207n3, 209, 213–15
Clark, P. B. 124, 127, 139, 208
Coase, R. H. 6, 29–30, 34, 40–1, 46, 53, 58, 60–2, 67–8, 78–9, 80n2, 82–5, 94, 99, 147–8, 191
Coe, N. M. 18, 30, 85
Coffee, J. 145, 190
Cohen, W. 198
Cohendet, P. 11, 125, 148
Cole, C. 68
Conley, J. M. 23, 112
Connelly, B. L. 180
Cyert, R. 27, 65

D'Agostino, L. M. 82
D'Arcy, S. P. 122, 125
Dale, R. 54
Danneels, E. 220
Davis, E. P. 2, 20
Davis, G. F. 26
Davis, K. E. 154, 180
Deakin, S. 14, 181
Demsetz, W. R. 57, 59, 60, 64
Dew, N. 220
Dewatripont, M. 13, 34, 61, 103–4, 113, 119, 153, 195
Diamond, D. 21, 145–7
Dicken, P. 38, 62, 82, 84
Diebold, F. X. 8
Dimson, E. 49
Dixon, A. D. 38, 63, 65, 77, 109, 119, 129, 142n7, 146, 165, 194, 203

Dore, R. 38
Durand, C. 11
Dutton, J. E. 219
Dworkin, R. 25

Easterbrook, F. H. 41, 58, 65, 86
Ebben, J. J. 220
Eisenberg, M. A. 121n4, 218
Eisenhardt, K. M. 218
El-Erian, M. 58
Ellis, C. D. 7, 216
Ellsberg, D. 18n4, 149
Engelen, E. 74
Epstein, G. 150

Fama, E. F. 6, 172
Faulconbridge, J. R. 11, 18n6, 56n4, 114, 120n3
Fehr, E. 207n5
Fischel, D. R. 41, 58, 65, 86
Florida, R. 61, 80n1
Foster, D. P. 212
Fox, C. 10, 150
Freeman, J. 29, 171
French, S. 18n6
Fried, C. 119, 212

Gabaix, X. 18n3
Galbraith, J. K. 24
Gans, J. 171
Gavetti, G. 219
Geithner 35n3
Gennaioli, N. 146, 206n1
Gertler, M. S. 24, 56n4, 66, 86, 188n4
Giertz, J. F. 122
Gilboa, I. 8
Gillette, C. P. 167n5
Gilson, R. 107, 110, 114, 188n6
Glaeser, E. L. 80, 122
Glasmacher, A. 74
Glasmeier, A. 66
Glode, V. 188n8
Glückler, J. 13, 34, 38, 47, 56n2, 60, 73, 82, 86, 105, 146–7, 175, 207n6
Gorton, G. 146, 148
Goyal, A. 145
Grabher, G. 127, 135, 198, 202
Granovetter, M. 123, 188n4
Greenwood, R. 216
Greif, A. 34
Grossman, G. M. 30, 34, 37, 41–2, 53, 55, 62, 85, 87–8, 95, 99
Grossman, S. J. 54, 83
Guyatt, D. 193

Hachigian, H. 147, 150, 207n7
Hagerman, L. 14, 123–4
Haldane, A. 4, 7, 19, 21, 173, 206
Hall, P. A. 109
Hannan, M. T. 29, 171
Harreld, J. B. 219
Hart, H. L. A. 25, 40, 59–60, 82, 86–7
Hart, O. 86, 168n7
Harvey, D. 53
Harvey, N. 101n5
Hawley, J. P. 40
Heath, C. 149
Hebb, T. 127
Helfat, C. E. 20, 31–2, 128, 146, 148, 189, 206
Helper, S. 12, 36n5
Helpman, E. 30, 34, 41–2, 53, 55, 62, 85, 87–8
Hilton, D. 56n1
Hirschman, A. 20
Ho, T. S. Y. 39, 56n1, 58, 59, 172
Holmström, B. 59, 82, 187n2
Hong, H. 58
Hurwitz, J. 141n3

Ibert, O. 198

Jackson, S. E. 219
Jenkinson, T. 146
Jensen, M. C. 27–8, 41, 85–6, 190, 207n4
Jensen, M. J. 27, 183
Johnson, A. C. 220
Jones, B. 49
Judge, K. 183

Kahneman, D. 6, 109, 116, 173
Katila, R. 220
Kay, J. 1, 111, 166
Kennedy, D. 109
Keynes, J. M. 7, 158
Kimel, D. 119, 153, 162, 168n8
King, R. G. 21, 23
Knight, E. R. W. 146
Knight, F. 7, 84, 158
Kőszegi, B. 168n6
Krugman, P. R. 60
Kurz, M. 18n4

La Porta, R. 120n2, 188n4
Laffont, J.-J. 181, 183
Laibson, D. 18n3
Lamont, M. 69
Lancaster, K. 27
Larson, Keith 128
Lavie, D. 218
Leahy, J. 188n9
Lee, S. B. 39, 56n1, 58–9, 172
Leiblein, M. J. 212
Levin, J. 95
Levine, R. 21, 23

Levinthal, D. 198
Levitt, D. A. 210
Levitt, S. D. 9, 109
Lewis, W. M. 220
Litterman, B. 7, 37, 59, 161, 172
Lo, A. 68, 108, 141, 167n3, 173, 179, 201
Lowe, M. 82
Lowenstein, L. 178
Lowenstein, R. 122, 127
Lubatkin, M. H. 217
Lucas, R. E. 61

McAfee, R. P. 175
Macauley, S. 13, 14
McCormick, R. 11, 114, 154
McKenna, R. 145
MacIntosh, J. 212
Macneil, I. R. 13, 34, 40
McNulty, T. 150
Malmberg, A. 82, 84
Manski, C. F. 18n4
March, J. G. 20, 26–7, 29–30, 65, 218
Marglin, S. 65, 78
Markowitz, H. 39, 172
Marshall, Alfred 30
Martimort, D. 181, 183
Martin, D. 167n2, 174
Martin, J. A. 218
Martin, R. L. 38
Maskell, P. 53, 59, 100n2
Maurer, B. 18n6
May, R. 4, 7, 19, 21, 173, 206
Mayer, C. P. 21, 28, 147
Mayer, K. J. 14, 137, 181
Meckling, W. H. 27, 183
Mellander, C. 80n1
Merton, R. C. 127, 149, 158–9, 160, 165–6, 169
Michie, J. 14, 181
Milgrom, P. 187n2
Milhaupt, C. J. 24
Mitchell, O. S. 39, 122, 139
Monk, A. H. B. 77, 87, 123–5, 127, 129, 139, 142, 188n3, 193–4, 203, 208, 214–15
Moore, J. 40, 60, 86–7, 168n7
Morrison, A. D. 20, 31, 211
Munnell, A. 122, 124, 140
Murdoch, J. 18n2
Muzio, D. 18n6

Nier, E. 21
North, D. C. 24, 26
Novy-Marx, R. 122, 127

O'Barr, W. M. 23, 112
O'Brien, R. 2, 53, 58, 75
O'Connor, K. 57n8
O'Hara, M. 58
O'Reilly, C. A. 217–18
Odean, T. 7, 8
Olson, M. 197, 207n5

Padgett, J. F. 206
Papke, L. E. 122
Peteraf, M. A. 146, 148
Pétermann, C. 22
Phalippou, L. 212
Pistor, K. 24
Ponzetto, G. A. M. 122
Porteous, D. 45
Posner, R. A. 24, 103–4, 111
Powell, W. W. 206
Pratt, J. 86, 183

Rajan, R. 43
Rapin, C. 22
Ratick, S. J. 100n1
Rauh, J. D. 122, 127
Rawls, J. 24
Reagans, R. E. 127
Riles, A. 23, 110, 113
Rivkin, J. W. 217
Robinson, D. T. 212
Roe, M. J. 25, 123, 149
Rook, D. P. 18n4
Rosen, S. 43, 61
Rosenberg, N. 160
Rosenkopf, L. 218
Rossi-Hansberg, E. 41–2, 85, 95, 99

Salais, R. 11
Samuelson, W. 207n2
Santamero, A. 146, 187n1
Schapiro, R. A. 123
Scharfstein, D. 216
Scheibelhut, T. W. 212
Schepker, D. J. 180
Schmidt, K. M. 207n5
Schneider, M. 150
Schoenberger, E. 86
Scott, A. J. 85
Scott, W. R. 23–4, 27, 59, 61, 160
Scott, W. R. 35n1
Sensoy, B. A. 212
Sharpe, W. F. 212
Sheffer, D. A. 210
Shiffrin, S. V. 14, 103
Shiller, R. J. 6, 35, 161, 173
Shleifer, A. 108, 145, 151, 161, 172–3
Shonfield, A. 24
Siggelkow, N. 217
Simon, H. A. 20, 26–7, 29–30

Sinn, W. 119
Slaatte, H. A. 220
Smith, Adam 12
Smith, R. S. 139
Soskice, D. W. 109
Spence, A. M. 46, 83, 188n7
Spulber, D. 147
Starks, L. T. 212
Steger, D. P. 25
Steil, B. 2, 20
Stewart, F. 123
Stiglitz, J. 7, 37
Storper, M. J. 11, 38, 56n4, 58, 73, 106, 135
Stout, L. A. 83
Summers, R. S. 110

Taylor, M. J. 38, 59, 85
Teece, D. J. 43, 65, 101n4, 209, 218–19
Thompson, W. 62
Thrift, N. 18n2, 58–9, 108
Thünen, J. H. 84
Tilba, A. 150
Tirole, J. 65
Torrance, M. 82
Triantis, G. 146
Tripsas, M. 219
Tushman, M. L. 217–18
Tversky, A. 6, 10, 149

Urwin, R. 4, 32, 99, 125, 138, 148, 152, 166, 170, 177, 179, 186, 206–7, 209, 213–14

Van Nunen, A. 169
Vayanos, D. 80n4
Venables, A. J. 38, 56n4, 58, 73, 106, 135
Viceira, L. M. 43, 172, 211
Vives, X. 21, 28, 147
Von Hippel, E. 48, 206

Wagner, R. K. 91
Wahal, S. 145
Wainwright, T. 102, 115–16
Warf, B. 53
Weber, L. 137
Weber, Max 23
Weitzman, M. 10, 18n5, 192
Wilcox, D. W. 122, 127
Wilhelm, W. J. 20, 31, 141n1, 211
Williams, A. T. 40
Williamson, O. E. 27, 30, 34, 36n5, 41, 43, 59, 60, 86, 87, 130, 148, 191, 199, 216
Wilson, J. Q. 23
Winton, A. 146, 148
Wójcik, D. 6–7, 9, 11, 18n6, 37–8, 56n5, 73, 75–6, 96–7, 102, 108–9, 115, 118, 120n2, 127
Woods, C. 83
Woolley, P. 80n4
Wrigley, N. 11, 41, 82

Yang, T. 122
Yates, J. F. 101n5
Yeung, H. W. 30
Yoo, S. W. 43
Young, H. P. 212
Youngdahl, J. 145

Zeckhauser, R. 86, 183, 197, 207n2
Zingales, L. 43

General Index

accounting 82, 105, 122, 127, 194
actuaries 16–17, 145, 153–4, 165, 191, 210, 212; actuarial services 154, 194
adaptive 68, 141, 167, 180; capacity 167, 179, 186; potential 28
adverse selection 183, 185, 187
Africa 58
Alaska 141n3
ambiguity 105, 146, 149, 157, 159, 162–6, 168n7, 168n8
America 140; *see also* North America; United States
American International Group (AIG) 35n3, 110
Amsterdam 73–4
Anglo-American equity markets 49; governments 39; institutions and markets 109; legal systems 110; pension-fund investment 127; world 2, 38, 125, 127
arbitrage 118
Arizona 142n9
Articles of Association 115–16
artificial intelligence 209
Asia 3, 58, 76; Asian financial crisis 3, 55, 172; *see also* financial crisis/crises
asset allocation 39, 44, 52, 63, 67, 68–71, 79–80, 81n6, 90, 92–3, 131, 140, 141n5, 153, 161, 189, 193, 210, 212, 214
asset classes 7, 13, 39, 43–4, 49, 67, 68, 70, 71, 74, 79, 81n6, 107, 111–12, 115–16, 118, 131–2, 140, 154, 161–2, 172, 192
asset consultants 16, 71, 76, 77, 79, 163, 177, 187
asset holders 20
asset management 11, 64, 70, 73, 80, 146, 166, 174, 176, 187, 209; managers 1, 3–6, 11, 15–16, 19–22, 40, 63, 69, 71, 80, 80n4, 116, 118, 151, 173–4, 188n3, 205, 207n6, 208, 210–12, 216, 222
asset owners 1, 3–6, 11, 15–16, 19–22, 28–9, 31, 33, 58, 63, 80n4, 116–19, 121, 145–6, 156, 161–6, 188n3, 190, 196, 204–5, 207n6, 208, 210–11, 216–17, 222; asset-owner investors 209, 222
assets under management (AUM) 15, 19, 29, 31, 43–4, 48, 50, 58, 63, 67–71, 73–7, 79, 80n3, 81n5, 82, 89–90, 92–3, 96, 107, 109, 112, 122, 125, 132, 135, 139, 146, 152, 169, 181, 190–1, 193, 213
Atlantic 14, 119
Australasia 11
Australia 113, 207n2
balkanize(d) 131, 140
Bank of England 114, 161
banking 20, 23, 38, 64, 107, 146, 176
banks 15, 19, 21–2, 28–9, 35n3, 38, 40, 48, 147–8, 165; shadow banks 206n1
beauty parades 3, 121n6, 129, 145
behavioural 27, 81, 111; biases 6; literature 69; paradigm 173; predispositions 80, 117; theory of the firm 27
benchmark(s) 45, 51, 79, 106–8, 112–13, 115–16, 161, 170, 191–2, 216; benchmarking 151, 161; industry 75
beneficial institutions 19, 203
bespoke agreements 117, 181, 186
big bang 39, 54
Blackrock 20
Black-Scholes model 57n6; theorem 3, 59, 127
Bloomberg 46, 92
Brexit 4, 161
BRICS 161
broken agency 210, 211
bull markets 162
bureaucracies 23, 26, 128
buzz 38–9, 47–8, 50–2, 54–5, 57n8, 59

California 125, 132
California Public Employees' Retirement System (CalPERS) 132, 135
California Teachers 125
Cambridge Associates 167n1
Canadian Office of the Superintendent of Financial Institutions Act 22
Canary Wharf 72
capabilities 3, 16, 20, 31–3, 69, 71, 79, 139, 146, 148–52, 155–7, 161, 166–7, 169, 181, 185, 189, 191, 194, 198–9, 201–2, 205, 209–10, 214, 218–21; competitive 213; dynamic 218, 220; governance 213; internal 156, 163, 212; managerial 195
capital 3, 32, 43, 54, 59, 61–2, 87, 202, 208, 210; expenditures 178; flows of 154; investment 213; capitalism 109; casino 119; cognitive 59; corporate 30; European 38; financial 39; industrial 37, 38, 39; modern 34; stock market 162; system 222
Carnegie Mellon University 27; Carnegie School 36n5
Cayman Islands 115

Certain Ltd Partners in Henderson PFI Secondary Fund II LLP (A Firm) v Henderson PFI Secondary Fund II LP 121n5
Cerulli Associates 46
charities 167n1
Chatham House 12
Chicago 45, 61, 72, 75, 124, 132, 136, 142n10
Chicago Park Employees' Fund 132, 135
Chicago Teachers' Fund 125, 132, 135
Chicago Transit Authority Trust 132
China 4; Chinese 4, 161; Chinese economy 208
City of Austin 125
close dialogue 12, 36n5
collaboration 17, 26, 104, 154, 170, 189–90, 193, 197–201, 204–5, 215–16; peer 221
collateralized debt obligation (CDO) 164
co-location 62, 73, 79
common law 60, 106, 176; English 22, 110, 120n2
communication technologies 30, 78, 84–5, 88, 99
competitive advantage(s) 209, 215, 217–18, 221; competitive strategies 191
complementarity 95, 153, 173, 178–9, 186, 192, 199
confidentiality 12–14, 103, 123, 131, 220
conflicts of interest 12, 46, 134, 159, 166, 175, 190
contract(s) 3–4, 11, 13–14, 16, 24, 29, 33–4, 40–1, 46, 51–3, 60, 64–5, 67–71, 74, 78, 82–3, 86–7, 93, 95, 97, 99, 100n2, 101n6, 102–7, 109–20, 120n1, 121n4, 121n5, 123–4, 129–33, 136–7, 139, 145–6, 151–9, 162–5, 167n4, 167n5, 168n5, 168n7, 174, 177, 179–82, 186–7, 188n6, 194–6, 198, 200, 204, 210, 212; ambiguous 159, 168n8; bespoke 120; bilateral 103–5, 116–19, 155, 195; commercial 129; complete 42, 56n3, 168n8; contract law 78, 104–5, 110, 117, 121n4; contract theory 86, 104, 155; discrete 40–2, 51, 56n3, 86–7, 94–5, 97, 101n3, 102, 105, 116, 153, 157; employment 33–4, 60, 86, 94, 98, 117, 128, 148, 169, 194, 205–6; financial 110; geography of 13, 102, 119; incomplete 40, 42, 95; itemized 158; labour 61, 65–6; legal 197; performance-oriented 157; private 13, 103, 110, 120n1, 121n4; relational 40–2, 56, 56n2, 86–7, 93, 97, 101n3, 102, 104–5, 116–19, 140, 157; role of 102; service 16, 29, 34, 123, 125, 128, 148, 155, 158, 169, 171, 194, 195; single 61; sociology of 14; standard 154–5, 167n4, 186; contract(s), standardized 113–14, 117, 146, 194; task-specific 68
contracting 13–14, 16, 34, 73, 99, 103–5, 107–8, 111–12, 118–19, 123, 130, 137, 139, 196, 198; bilateral 62; conventional 216; parties 101n3, 104–5
contractual 11, 13–14, 52, 55, 64, 78, 87–9, 102–5, 109–12, 114, 118–19, 123–4, 132, 140, 146, 154, 159, 167n5, 183, 188n4; agreement 180; dispute 121n5
cooperation 17, 26, 34, 43, 56, 61, 65, 94, 189–90, 193, 196–8, 200–1, 204–5, 207n5, 215–16; and collaboration 17, 189–90, 193, 196–7, 200–1, 205, 216; cooperative ventures 199
corporation(s) 24, 28, 30, 36, 38, 74, 109, 152, 171, 175; corporate strategy 28, 51, 175; large 185
costs of production 41, 191
credit unions 21
currency/currencies 53, 58, 173, 193
custodial 48; services 131, 194
customization 156

Datastream 57n7
decision rights 27, 42–3, 179; transparent 178
decision-making 3, 5, 16, 18, 24–5, 27–8, 32, 35, 37, 43, 54, 62, 64, 69, 78, 82–3, 85, 90–1, 101n5, 107, 114, 145, 148, 151–3, 156–61, 163–5, 170, 173–5, 180, 190, 192, 197–8, 202–3, 205, 213–14
defined benefit (DB) 122, 124, 127, 141n4
defined contribution (DC) 122, 124, 141n4
Delaware 114
delegated chief investment officer (DCIO) 169
Denver School 125
deregulation 39, 172
Detroit 122
developing economies 40, 54, 173
digital economy 42
diversity 16, 62, 123, 133, 137, 139, 171
divide-and-conquer (DAC) 15, 65, 71, 74
domain-specific skills 64, 106, 174
domestic equities 44, 75–6
Dublin 73, 115

East Asian 75, 109
economies of scale 6, 44, 46, 62–3, 73, 81n5, 93, 106, 125, 174, 189, 195; and scope 174, 185, 191
Edinburgh 73
efficiency 9, 37, 62, 85, 87, 101, 104, 208, 218–20

efficient market hypothesis (EMH) 3, 6, 7, 37, 39, 127
emerging economies 173
emerging markets 4–5, 49–51, 55, 76–80, 131, 161, 163, 196
Employee Retirement Income Security Act (ERISA) 122, 126, 141n1
endowments 1, 3, 5, 15, 20, 22, 145, 150, 160, 164, 208–9, 220; university 222
England 16, 110, 115–16, 154; English 22; English courts 110; *see also* United Kingdom; Wales
entrepreneur 30, 40, 61, 80n2, 83–4; coordinator 60–1, 64, 78, 83, 85
euro 4, 39, 55, 173, 196, 206; crisis 4, 55, 96, 161, 196, 206
Europe 11, 13, 16, 39–40, 46, 102, 113–15, 117–19, 154, 167n1; European 14, 38, 40, 73, 103, 107, 109, 114–15, 117–18, 120, 120n2
expertise 8, 91
exploration and exploitation 218, 220

factors of production 60, 62, 84, 100n2
factory visits 12
family offices 1, 5, 15, 20, 150, 160, 164, 167n1, 222
Federal Reserve 21, 25, 35n3, 49, 124
fiduciary/fiduciaries 106, 216; duty/duties 31, 39, 46, 83, 127, 133, 135, 138, 141n1, 176; management (FM) 163, 169
fieldwork 11–14, 103, 123, 217
finance theory 127
Financial Accounting Standards Board 127
financial crisis/crises 3, 18n2, 35n3, 49, 160, 221; *see also* Asian financial crisis; global financial crisis (GFC)
financial institutions 6, 10–14, 19–24, 26–8, 31–2, 34–5, 37–40, 43, 46–55, 58–9, 62–3, 66–7, 71–3, 75, 78–9, 80n3, 82–3, 85, 89–90, 92, 95–6, 98–9, 101n2, 102–3, 105–9, 112, 114–15, 117–20, 122, 145, 165–6, 188, 188n3, 189, 193–4, 196–8, 201, 203, 205–6, 207n2, 207n7; large 74, 100, 185; and small 76, 99; local 194; offshore 115; private-sector 126; small 67, 74–5, 79, 96, 194
financial markets 1–7, 9–11, 13, 15–17, 20, 22, 26–8, 32, 34, 37–8, 40, 44–5, 53–5, 58–9, 62–4, 67–71, 74, 78, 81n4, 85, 89, 97, 102, 108–9, 124, 130, 136, 142n7, 150, 158–60, 167n3, 172–3, 187, 189, 192, 205–6, 209–10, 213, 217, 222; developed 173; global 106, 111, 114, 120n2, 123, 131, 193; *see also* global financial markets
financial services 6, 11, 13–14, 16, 22–3, 33–4, 45–7, 53, 55, 58, 61, 67–8, 70, 72–4, 89, 93–4, 96–7, 100, 102, 106, 110–12, 114–15, 117–18, 122–4, 128–31, 136–7, 140, 145, 150, 154, 165, 168n7, 171, 176–7, 183, 185, 187, 187n1, 188n5, 188n9, 190–1, 210; global 113–14, 118–19, 120n2, 127, 145, 159, 164–5, 168n5, 174, 182–3, 185, 187, 187n1, 188n5, 189; market for 203; *see also* global financial services
financial theory 6, 39, 53, 147
Florida Retirement System 125
formalism 197
foundations 3, 5, 20, 22, 145, 150, 167n1, 209; charitable 222
Frankfurt 45, 73
freedom of information (FOI) conventions 141n2; requests 14, 123, 132
FTSE 100 index 57, 192

gamesmanship 103
general partners (GPs) 204
geography 7, 11, 13, 24, 30, 60, 82, 102, 114, 119, 165, 202; economic 1, 11, 12, 38, 59, 82; end of 2, 53, 58; relational economic 13, 56n2
global 1–7, 11, 13–14, 16, 24–5, 28, 30, 34–5, 39–40, 45–6, 51, 54–5, 56n4, 58–9, 62–3, 99, 103, 106, 108–9, 111, 113–15, 118–19, 120n2, 120n3, 122–5, 127, 131, 145, 159, 164–5, 168n5, 169, 173–5, 182–3, 185, 187, 189, 193, 203, 205, 208; downturn 196; economy 95, 192, 206, 213; equity 70, 76–7, 127; financial centres 74, 79; financial crisis (GFC) 4, 7, 19, 25, 39, 59, 96, 110, 122, 124, 162, 164, 170, 173, 196, 206, 208, 213, 221; financial integration 2; financial markets 74; financial services 11, 13, 70–3, 75, 79, 89, 95–8, 103, 113–14, 118, 154, 187–8; financial system 52, 99, 206; integration 162; investment houses 100; global market(s)/marketplace 2, 11, 19–20, 34, 37–8, 40, 51, 53, 63, 70, 100, 108, 161, 163, 189, 206
globalization 30, 49
Goldman Sachs 161–2, 173
governance 4–5, 10–12, 14, 16–17, 35, 37, 41–5, 53–5, 82, 85–7, 89–100, 102, 114–19, 123, 126, 138–9, 150–3, 158, 170–1, 175–6, 179, 183, 185, 197–8, 200–1, 205, 207n7, 209, 213–15, 217, 220–1, 222n1; best-practice 138; budgets 213, 214, 220; corporate 114
governing boards 31, 139
Government Accountability Office (GAO) 124, 141

health care benefits 122
hedge fund(s) 52, 55–6, 68, 106, 113, 115, 118, 202
herding 7, 56n1, 109
Hong Kong 75–6, 113, 202
horizontal process of incorporation (HPI) 65–6, 68, 71, 74
household saving 38
Houston Firefighters 142n9
hub-and-spokes model 29, 33, 129, 169–71, 175, 178–80, 182–3, 185–6
human capital 5, 15, 32–3, 37, 43, 54, 59, 61, 64, 80n1, 82, 85, 90–3, 95, 97, 99, 142n7, 211

Illinois 124–5, 132, 136, 138, 142n10
Illinois Municipal Retirement Fund 125, 132, 135–6
Illinois State Board of Higher Education 136
Illinois Teachers 125
Illinois Universities Retirement System 125, 132, 135–6
incorporation 15, 54
industrial revolution 23, 38
inflation 63, 66–7, 162
information asymmetries 37, 51, 55, 84, 183, 187n1; flows 38, 47; systems 15, 32, 37, 48, 50, 174; technology (IT) 92, 120n1
innovation 3, 5–6, 9, 12, 17, 22, 26–8, 35, 41, 60, 80n1, 106, 128, 138, 145–7, 149, 156, 160, 162–4, 166, 167n4, 169, 181, 188n3, 188n6, 189, 196–202, 204–6, 209, 211, 213–22; catalysts for 214; internal 215; investor 213; organizational 197, 207n4, 209; policy/policies 213, 217; product 164, 206
insider trading 79
insource/insourcing 4–5, 16–17, 20, 29, 31, 33–4, 37–8, 43–4, 50–1, 68, 74, 76, 82–4, 87, 89, 93–100, 101n6, 128, 145, 148, 152, 160, 163, 166, 169, 171, 173–6, 185–6, 188n3, 194, 201, 206; *see also* outsource/outsourcing
institutional investors 1–5, 7, 11–12, 14–17, 20–3, 25, 115, 148, 157, 159–60, 170, 190, 192, 208–15, 217–19, 222
institutionalism 23, 26
insurance companies 1, 5–6, 19, 22, 35, 39, 48, 63, 74, 164, 207
Insurance Companies Act 22
intermediation 3–6, 15–17, 26, 28, 33–4, 46–7, 63, 107, 117, 145–9, 154, 164, 187n1, 212; disintermediation 4–6, 17, 20, 167, 169, 185; financial 165; reintermediation 4–6, 17, 20, 33, 166–7, 169, 185; theory of 146–7, 149
international equities 75
investment advisers/consultants 112, 143, 145–6, 148, 150–67, 167n1, 168n6, 170, 172, 191, 195; clubs 204; counselling 22
investment management 3, 5–6, 14, 16, 21, 32, 52–3, 58–9, 67, 70, 73, 75, 94, 102, 114, 116–17, 119–20, 121n5, 123, 131, 136, 140, 151–2, 154–6, 159, 171–4, 176, 179–86, 188n2, 189, 195–6, 203–5, 210
investment management agreements (IMAs) 14, 111–20, 123–5, 132–40, 141n2, 142n9, 181; bilateral 118
Investment Management Consultants Association (IMCA) 131
investment managers 3, 55, 91, 107–9, 111–12, 114, 116–18, 121n7, 134, 136, 140, 146, 154–5, 170, 173, 204; external 191
investment portfolio 44, 75
investment returns 1, 5–6, 10, 15, 17, 58–9, 62–4, 67–8, 70, 74, 78–9, 89, 99, 124, 148, 155, 162, 164, 175, 190, 195, 198, 215, 222
investment strategies 1, 4, 9, 15–17, 19, 29, 31, 33, 35, 37–9, 43–4, 49–52, 54–5, 58, 63, 68, 71–2, 75–7, 79, 90–3, 112, 115–16, 118, 121n5, 126, 131, 140, 145, 147, 150–3, 156–7, 159–65, 169, 171–8, 180, 182–3, 185–7, 188n2, 191–5, 211, 213–14, 221

Japan 2
joint ventures 77, 128
JP Morgan Chase 20
jurisdiction(s) 2, 7, 9, 11, 13–14, 19, 35, 38–9, 42, 66, 74, 76–7, 82–5, 88, 98, 101–3, 110, 115, 117, 119, 120n2, 121n4, 121n6, 121n7, 122–3, 127, 135, 137–8, 140, 150, 165, 167n1, 169, 171, 176, 182, 190, 193–4, 200, 202–3, 206n1, 207n2; choice of 14, 102–3, 109, 112; offshore 115–16, 118

Kansas PERS 132
Kentucky PERS 142n9
Kentucky Teachers 131

LA County PERS 131
La Porta 119, 154
labour 41, 43, 60–1, 64, 78, 80n1, 93, 174; costs 62; division of 104; internal markets 86; market 74; productivity 192
LACERS 132, 135
Latin America 3, 58; Latin American 109
law(s) 34, 35n2, 104–5, 110, 120n2, 123, 141n2, 182; company 22; contract 14, 78, 104; firms 113–14, 120n3, 167n4; of

England and Wales 16, 116, 154; role of 105; state 133, 136; theory of 25; trust 176; UK 114; *see also* common law; contract law; legal; rule of law
learning by doing 9, 10, 192, 200
legal advisers 110, 113, 121n4, 154, 165; services 11, 56, 163, 166; system(s) 104, 110, 113–14, 154
Lehman Brothers 35n1
liberal democracy 101n3
limited partners (LPs) 204, 212
Local Government Employee Benefit Trust Fund 138
London 2, 39, 45–6, 54, 56n3, 58, 74, 106, 112, 114–15, 118–20, 121n6, 172, 202–3; City of 72, 114
Long-Term Capital Management (LTCM) 3, 55, 172
long-termism 219
loose coupling 127, 135
Los Angeles 45; Los Angeles PERS 131
Louisiana State Employees 135
Luxembourg 115

Maine Local 125
Maine PERS 142n9
make-or-buy option 16, 20, 29, 31, 33, 44, 128, 148, 189, 194, 196, 204–6, 222
management innovation 166, 217
management science 147–8
Manchester 45
manufacturing industries 107
market capitalization 194; density 129; disjuncture 160, 162; information 9, 32, 41, 44, 47, 54, 56, 73, 92, 98, 161; integration 75, 79; irrationality 158; liberalization 39; performance 9, 45–6, 59, 92, 109, 111, 159–61, 192; signalling 83; volatility 49, 111, 159, 162, 177, 200
markets 1–7, 9–10, 15, 18, 25, 27–8, 30, 35, 37–43, 46, 49–52, 54–5, 57–61, 63–4, 69, 74–7, 79–81, 84, 86, 91, 95, 97–8, 100, 105–6, 108–9, 113, 118, 123, 140, 142n7, 151, 158, 161, 173, 190, 192, 194, 200–1, 206, 210, 218; bull 210; developed 108; financial 111, 158, 172, 173, 210; theory of 148
Massachusetts 124
Melbourne 45
memorandum of understanding (MoU) 197
Mercer 46, 167n1
mergers and acquisitions 190
Metropolitan Water Reclamation Fund 132
Miami 45, 72
Michigan 141n3
Middle East 11
Minnesota Teachers' Fund 132
Missouri Local Government 141n2, 142n9
Missouri SERS 132
Missouri's Sunshine Law 141n2
mix-and-switch strategy 68, 71, 73, 75–6, 79
modern portfolio theory (MPT) 3, 39, 55, 59, 172, 179
moral hazard 183, 185, 187
Morgan Stanley 35n3
mortgage companies 21
multinational firms 54, 106, 113, 120n3; service providers 120
Munich 45
mutual fund 58, 68, 81n5

National Association of State Retirement Administrators 142n6
National Conference of Commissioners on Uniform State Laws 141n1
nation-states 2, 19, 24, 109, 119
neoclassical economic theory 158
networks 12, 30, 54–5, 73, 75, 78, 88, 97, 104, 128, 153, 196, 206, 207n6; electronic 41, 47, 58, 106; informal 38; local market 52; of suppliers 41, 42; tailor-made 48
Nevada 131; Nevada PERS 135
New Mexico Education Board 135
New York 2, 39, 45, 58, 72, 74–5, 106, 121n6, 172, 203
New York State and Local 125
New York State Highways Authority 26
norms and conventions 5, 24, 34, 56n3, 62, 66, 88, 106, 114, 121n4, 127, 154, 159, 161, 165, 168n7, 191; academic 13; community 60, 214; contractual 14, 123; industry 46, 64, 146–7, 151, 154, 156, 158, 162–6, 169, 188n6, 196, 205; investment 3; social 105, 197
North America 11, 16, 113, 167n2; *see also* America; United States
North Dakota Investment Office 142n9

OCIO 176–7; management 170, 176–88; managers 178–81, 184–7
offshore 7, 16, 30, 42–3, 51–2, 55, 66, 72, 77, 85, 97–8, 101n7, 102, 112, 115–20, 121n6, 121n7, 206n1; offshoring 34, 37–8, 42, 53–5, 82, 85, 87–9, 95–6, 98–100; *see also* onshore
Ohio 125; Ohio PERS 142n9; Ohio Police and Fire Pension Fund 132, 135
Ombudsman 114
onshore 206n1; onshoring 83, *see also* offshore
opportunism 1, 56, 111, 116, 119, 130, 180
Oregon 124, 128, 138

Oregon Investment Corporation (OIC) 124, 138, 139
Oregon Investment Council 138, 142n11
Oregon Laws and Resolutions 142n11
Oregon University System Fund 138
Organization for Economic Cooperation and Development (OECD) 21, 172
organizations 1, 5, 11–13, 15, 17, 19–23, 25–30, 32–5, 35n1, 36n5, 37, 63–6, 70, 103, 116, 127–8, 145–7, 149–51, 153–6, 159–60, 164–6, 167n1, 169–70, 177–8, 182–3, 186–7, 188n3, 190, 193, 195, 202, 208, 210–11, 213, 215–18, 220–2; ambidexterity of 218–21; ecology of 29; financial 148, 158, 167n3; investment 213, 217; large 207n4; relational theory of 60; small 69; theory of 34
outsource/outsourcing 6, 16, 20, 28–31, 33–4, 37–8, 41, 44, 51–2, 54–5, 62–3, 65, 68, 70, 74, 76, 82, 84–5, 87, 89, 94–100, 100n1, 101n6, 128–9, 145, 147–8, 160, 163, 166, 167n2, 169, 171, 173–6, 178, 180, 185–6, 188n3, 191–2, 194, 199–201, 205–6, 207n3
outsourced chief investment officer (OCIO) 17, 169–70, 176–87, 188n5
Oxford 12

Pareto optimal 42, 61, 195, 207n5
participant observation 11
Pennsylvania PSERS 141n2, 142n9
Pennsylvania Right-to-Know law 141n2
Pension Benefit Guaranty Corporation (PBGC) 127
pension funds 1, 3, 5–6, 15, 19–20, 22–3, 26, 28, 39, 43, 48, 63, 80n3, 123, 126, 130, 132, 145, 149–50, 155, 157, 160, 162–4, 169, 171, 173–7, 181–3, 185, 187, 190, 206n1, 207–11, 216, 220, 222; global industry for 186; governance of 125, 169–70, 172, 175, 177–8, 185–6; management of 141, 169–70, 173; private 13; public-sector 45, 128–30, 137, 140, 167n1, 205; small 63, 125, 163, 169, 183, 185–6; state and local 16, 123, 127, 132, 137–8, 140
pension plans/schemes 48, 124–6, 128, 136–7, 186; public-sector 63, 122, 127–8; state and local 123–4, 127; workplace 38
Phoenix PERS 125
pipelines 38, 40, 47, 48, 50, 51, 52, 54, 55, 56n5, 57, 57n8
Pittsburgh 36n5
portfolio diversification 3–4, 151; investment 39, 44, 46, 48, 94, 101n4, 101n7; investment teams 51, 90, 92; management 22, 37; theory 127
portfolio managers 7, 9, 37, 40, 43–5, 50, 52–5, 63, 65, 68–70, 73–4, 77–9, 81n5, 91, 93–4, 97–8, 107, 112, 152, 193–5, 200, 205, 214; external 51, 55–6, 70, 75, 195–6, 198, 203; internal 44, 46, 52, 55, 69–70, 75, 195–6, 198; talented 200
predatory behaviour 190
price mechanism 83
principals and agents 111, 115, 182–3, 211; principal-agent model 170, 183; principal-agent problem 27, 181–4, 187, 188n2, 188n9; principal-agent relationships 210, 222
private equity 52, 70, 192, 204
private property 24
procurement policies 128, 131, 138–9
production platforms 30
public employee retirement systems (PERS) 14, 122–5, 128, 131–2, 135–6, 138–9, 141n2
Public Employees Retirement Fund (PERF) 138
Public Fund Survey 57n7
Public Safety System 142n9
public-private partnerships (PPPs) 207n7

quantitative easing 124, 196

R&D 219
rates of return 7, 16, 19, 31–2, 34–5, 38, 44, 49, 52–6, 107, 109, 115, 118, 140, 148, 191–2, 194, 197; risk-adjusted 7, 15–16, 19, 28–9, 31, 34, 43, 77, 90–2, 99, 173–4, 182, 191–4, 197; targets 43–5, 48–9, 51, 67, 93, 96, 203
rational expectations equilibrium (REE) 10, 18n5
raw materials 61–2, 78
Red Cross 26
reflexivity, importance of 147
relational 56
rent-seeking behaviour 149, 190, 195
request for proposals (RFPs) 14, 123–4, 129–33, 137–40, 142n9
research clubs 12, 201–2
resources 2–3, 13, 16, 20, 31–3, 37, 61–2, 69, 71, 77, 79–80, 82–4, 90, 93, 95, 107, 110, 117, 120, 125, 146–52, 155–7, 161, 166–7, 169, 177–8, 181, 185, 189, 191, 194, 197–9, 201–2, 205, 206n1, 211, 213–21; human 95, 212; internal 156, 163, 213, 216, 218; managerial 195; scarce 147, 161, 214
returns to scale 30, 60, 84, 100, 112
Reuters 46
Rhode Island 141n3

risk/risks 2–4, 9, 15, 35n3, 39, 45, 48–9, 51–3, 55, 56n1, 56n5, 57n6, 58, 68, 75–7, 83–5, 90, 92–3, 95, 102–3, 107, 111–13, 115, 117, 119, 125, 141, 141n5, 146–7, 149, 158, 161, 164, 167n4, 172–3, 177–9, 185, 189, 192, 196, 199–200, 203, 205, 210–12, 221; and uncertainty 1, 7, 9, 11, 13, 20, 27, 34, 68, 84, 90, 93, 117; aversion 71, 76; budget 213–14, 222n1; risk/risks career 77, 191, 221; diversification 59, 162; investment 170, 172; management 2–4, 8, 170, 178, 221; market 20, 59, 68, 90, 93, 117, 119, 147, 179, 195, 198; models 8, 108; pricing 4, 57n6, 76, 127; sharing 168n5
rogue trader phenomenon 45
rules 2–3, 8, 12, 23–4, 26, 110, 116, 121n7, 123, 127, 138, 140, 141n1, 197; and regulations 140; as institutions 24–5; legal 171; liberalization of 172; of the game 24, 26; public procurement 124; rulebooks 42, 52–3, 55, 59, 129; rule of law 110; rules-based logic 85; statute-based 46; systems of 24

San Diego County 142n9
search costs 41–2, 46, 53, 73, 76, 83–4, 105, 149, 195
Second World War 2, 30
seeding start-up ventures 202
Senate Bill 120, 138
Senate Finance and Revenue Committee 128
senior managers 6–7, 12, 14–15, 17, 20, 28, 31–3, 37, 42–5, 50–2, 54, 58–9, 61, 63–5, 68, 70–1, 73–4, 76–80, 81n4, 83, 85, 90 1, 93 4, 101n6, 123, 146, 148, 156, 189–90, 192–4, 196–206, 210
service providers 3–4, 7, 11, 13–14, 29, 47–8, 54, 63, 67, 73–5, 94–5, 102–3, 107, 111–12, 114–16, 118, 120, 120n1, 123, 125, 129–30, 132, 145, 151, 153–5, 160, 163, 165, 174, 177, 179, 181, 189, 210–11, 215; external 196, 203, 216, 221
Shanghai 45, 75, 76
Sharpe ratio 3
Silicon Valley 202
Singapore 45, 75, 76
skills 10, 43, 44, 55, 87, 91, 107, 129, 214, 219; and expertise 8, 15, 31–2, 43, 59, 61–2, 64, 66, 78–9, 83, 85, 90–2, 97, 101n5, 106, 108–9, 116, 125–6, 146–8, 153, 155–6, 158–9, 162, 164, 167, 169, 171, 174, 176, 178, 183, 192, 194, 196, 202, 215; financial 31, 73; organizational 213
sovereign development funds (SDFs) 215
sovereign funds 190, 208–9, 211, 220, 222
sovereign wealth funds 1, 5, 12–13, 19–20, 22, 26, 28, 48, 99, 145, 150, 160, 164, 166
standardization 93, 110, 117
standards of conduct 24, 128
Stanford University 12, 141n2
State Street 20
status quo bias 195
stock market 161–2, 172–3, 196
Stockholm 73
Studebaker 126
success syndrome 218
sunk costs 41, 87, 99
supply chains 30, 55
Swiss Financial Institutions Act 22
Swiss government 22
Sydney 45, 75

tacit knowledge 6, 56n4, 86
talent 43–4, 59, 61, 80n1, 107, 190, 210, 214; market for 62, 94, 194, 196
target rates of return 32, 43–4, 64, 94, 107, 109, 113, 194, 200
tax benefits 121n6
terrorist attacks 4
Texas Municipal Fund 132
Texas Teachers 125
theory of the firm 34, 37, 58, 60, 62, 86, 99, 147
Thomson Reuters 46, 92
TMT bubble 3, 55, 161
Tokyo 2, 45, 58, 75
Toronto 74
trade 9, 30, 41, 58, 88, 104, 207n5, 208; publications 129
transaction costs 27, 34, 41, 60, 86, 94–9, 107, 110–11, 113–14, 117, 119, 123, 125, 129, 140, 148, 154–5, 158–9, 168n6, 174, 177, 179–80, 193, 196, 200; theory of 36n5, 147
Transit Authority 132, 136
transparency 7, 79, 113, 115, 134, 178, 204, 212, 215; fees and cost 215

uncertainty 4, 9–11, 13, 18n2, 20, 27, 59, 68, 83–5, 90, 93, 102–3, 111, 117, 119, 125, 141, 146–7, 150, 158, 179, 189, 192, 209; market 195, 198; *see also* risk/risks
Uniform Management of Public Employee Retirement Systems Act 141n1
Unilever Superannuation Trustees Ltd v Mercury Asset Management 121n5
United Kingdom 1, 11, 13, 16, 24, 38–9, 48, 102, 110–11, 113–15, 117, 121n5, 121n7, 153, 161, 167n2, 207; *see also* England; Wales

United States 4, 13–14, 16, 21, 24–5, 35n3, 38–9, 45, 49, 57, 62, 72, 110, 114, 120n1, 121n7, 122–8, 131–2, 136–7, 139, 141, 141n1, 142n10, 161, 164, 186, 205; *see also* America; North America
United States Steel 26

value chain 17; investment 178
Vermont State Employees 125

Wales 16, 110, 115–16, 154; *see also* England; United Kingdom
Wall Street 210, 216
war on terror 4
Willis Towers Watson 46, 167n1
Wilson Report 38
Winterthur 74

Zürich 74

The manufacturer's authorised representative in the EU for product safety is Oxford University Press España S.A. of el Parque Empresarial San Fernando de Henares, Avenida de Castilla, 2 – 28830 Madrid (www.oup.es/en or product.safety@oup.com). OUP España S.A. also acts as importer into Spain of products made by the manufacturer.

www.ingramcontent.com/pod-product-compliance
Lightning Source LLC
LaVergne TN
LVHW011753200926
848484LV00003B/693
9780198793212